G000054311

Hong Kong, China
Growth, Structural Change, and
Economic Stability During the Transition

John Dodsworth and Dubravko Mihaljek

INTERNATIONAL MONETARY FUND
Washington DC
August 1997

© 1997 International Monetary Fund

Cataloging-in-Publication Data

Hong Kong, China : growth, structural change, and economic stability
during the transition / John Dodsworth and Dubravko Mihaljek.
p.   cm. — (Occasional paper ; 152)
Includes bibliographical references (p.)
ISBN 1-55775-672-4
1. Hong Kong (China)—Economic conditions 2. Hong Kong
(China)—Economic policy   3. Hong Kong (China)—Politics and government.
I. Mihaljek, Dubravko. II. Title. III. Series: Occasional paper (International Monetary Fund) ; 152.
HC470.3.D63 1997
338.95125—DC21

Price: US$15.00
(US$12.00 to full-time faculty members and
students at universities and colleges)

Please send orders to:
International Monetary Fund, Publication Services
700 19th Street, N.W., Washington, D.C. 20431, U.S.A.
Tel.: (202) 623-7430   Telefax: (202) 623-7201
E-mail: publications@imf.org
Internet: http://www.imf.org

recycled paper

Contents

The following symbols have been used throughout this paper:

. . . to indicate that data are not available;

0.0 to indicate that the figure is zero or less than half the final digit shown;

n.a. to indicate that the item does not exist;

– between years or months (e.g., 1994–95 or January–June) to indicate the years or months covered, including the beginning and ending years or months;

/ between years (e.g., 1994/95) to indicate a crop or fiscal (financial) year.

"Billion" means a thousand million.

Minor discrepancies between constituent figures and totals are due to rounding.

The term "country," as used in this paper, does not in all cases refer to a territorial entity that is a state as understood by international law and practice; the term also covers some territorial entities that are not states, but for which statistical data are maintained and provided internationally on a separate and independent basis.

Preface

Hong Kong, China, returned to Chinese sovereignty in July 1997 as one of the world's freest and most vibrant economies. Hong Kong's economic success, documented and analyzed in this occasional paper, has been particularly notable against the background of its structural transformation, one of the world's swiftest and most profound over the past half century, and its unique political transition from an overseas dependent territory of the United Kingdom to a special administrative region of the People's Republic of China. Although the circumstances in which growth in Hong Kong has evolved are in many ways unique, the lessons are universal.

The Hong Kong authorities have consistently encouraged free trade, free flow of capital, open competition, and market flexibility by following a transparent, rules-based policy framework. Key macroeconomic policies—a linked exchange rate, prudent fiscal policy, firm financial regulation, and a noninterventionist stance vis-à-vis the goods and factor markets—have facilitated quick adjustment to shifts in comparative advantage, which have become common in an era of world wide economic liberalization and rapid technological change. These policies have also encouraged Hong Kong entrepreneurs and workers to take advantage of—rather than resist—the forces of globalization. The movement of local industries to mainland China has not hurt Hong Kong's economy—on the contrary, it has left room for new activities in the territory and allowed both Hong Kong and China to benefit from their respective comparative advantages. Hong Kong has thus demonstrated that, with appropriate policies, the forces of globalization and integration into the world economy can bring significant economic benefits to large segments of the population.

Sound institutions and good governance have been another critical ingredient of Hong Kong's economic success. By safeguarding the rule of law and impartiality of the judiciary, improving the efficiency and accountability of the public administration, tackling corruption, and ensuring a free flow of information, the authorities have created an environment which rewards hard work, initiative, and risk taking. As Hong Kong, China, embarks on its historic voyage under the "one country, two systems" approach, these institutions and values remain key to its future stability and prosperity. The Joint Declaration and the Basic Law, as well as the arrangements for the mutually independent monetary relationship between Hong Kong and China, provide assurance that this framework will continue.

Confidence concerning Hong Kong's economic future appears well justified given the ongoing commitment to sound macroeconomic policies and institutions. As argued in the paper, Hong Kong is well positioned to benefit from the outlook for solid and more stable growth in China as well as encouraging prospects for regional and global economic expansion. As China gradually liberalizes capital account transactions, Hong Kong will be able to play a vital role in the subsequent rise in financial flows into and out of China. More generally, Hong Kong's position as a preeminent international financial center will enable it to intermediate the huge saving and investment flows within Asia, which are presently to a large extent intermediated outside the region. These opportunities are likely to increase the ability of Hong Kong firms and financial institutions to initiate and manage commercial activity across international borders.

Hong Kong's ambitions to develop further as an international financial center will require that the Hong Kong Special Administrative Region assume increased responsibilities before the international financial community. In addition to continuing its record of sound macroeconomic management and firm financial regulation, Hong Kong will need to strengthen economic cooperation with Asian and OECD countries. Growing cooperation among Asian central banks, membership in the Bank for International Settlements, and the Hong Kong Monetary Authority's participation in the IMF's New Arrangements to Borrow are examples of actions that demonstrate Hong Kong's willingness to take on new responsibilities commensurate with its evolving status.

Hubert Neiss
Director
Asia and Pacific Department

Acknowledgments

As the first publication on Hong Kong in this series, this occasional paper builds on the work of numerous current and former staff of the Asia and Pacific Department of the IMF. The authors acknowledge the valuable comments and ideas provided by David Goldsbrough, and would like to thank Bijan Aghevli, Charles Adams, Hoe Ee Khor, Guy Meredith, and Wanda Tseng for providing guidance for research on Hong Kong over recent years. Parts of this paper are based on contributions originally prepared by our colleagues Aasim Husain (financial market infrastructure and institutional development, financial system and regulatory framework), Jan Kees Martijn (transportation infrastructure, social policies, competition policy), and Ichiro Oishi (competition policy). The authors would also like to acknowledge past contributions by Lynn Aylworth, Bankim Chadha, Kenneth Miranda, and Kenji Okamura.

Aung Thurein Win and Youkyong Kwon provided excellent research assistance. The authors are also grateful to David Driscoll and Marina Primorac of the External Relations Department, who edited the paper for publication and coordinated production. Lastly, the authors are indebted to the Hong Kong authorities for their outstanding cooperation.

The views expressed here, as well as any errors, are the sole responsibility of the authors, and do not necessarily reflect the opinions of the Hong Kong authorities, the Executive Directors of the IMF, or other members of the IMF staff.

Glossary of Abbreviations

APEC   Asia-Pacific Economic Cooperation Council
BIS   Bank for International Settlements
GMM   generalized method of moments
HKMA   Hong Kong Monetary Authority
HKSAR   Hong Kong Special Administrative Region
SSA   social security allowance
TFP   total factor productivity
WTO   World Trade Organization

1 Introduction and Overview

As Hong Kong, China, enters a new stage of development with the return to Chinese sovereignty, it can take confidence from its long-term evolution and its resilience to adverse developments over the past half-century. The ability of Hong Kong to prosper amidst change has intrigued economists for a long time. Nearly 40 years ago, a pioneering study of the economic growth of Hong Kong (Szczepanik (1958)) noted

> On 30 August 1945, when Hong Kong was liberated after four years of occupation, its economy was in ruins. Ten years later, the Colony achieved the fame of being one of the most prosperous territories in the Far East. It is difficult to find a comparable example of economic growth. The question which immediately arises is how to explain this fascinating case of economic development (p. 3).

Yet, fascinating as it may have seemed, the progress made during the 1950s pales in comparison with what was realized during the subsequent decades, especially since the 1970s. As one observer (Smith (1997)) summed up the state of the economy at that time,

> When I arrived in the territory in 1970, Hong Kong's reputation was as a low-cost manufacturer of cheap clothing, wigs, plastic goods and toys. Although the Hongkong and Shanghai Bank, Standard Chartered, and Citibank were present in Hong Kong with a group of relatively weak local banks, Hong Kong was in no sense a financial centre, let alone an international financial centre. If a trading company were to have asked its bankers for a price for U.S. dollars two weeks hence, it would most likely be told: "If you want dollars in two weeks' time, come back then—I'm sure we will have some" (pp. 1–2).

In 1997, Hong Kong belongs to a very different world. It has transformed itself into one of the world's premier trade, business, and financial centers. Although relatively small in terms of population—about 6.4 million people, slightly smaller than Switzerland—and area—1,095 square kilometers, approximately a third larger than New York City— Hong Kong has grown into an economic powerhouse, with GDP equivalent to US$155 billion, total trade worth over US$440 billion, and bank assets valued at over one trillion U.S. dollars in 1996. With integration into the global service economy, by 1996 Hong Kong had become

- the world's seventh largest trading entity and seventh largest stock market
- the world's fifth largest banking center in terms of external financial transactions and fifth largest foreign exchange market in terms of average daily turnover
- the world's fourth leading source of foreign direct investment
- the world's busiest container port, and
- one of the world's most prosperous economies, with per capita GDP of US$24,500 comparable to all but the wealthiest industrial countries.

These achievements have been realized within a stable, noninterventionist economic policy framework, where the government has performed the classical role of providing a legal and administrative framework and parts of the physical infrastructure, and the private sector has decided on its own how to allocate resources on the basis of clear market signals. Within this setting, private firms have adapted quickly to shifts in comparative advantage and have maintained competitiveness, while the economy as a whole has demonstrated remarkable strength and resilience in the face of economic and political shocks. Indeed, Hong Kong's performance contains important messages for policymakers everywhere. First, it underscores that economic success in today's world is less a question of relative resource endowments and more a question of the market perception of the orientation and predictability of economic policy. Second, more than any other economy in the world, Hong Kong has harnessed, rather than resisted, the forces of globalization and has thereby demonstrated the economic gains that can be achieved, with the right policies, as the integration of the world economy continues through trade, financial flows, and the exchange of technology and information.

This paper aims to explore some of the reasons for Hong Kong's successful economic performance and assess future economic prospects in the context of existing institutions and arrangements for economic policymaking that are expected to be in place after July 1, 1997. A discussion of the post-1997 arrangements complements this review by highlighting the extent to which the existing institutions and economic policies are expected to be preserved under the "one country, two systems" approach envisaged for the Hong Kong Special Administrative Region (HKSAR) of the People's Republic of China. The following is a summary of the main conclusions reached in the paper.

Longer-Term Trends

Since 1980, Hong Kong's economy has expanded by 6½ percent annually and evolved through three business cycles. The growth pattern over these cycles has taken three distinct forms: export-led growth (from 1980 to 1989), domestic demand-driven growth (from 1990 through the first half of 1994), and consolidation (from the second half of 1994 through the first half of 1996). During each phase, growth rates of real GDP have become progressively lower and more stable, reflecting the maturing of the economy and a structural shift from manufacturing to services.

The opening up of China to foreign trade and investment in the late 1970s has had a profound impact on Hong Kong's economy. For much of its history, Hong Kong's main economic function was as China's entrepôt. That function, however, virtually ceased between 1949 and 1978. During that period, Hong Kong developed labor-intensive manufacturing industries and began exporting its products overseas. By the late 1970s, manufacturing matured to the point where Hong Kong entrepreneurs were ready to set up production facilities abroad. China had abundant land and labor resources, but still lacked well-functioning transportation, telecommunications, and financial sectors. These complementary factor endowments were the impetus for much closer economic integration and the main force behind Hong Kong's remarkable structural transformation. Thus, between 1988 and 1995, the share of manufacturing in Hong Kong's GDP fell by 12 percentage points, with an approximately corresponding rise in the share of trade, transportation, financing, real estate, and business services. By 1995, the share of manufacturing in Hong Kong had declined to less than 9 percent of GDP. In the process, Hong Kong's traditional entrepôt role was resurrected, but this time within a much broader setting—Hong Kong firms no longer served just as intermediaries,

but as initiators of international business activity. This role has allowed Hong Kong to play a small but important role in the enterprise reform in China, as economic integration with Hong Kong has provided additional flexibility for China selectively to open, develop, and deregulate its domestic markets. For Hong Kong, increasing integration with mainland China has meant that its business cycle has become more synchronized with that of China. Given the linked exchange rate system between the Hong Kong and U.S. dollars, this has implied, on occasion, that monetary conditions—determined essentially by those in the United States—have not been in line with Hong Kong's economic cycle. However, owing to the flexibility of Hong Kong's factor markets, the necessary adjustments have taken place through a rapid reallocation of resources.

Adjustment in the Mid-1990s

During the early 1990s, Hong Kong experienced a boom in personal consumption, reexports, and asset markets. Stock prices doubled during 1993, and residential property prices rose by a third during the first quarter of 1994 alone. Inflation approached double-digit levels and the external balance deteriorated sharply. Successive increases in U.S. interest rates in 1994 and the implementation of stabilization measures in China gradually cooled off demand in Hong Kong and led to a prolonged consolidation in its asset markets. Between early 1994 and early 1996, growth slowed from about 6 percent to 3½ percent a year. In 1995, as the unemployment rate rose above the 3 percent mark for the first time in more than a decade, consumer sentiment was profoundly affected. However, the underlying fundamentals were sound and investor confidence remained strong. Real wages and property prices fell rapidly between late 1994 and early 1996, while firms upgraded their office and production technology and cut costs, thus creating the necessary conditions for lower domestic inflation and resumption of growth. Without this adjustment, Hong Kong's economy would have approached the transition with growing macroeconomic imbalances and uncertain prospects about stable growth after 1997.

Macroeconomic Policies

As frequently observed, one of the "secrets" of Hong Kong's economic success lies in a clear division of roles between the private and public sectors. Within the public sector, institutional factors, such as a sound and transparent legal system, independent judiciary, neutrality of the civil service, free flow of information, and small and efficient administration, have contributed toward creating an atmosphere conducive to steady economic expansion. Equally important have been Hong Kong's predominantly "rules-based" macroeconomic policies and a firm regulatory framework. Consistent with a noninterventionist approach, the authorities have maintained a coherent set of fiscal, monetary, and exchange policies that have helped limit the size of the public sector to under 20 percent of GDP, and have preserved the flexibility of factor and goods markets.

Fiscal policy has traditionally aimed at maintaining a simple and stable tax system with low tax rates, limiting current spending increases in line with GDP growth while providing adequate funding for infrastructure projects and keeping sufficient reserves to deal with contingencies. The authorities have refrained from the use of fiscal subsidies or preferential tax treatment to promote particular sectors or industries. In addition, social welfare benefits have been narrowly targeted and labor market policies have focused on providing assistance for retraining rather than for unemployment insurance. However, the authorities have also had a substantial involvement in sectors such as public housing and port and airport development, and through the release of land for development.

Monetary and exchange rate policies have been determined by currency board rules during most of Hong Kong's history. Under the linked exchange rate system established in 1983, monetary policy has a single, transparent objective: to maintain a stable exchange rate between the Hong Kong and U.S. dollars. The link, together with the freedom from controls on capital flows, implies that Hong Kong's interest rates are essentially determined by U.S. monetary conditions. While the Hong Kong Monetary Authority (HKMA) has some limited tools to influence interbank liquidity and thereby affect local short-term interest rates, these instruments have been used sparingly, mainly to smooth the occasional volatility in overnight interest rates. Such operations, however, have been very much a secondary objective to the primary goal of defending the exchange rate link, which has served Hong Kong well and has provided a firm anchor for financial policies.

In support of the exchange rate link, the financial regulatory framework has been overhauled since the banking crisis of the early 1980s and the authorities have placed priority on maintaining high standards of prudential supervision in line with best international practices. Their strategy in this area has been to promote a freer flow of information about the financial sector by enhancing banks' disclosure requirements, to supplement on-site bank examinations with off-site review and analysis, and to ensure

that banks' internal risk management systems function well.

The authorities have played a limited, hands-off role in developing the financial sector, concentrating on providing a suitable institutional and regulatory framework and leaving the development of financial products to the market. In this context, recent initiatives have included the establishment of a longer-term benchmark yield curve, the introduction of a Mortgage Corporation, and bringing interbank clearing into the Monetary Authority through the introduction of a Real Time Gross Settlement system.

The existing macroeconomic policy framework has served Hong Kong extremely well. There has been no buildup of unsustainable macroeconomic pressures over the years. Occasional bouts of inflation and trade balance deterioration led to pressures to reduce costs and restore competitiveness. The absence of policy distortions has helped promote flexible markets and ensure that factors of production move smoothly across sectors in response to changes in market conditions. Prudent budgetary management has resulted in the accumulation of substantial fiscal reserves (equivalent to 14 percent of GDP at the end of FY1996), and, along with growing confidence in the Hong Kong dollar, has underpinned the strong growth of foreign exchange reserves, which reached US$64 billion at the end of 1996.

In the financial sector, the banking system has become profitable and the banks have become highly capitalized—the risk-weighted capital adequacy ratio for the entire banking system was almost 18 percent in 1996. The use of conservative loan-to-value ratios and variable loan rates has enabled the banks to withstand substantial asset market shocks. As banks' assets and liabilities are repriced quickly, changes in interest rates have generally had a small and short-lived impact on lending and deposit interest rate spreads.

In the nontraded goods markets, a steady program of deregulation is under way. There is, however, a need for the authorities to take further steps to increase competition in certain service industries, which would further enhance Hong Kong's position as an international business and financial center.

Competitiveness

Concerns about the ability of Hong Kong's service industries to keep pace with their competitors in the emerging regional centers, such as Singapore, Shanghai, and Kuala Lumpur, have been heightened in recent years by rising labor and property costs and uncertainties associated with the transfer of sovereignty. The issue of competitiveness has stimulated a wide-ranging debate and has emerged as a key public policy issue on the eve of Hong Kong's transition in 1997. Many observers have argued that, with Hong Kong entering a new era, a fresh look should be taken at the government's hands-off approach to industrial policy. The discussion has been hampered by the lack of sectoral data in constant prices, which has made it difficult to assess whether the services sector has a competitiveness problem.

To address some of these issues in an analytical framework, the study presented in Section V constructs estimates of competitiveness for Hong Kong's manufacturing and services industries from highly disaggregated production-based GDP data for 1982–94. These estimates indicate that Hong Kong's service industries, especially those producing tradable goods and services, are highly competitive, and that markets have performed well in channeling resources toward more efficient uses. Wholesale trade, import/export trade, transportation, communications, financial, and business services all expanded, on average, at double-digit annual rates in real terms and recorded high growth rates of labor productivity since the early 1980s. Responding to relative price changes and relative wage differentials, labor and other resources have moved in a clear, predictable pattern from manufacturing and certain declining service industries to the rapidly growing sectors, such as trade, transportation, financing, and business services.

There has been a marked difference in the performance of tradable and nontradable industries. Manufacturing and tradable services (import/export trade, most transportation industries, financing) expanded on average twice as fast as nontradable services (retail trade, restaurants and hotels, domestic passenger transportation, real estate, and social and personal services). At the same time, prices of nontradables increased twice as fast as prices of tradables. As employment growth in nontradable industries outpaced that of tradables by a huge margin, productivity growth in the tradable industries has been much faster than in nontradable industries. This productivity differential accounts for almost the entire inflation differential between Hong Kong and the United States, suggesting that the real exchange rate of the Hong Kong dollar did not become overvalued. These results confirm the view that inflation under Hong Kong's linked exchange rate system has been an equilibrating response to the relatively strong productivity growth in tradable industries.

Transition and Future Prospects

Uncertainties over the implications of Hong Kong's return to Chinese sovereignty have gradually narrowed with the approach of the transition. The in-

stitutional arrangements expected to be in place after 1997, which are summarized in Box 1, are described in detail in Section VI. Under the arrangements, policymakers will retain considerable independence and autonomy in economic management. The fundamental elements of the existing policy framework—openness, freedom from foreign exchange and trade controls, small government, and the avoidance of budget deficits—are embedded in the Joint Declaration and the Basic Law. Under the Basic Law, budgets are to be independently set by Hong Kong policymakers. In the monetary areas, China and Hong Kong will continue to have two separate monetary systems, two currencies, and two independent monetary authorities. Hong Kong will also continue to participate in international organizations and subscribe to international treaties.

Continuation of the institutions and the rules-based policy framework that have contributed to Hong Kong's past success augurs well for maintaining confidence and stability in the coming years. In the area of fiscal policy, the authorities envisage budget surpluses to continue over the medium term. While some concerns have been expressed that the budget surpluses, along with a high level of fiscal reserves, will intensify political pressures for more interventionist policies, the tradition of small government appears well entrenched in Hong Kong, and continued moderate budget surpluses appear appropriate from the viewpoint of macroeconomic policy. Continuity of the current exchange rate arrangement will also be important for maintaining confidence, and policymakers are well placed to maintain the link between the U.S. and Hong Kong dollars. Past experience suggests that the adaptability of Hong Kong's firms and the flexibility of factor and commodity prices—even during a period of massive structural change—are sufficiently high to preserve competitiveness and continued strong macroeconomic performance.

Within the context of a sound economic policy framework, Hong Kong's medium-term prospects appear highly favorable. On the domestic side, recent public infrastructure investment and the related large imports of capital goods have raised the productive capacity of the economy. In addition, with many emigrants returning to Hong Kong, the labor supply has become more abundant after a decade of labor shortages. On the external side, the recent "soft landing" of the Chinese economy suggests that China will be able to sustain solid and more stable growth over the coming years, which will be highly beneficial for Hong Kong. In addition, Hong Kong has strong potential to develop further as an international trade, business, and financial center. As China liberalizes its controls on capital account transactions, Hong Kong will be able to play a central role

Box 1. Institutional Arrangements for Hong Kong After 1997

The constitutional framework for the Hong Kong Special Administrative Region has been laid down in the Sino-British Joint Declaration (1984) and the Basic Law of the Hong Kong Special Administrative Region of the People's Republic of China (1990). Under this framework, the Region is to remain autonomous in all but two areas—foreign affairs and defense—for 50 years after July 1, 1997.

Key provisions with respect to the **economic and legal system** of the Hong Kong Special Administrative Region are these.

- The socialist system and policies shall not be practiced in the Region, and the previous capitalist system and way of life shall remain unchanged for 50 years.
- The rights of private ownership of property and investments shall be protected by law.
- The land and natural resources within the Region shall be state property and shall be managed by the Government of the Hong Kong Special Administrative Region.
- The laws previously in force in Hong Kong—the common law, rules of equity, ordinances—shall be maintained, except for any that contravene the Basic Law.

On **public finances,** the Joint Declaration and the Basic Law guarantee:

- Independent finances of the Region and use of its resources exclusively for its own purposes.
- Freedom from taxation by the Central Government of China in the Region.
- Independent tax system and own tax laws of the Region, taking the low tax policy as reference.
- Prudent budgetary principles consisting of: (i) keeping expenditure within the limits of revenue in drawing up the budget; (ii) striving to achieve fiscal balance; (iii) avoiding deficits; and (iv) keeping the budget commensurate with the growth rate of GDP.

On the **monetary and exchange rate system,** the key provisions are the following.

- Independence of the Region in monetary, financial, regulatory, and supervisory policies.
- The Hong Kong dollar shall remain the legal tender and a freely convertible currency fully backed by foreign exchange.
- Freedom from all foreign exchange controls in the Region.
- Free movement of capital within, into, and out of the Region.
- Management and control of the Exchange Fund by the Government of the Hong Kong Special Administrative Region primarily for regulating the exchange value of the Hong Kong dollar.

In addition, in September 1996, the Chinese authorities defined the monetary relationship between China and Hong Kong under the concept of "one country, two systems" as one country with two currencies, two monetary systems, and two monetary authorities that are mutually independent.

The Hong Kong Special Administrative Region shall also maintain autonomy in its external economic relations (including the status of a free port and a tariff-free zone, separate customs territory, and participation—in an appropriate capacity—in relevant international organizations), immigration controls on foreign persons (entry of people from the other parts of China will be controlled by the Central Government in consultation with the Government of the Hong Kong Special Administrative Region), and other policies (land leasing, shipping, civil aviation, social services).

in the subsequent rise in financial flows into and out of China. More generally, Hong Kong can benefit as an intermediary for saving and investment flows within Asia, as these are presently to a large extent intermediated outside the region. These opportunities are likely to develop further the ability of Hong Kong firms and financial institutions to initiate and manage commercial activity across international borders. Thus, while growth is unlikely to reach the levels of the 1980s, Hong Kong appears to be well positioned to mature further as a services-based economy with development of trading and financial links both to the rest of China and to the rest of the world.

II Growth, Structural Change, and Economic Integration

Hong Kong enters the new era in its history with an exceptionally strong record of economic performance. Since 1980, real GDP growth has averaged 6½ percent annually, while per capita GDP has increased fourfold (Table 1).[1] Over this period, Hong Kong's economy has undergone a dramatic structural change as it has become increasingly linked through trade and investment to China and the rest of Asia. While the importance of the manufacturing sector and domestic merchandise exports has declined, Hong Kong has emerged as a mature services-based economy. It has done so with relatively little of the disruption in employment that has accompanied such shifts in other parts of the world,

primarily by taking advantage of—rather than resisting—the opportunities for relocation of production bases and globalization of trade, business, and financial operations. Hong Kong's history, geographic location, openness to trade, and importance as a financial center all point to its critical interest in and ability to benefit from continued global integration. This section reviews longer-term trends in Hong Kong's economy.

Structural Transformation

For much of its history, Hong Kong has served as China's entrepôt, with the important exception of the 30-year period from 1949 to 1979. During those years, the economic embargo that was imposed on China at the outbreak of the Korean War forced Hong

---

[1]The data reported in this paper are based on information available as of the end of May 1997.

Table 1. Basic Indicators
(Annual percentage changes)

| | Period Average | | | | 1996 |
	1980–96	1980–85	1986–90	1991–95	
Real GDP	6.4	6.3	7.5	5.5	4.7
GDP deflator	8.2	9.2	8.4	7.3	5.4
Consumer price inflation[1]	8.9	10.4	7.1	9.3	6.0
Employment	2.2	3.4	1.3	1.4	3.5
Unemployment (percent)	2.6	3.8	1.6	2.2	2.8
Nominal wages	10.2	11.4	10.1	9.9	6.3
Real wages	1.2	0.6	2.9	0.4	0.4
Labor productivity	4.1	2.8	6.1	4.1	1.2
Unit labor costs	6.0	8.4	3.8	5.6	5.1
Nominal effective exchange rate	−1.4	−2.2	−4.0	1.1	3.5
Real effective exchange rate	2.1	1.3	−0.9	5.3	5.9
Per capita nominal GDP, in U.S. dollars[2]	...	5,630	7,250	14,950	24,520

Sources: Census and Statistics Department, Estimates of Gross Domestic Product, 1961 to 1996, and Monthly Digest of Statistics (various editions); IMF, Information Notice System; and IMF staff estimates.

[1]Based on consumer price index (A), which is based on expenditure patterns of about 50 percent of households.

[2]Data shown are as of 1980, 1986, 1991, and 1996.

Kong to move away from its entrepôt role and develop its own manufacturing industries. Hong Kong began to specialize in the production of labor-intensive consumer goods, drawing on an abundant supply of inexpensive labor and the entrepreneurial skills of its own merchants and industrialists, who arrived from Shanghai and other areas of mainland China.

By the time China changed course at the end of 1978 to adopt the policies of economic reform and greater openness, Hong Kong had developed a large, internationally competitive manufacturing sector, which began to look for production bases abroad. Hong Kong manufacturers were thus quick to take advantage of the resources across the border, where labor costs were initially up to 15 times lower, and land and facility costs up to 10 times lower, than in the territory. Over the next 15 years, the expansion of outprocessing operations, as well as the sustained rapid increase in China's export activity, boosted the development of supporting service industries in Hong Kong and resulted in a dramatic structural shift of the economy. The manufacturing sector's share declined from about one-fourth of GDP in 1980 to less than 9 percent in 1995, while the combined share of services rose from two-thirds of GDP to about 85 percent (Figure 1). The change in the structure of employment was even more dramatic: employment in manufacturing fell from 41 percent of total employment in 1980, to 13 percent in 1995, while the share of four key service sectors rose from 37 percent of the total in 1980 to 63 percent in 1995 (Figure 2).

The turning point in this process appears to have occurred around 1988. The emergence of competitors in the region put downward pressure on prices in manufacturing industries in which Hong Kong previously enjoyed a comparative advantage (see Section V). Until 1987, adjustments in manufacturing wages relative to productivity increases were moderate, allowing home-grown industries to maintain competitiveness and their share in GDP:

	1980–95	1980–87	1988–95
	(In percent of GDP)		
Change in sectoral share of GDP			
Manufacturing	−14.9	−1.7	−11.7
Utilities	1.0	1.3	0.0
Construction	−1.7	−2.0	0.2
Trade and tourism[1]	6.0	2.9	2.3
Transportation and communications	2.4	1.2	0.7
Financing, real estate, and business services	1.9	−5.1	6.0
Of which: Banks	2.6	−0.6	3.1
Community, social, and personal services	5.0	2.4	3.2

[1]Includes wholesale, retail, import/export trades, restaurants and hotels.

However, forces unleashed by the opening of China's economy and the expansion of low-cost labor-intensive manufacturing elsewhere in the region resulted in a secular decline in the relative price of manufacturing goods that the factor markets in Hong Kong could not accommodate. At the same time, the advantages of Hong Kong's location gained new significance as regional trade expanded and the demand for the provision of trade, business, and financial services to China increased.

A remarkable aspect of Hong Kong's structural transformation is that it took place without disruption in the pace of economic activity or a significant pickup in unemployment. Indeed, growth of real GDP remained strong throughout the period, and more than 700,000 jobs were created in service industries since 1988, offsetting the loss of nearly half a million manufacturing jobs. Labor productivity growth averaged close to 4½ percent a year during the 1980s. Even in the 1990s, as Hong Kong became an increasingly services-based economy, productivity gains have averaged almost 4 percent annually. Estimates of total factor productivity growth in Hong Kong during the 1980s range from 1¾ percent a year (Young (1995)) to 4½ percent (Hawkins (1995)), well above the pace experienced in most OECD countries over the same period.

During the process of structural change, Hong Kong has grown to become an important international financial center. As of early 1997, over 500 banking institutions were present in Hong Kong, including 82 of the 100 largest banks in the world. The external assets held by banks and deposit-taking institutions exceeded US$600 billion, making Hong Kong the fifth largest banking center in the world. Over 70 percent of banking business is denominated in foreign currencies, and Hong Kong ranks fifth in the world in terms of foreign exchange market turnover. Hong Kong's stock market is the seventh largest in the world and second largest in Asia in terms of market capitalization.

Given the openness and external linkages of Hong Kong's economy, the future pace of structural transformation will depend to a large extent on developments in China and the global economic environment. However, it is safe to predict that the process as a whole will continue. Despite increasing regional competition in providing international business services, it seems most unlikely that a possible fall in the relative price of such services would trigger a shift in comparative advantage in Hong Kong back toward the manufacturing sector.

Figure 1. Output By Sector
(In percent of GDP)

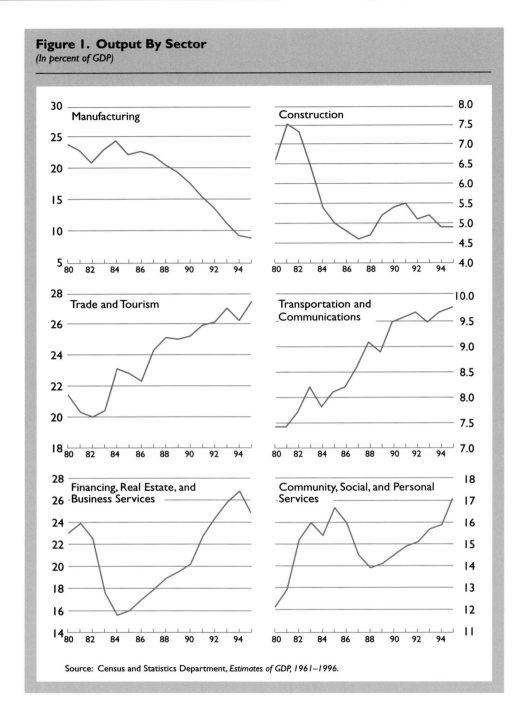

Source: Census and Statistics Department, *Estimates of GDP, 1961–1996.*

Economic Integration of Hong Kong and China

The economies of Hong Kong and southern China have been closely linked throughout history via trade and movements of people. China has traditionally supplied most of Hong Kong's food and water, and Hong Kong has traditionally served as China's main port. Since 1978, the links between the two economies have been extended to production, investment, provision of services, and financial relations (Figure 3). At the same time, Hong Kong's economic links with other countries in East Asia also have been strengthening rapidly.

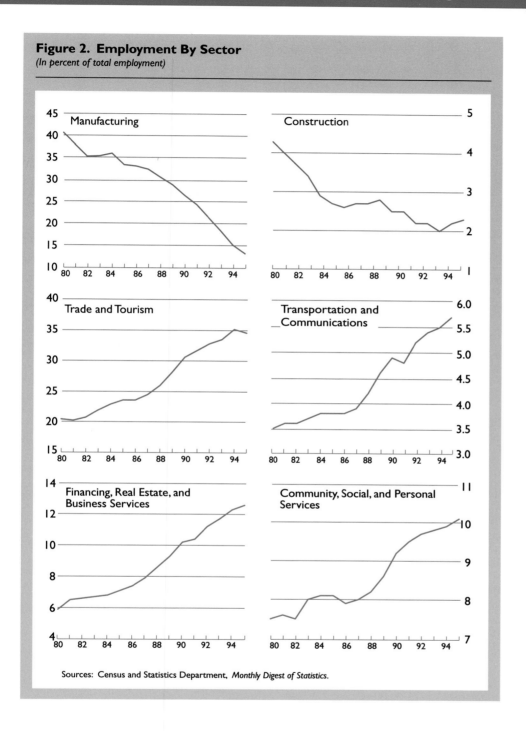

Figure 2. Employment By Sector
(In percent of total employment)

Sources: Census and Statistics Department, *Monthly Digest of Statistics*.

Trade Links

China is Hong Kong's largest trading partner and Hong Kong is China's third largest. In 1996, China purchased one-third of Hong Kong's total exports and provided 37 percent of its imports. Hong Kong, in turn, was the destination for one-fifth of China's exports and the source of 6 percent of its imports.

The trade flows between Hong Kong and China are complex. About one-half of Hong Kong's total exports to China are the inputs to outprocessing activities by Hong Kong firms in China, and three fourths of Hong Kong's imports from China are the outputs of these operations, which are subsequently reexported by Hong Kong to the rest of the world, particularly the United States, Japan, and the European Union:[2]

	(In percent)		
	Share in Total	Consumed in China	Used in Outprocessing Plants
Exports to China			
Domestic exports to China	14	29	71
Reexports to China	86	55	45

	Share in Total	Output of Outprocessing Plants	China's Domestic Exports
Imports from China			
Retained imports from China	7	...	...
Reexports of China origin	93	82	18

These reexports incorporate a wide range of service inputs (transportation, insurance, financial and business services) and ancillary production processes (design, pricing, quality control, packaging) added by Hong Kong firms, equivalent on average to 16–17 percent of GDP.

Adding to the complexity of trade links between Hong Kong and China is the growing importance of transhipments—goods transported from China to their final destination under a single bill of lading.[3] Transhipment cargoes increased from 4 million metric tons in 1991 to over 9 million metric tons in 1995, and there are indications that they may be replacing some reexport trade. While transhipments involve a lower degree of value added than reexports, they still generate value added in the transportation, communication, and banking sectors, which is captured in Hong Kong's services trade statistics. With a gradual streamlining of shipment procedures and improvement in operation of port facilities in China, the shift from reexport trade to such offshore trading is expected to continue.

Production and Investment Links

Outprocessing activities by Hong Kong manufacturers in China involve contracting with firms in China to produce semimanufactures or finished manufactured goods that are subsequently imported into Hong Kong for reexport to third markets. Initially, these activities were confined to special economic zones in southern China. As the Chinese authorities have opened up cities and whole economic regions to

Figure 3. Economic and Financial Integration Between Hong Kong and China

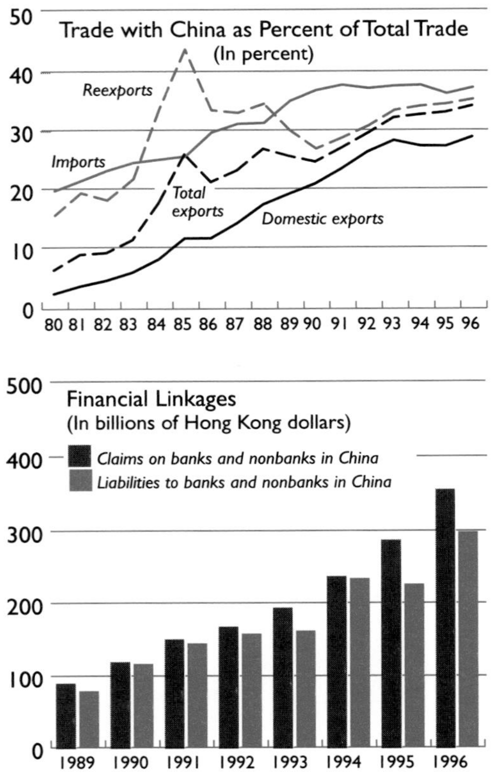

Sources: Census and Statistics Department, *Monthly Digest of Statistics;* and HKMA, *Monthly Statistical Bulletin.*

foreign trade and investment, the location of Hong Kong's outprocessing activities has moved to other parts of China. It is estimated that, by the end of 1991, Hong Kong firms operated about 14,000 foreign-funded enterprises, which employed about 3 million workers, in Guangdong Province alone (OECD (1993)). Inputs into outprocessing activities in China were valued at US$29 billion in 1996; the output of outprocessing plants amounted to US$59 billion; and reexports of these goods from Hong Kong to third countries were valued at US$71 billion.

The pace of relocation of manufacturing industries from Hong Kong appears to have peaked in the early 1990s, in part because of rising wages in southern China.[4] However, Hong Kong manufacturers have

---

[2]Some exports from southern China to Hong Kong are reexported back to other regions of the mainland.

[3]Reexports enter Hong Kong under one bill of lading and leave with another one, identifying Hong Kong as a transfer point.

---

[4]The wage differential between southern China and Hong Kong is presently estimated at 1:5.

started relocating higher-value-added and more complex production processes, expanding their existing facilities in southern China, and moving lower-value-added processes to northern and western provinces where costs of labor and land are still low.

A new pattern of economic integration—outsourcing of services to China—has emerged in recent years. Outsourcing, which involves contracting with firms in China to provide noncore services traditionally provided internally, has so far been limited to such labor-intensive activities as data processing, financial back-office operations, and printing. Nevertheless, the potential for expansion of outsourcing in Hong Kong's services-based economy is large, and this has raised some concerns about competitiveness of services industries.

The total number of Chinese firms operating in Hong Kong is estimated at about 2,000. Chinese firms have mostly been active in Hong Kong's trade and retail sectors.

Hong Kong has been the source of almost 60 percent of inward foreign direct investment in China since 1979. In 1995, such investment realized by Hong Kong firms in China was estimated at US$20 billion, bringing the cumulative total to US$80 billion. China was, in turn, the second largest external direct investor in Hong Kong, with a cumulative total reaching US$14 billion by the end of 1995.

Financial Integration

As a result of close production and trade linkages between Hong Kong and China, financial business between the mainland and Hong Kong has increased rapidly over the past decade. One visible aspect of these linkages has been the use of Hong Kong currency in China: it is estimated that about one-fourth of total Hong Kong dollar currency issued circulates in southern China. The amount of renminbi in circulation in Hong Kong is very small, but the Chinese currency can be exchanged easily.

Banks in Hong Kong conduct extensive and rapidly growing banking business with China from their offices in Hong Kong. At the end of 1996, liabilities of banks in Hong Kong to banks in China amounted to HK$287 billion (US$37 billion), with an equivalent in claims of banks in Hong Kong on banks in China. Hong Kong dollar deposits of Chinese banks comprise more than half of all such deposits by foreign banks in Hong Kong, while Hong Kong dollar claims on Chinese banks comprise about 35 percent of such claims by Hong Kong banks on foreign banks. Hong Kong banks operate a network of over 50 branches and representative offices in China; at the same time 35 Chinese banks had operations in Hong Kong in 1996. Unlike other locally incorporated but foreign-owned banks,

which are primarily active in the offshore bank market (notably in external interbank activity and syndicated lending), Chinese banks, including the Bank of China and its "12 sisters," are engaged mainly in retail banking, and hold 29 percent of the Hong Kong dollar deposits and 16 percent of the foreign currency deposits of all banks in Hong Kong. In 1994, the Bank of China became Hong Kong's third note-issuing bank, and presently issues about 14 percent of Hong Kong dollar banknotes.

The rapid growth of China's economy in the 1990s and its underdeveloped domestic capital markets have prompted Chinese enterprises to seek capital abroad. Initially, some Chinese enterprises entered the Hong Kong stock market by purchasing listed Hong Kong companies and using them as shell companies to raise equity finance in Hong Kong. In 1993, Chinese companies issued H shares for the first time on the stock exchange of Hong Kong.[5] In addition to the 28 enterprises that issued H shares, it is estimated that about one-fourth of companies listed on the stock exchange are closely related to China in terms of ownership, location of operations, or origin of their profits. Listing on the stock exchange exposes Chinese premier state-owned enterprises to international competition, and at the same time raises the international profile of the stock exchange, allowing it to diversify into industrial stocks and thus reducing the weight of property and financial sectors in its market capitalization.

Hong Kong's links with other economies in the East Asia region are also strong.[6] The region accounted, on average, for 28 percent of Hong Kong's total trade over 1990–96 (20 percent of domestic exports, 17 percent of reexports, and 38 percent of imports). In addition, more than a third of Hong Kong trading companies are now engaged in offshore trade, most of it arranged by Hong Kong trading companies among countries in Asia:

	1988	1991	1995
Origin of exports handled by Hong Kong trading companies, in percent			
Made in Hong Kong	35.8	22.1	11.2
Made in China	35.8	57.6	58.7
Made in third countries	28.4	20.3	30.1

Source: Hong Kong Trade Development Council.

[5]H share companies are companies incorporated in the People's Republic of China and have been nominated for listing in Hong Kong by the Chinese government. Since the listing of the first H share company in July 1993, there have been 28 H share companies listed on the Stock Exchange to date, raising a total of HK$39 billion at launch.

[6]The East Asia region is defined here to include Indonesia, Japan, Malaysia, the Philippines, Singapore, South Korea, Taiwan Province of China, and Thailand.

Hong Kong has been one of the principal sources of foreign direct investment in a number of East Asian economies, including Indonesia, Taiwan Province of China and the Philippines (third largest), and Singapore (fourth largest). Reciprocally, Japan, Singapore, and South Korea have been among the top ten foreign investors in Hong Kong. The trend of increasing economic liberalization and deregulation in the region is expected to provide further impetus to regional economic integration.

Patterns of Growth

Since the mid-1980s, growth in Hong Kong has evolved through different phases: export-led growth (from 1986 to 1988), which ended in a brief recession in 1989; domestic demand-driven growth (from 1990 through the first half of 1994); and consolidation (from the second half of 1994 through the first half of 1996). The economy began to recover in the second half of 1996 with revival of consumer confidence, increased private sector investment, and improved investor sentiment in asset markets. These positive developments are expected to broaden and strengthen further during 1997.

The period 1986–88 was one of the most successful in Hong Kong's economic history. Real GDP grew by over 10 percent per year, and merchandise exports and trade-related services industries expanded by 25–30 percent per year. The main impetus to this strong expansion came from the rapid real depreciation of the Hong Kong dollar along with the U.S. dollar in the mid-1980s. Low domestic inflation and moderate wage increases kept business costs low, while expanding employment led to strong consumption growth. This growth stage ended in mid-1989, when the labor market tightened considerably owing to large-scale emigration of skilled workers and professionals, and inflation rose to double-digit levels. At the same time, the Hong Kong dollar began to appreciate rapidly in real terms.

The 1989 recession, however, was short lived. Growth resumed in mid-1990, and for the next four years it averaged about 5¼ percent a year. Unlike the 1980s, the early 1990s were a period of domestic demand-led growth:

	1986–89	1990–94[1]	1994–96[2]
	(Average of annual percentage changes)		
Real GDP growth	8.5	5.5	4.7
Domestic demand	6.7	8.0	6.3
External sector	1.9	–2.5	–1.6

[1]Through the first half of 1994.
[2]From the second half of 1994.

Rising real wages and negative real interest rates boosted private consumption, while the government started a massive program of infrastructure development. Robust domestic demand led to rapid increases in imports and a widening of the merchandise trade deficit. The external sector's contribution to real growth thus became negative despite relatively strong export growth during this period.

The acceleration in economic activity was accompanied by substantial gains in asset prices: stock prices more than doubled through 1993, while property prices rose by about 40 percent on average between the end of 1992 and early 1994. A key factor underlying these developments was increased optimism among domestic and international investors regarding long-term growth prospects for Hong Kong and the southern China region. In 1993 and early 1994, the initial public offerings of Chinese companies' shares on the Hong Kong stock exchange were typically several hundred times oversubscribed, investment income from outprocessing operations in China flowed into the residential property market, and multinational companies vied to establish their presence in Hong Kong.

Successive increases in U.S. interest rates in 1994 and early 1995 and a reassessment by investors of the fundamentals in China and Asian markets in general led to a prolonged consolidation in Hong Kong's asset markets. Higher interest rates, falling property prices, and rising unemployment weakened household confidence and dampened spending, which barely increased in 1995. As a result, real GDP growth decelerated steadily from over 6 percent in 1993 to 4 percent in the first half of 1996. During the second half of 1996, however, investor and consumer confidence improved, and by the end of the year real GDP resumed growth at an annual rate of about 5½ percent per year.

Fluctuations in Aggregate Output

Figure 4 illustrates the growth of actual and potential output in Hong Kong since the late 1970s. Growth rates of potential output have declined steadily, from over 8½ percent in the late 1970s to about 5–5½ percent in 1996.[7] Hong Kong experienced three business cycles over this period. The amplitudes of the first two cycles were large, with output gaps of up to 5½ percent of potential GDP

_____
[7]Potential output was estimated by applying the Hodrick-Prescott filter to annual GDP data in constant prices over 1961–96. The estimated current growth rate of potential GDP is sensitive to the endpoints of the data series, and is hence given as a range rather than a point estimate.

Figure 4. Business Cycles

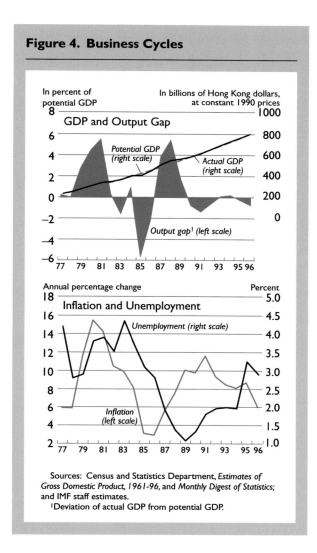

In percent of
potential GDP

In billions of Hong Kong dollars,
at constant 1990 prices

GDP and Output Gap

Potential GDP
(right scale)

Actual GDP
(right scale)

Output gap¹ (left scale)

Annual percentage change

Percent

Inflation and Unemployment

Unemployment (right scale)

Inflation
(left scale)

Sources: Census and Statistics Department, *Estimates of Gross Domestic Product, 1961-96*, and *Monthly Digest of Statistics*; and IMF staff estimates.
¹Deviation of actual GDP from potential GDP.

Table 2. Business Cycles in Hong Kong
(In percent of potential GDP)

	Cycle 1		Cycle 2		Cycle 3	
	Year	Output gap¹	Year	Output gap¹	Year	Output gap¹
Duration	1978–85	...	1985–91	...	1991–96	...
Peak	1981	5.3	1988	5.2	1994	0.1
Trough	1985	–5.4	1991	–1.3	1996	–1.1

Source: IMF staff estimates.
¹Deviation of actual GDP from potential GDP, in constant 1990 prices.

consumer prices rose steadily in the late 1980s (Figure 4, lower panel). Following the 1989 recession, however, the unemployment rate stayed low and inflation continued to rise although the output gap became negative. The tightness in the labor market mainly reflected labor shortages induced by large-scale emigration of Hong Kong residents. Labor market conditions remained tight until 1995, when employment growth slowed and the labor supply improved owing to increased immigration. Since then, wages and domestic inflation have been moving once again in line with the output gap.

Hong Kong's business cycle has become more synchronized with that of China over the years (Figure 5). Until the mid-1980s, the correlation between the output gaps in Hong Kong and China was negative, suggesting that different factors were driving growth in their economies at the time (Table 3). In the second half of the 1980s, however, as Hong Kong's manufacturing sector became more integrated with that of southern China, Hong Kong began to follow China's business cycle more closely, especially after 1987. Broadening and deepening of economic integration since 1991 led to further synchronization of the two economies' business cycles. However, structural change in Hong Kong's economy—that is, the shift toward a services-based economy, which is less prone to large output fluctuations—has dampened the amplitude of the business cycle in Hong Kong relative to China. The correlation between business cycles in Hong Kong and the United States also increased in the second half of the 1980s, though, since 1991, the two cycles have become slightly less synchronized (Table 3).

The relationships between the business cycles of Hong Kong, China, and the United States have im-

(Table 2). The most recent cycle started in 1991, peaked in 1994, and bottomed out in mid-1996. Unlike the previous cycles, the 1991–96 cycle was relatively shallow, as actual GDP fell only about 1 percent below its estimated potential. However, as the most recent downturn was relatively long (from mid-1994 to mid-1996), the *level* of actual output was still slightly below the level of potential output at the end of 1996.

Movements in other indicators of the cyclical position of the economy, such as the unemployment rate and inflation, have been broadly consistent with movements in the output gap. Rapid economic expansion in the second half of the 1980s brought the economy to a very high level of resource utilization. As labor market conditions tightened progressively, the unemployment rate fell from 3–4 percent in the first half of the decade to an average of less than 1¼ percent in 1989–90. As a result, wages and

Figure 5. Business Cycles in Hong Kong, China, and the United States

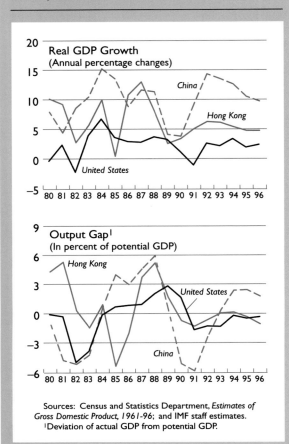

Sources: Census and Statistics Department, *Estimates of Gross Domestic Product, 1961-96*; and IMF staff estimates.
[1] Deviation of actual GDP from potential GDP.

Table 3. Hong Kong: Interactions with Business Cycles in China and the United States

	1978–85	1985–91	1991–96
Correlation between the output gaps			
Hong Kong–China	–0.51	0.07	0.63
Hong Kong–United States	0.13	0.43	0.34
China–United States	0.67	0.75	0.88
Standard deviation of the output gap			
Hong Kong	3.17	3.36	0.54
China	2.99	3.92	3.02
United States	2.61	1.31	0.57

Source: IMF staff estimates.

plications for macroeconomic conditions in Hong Kong. In particular, while economic activity in Hong Kong is often affected by cycles in China, monetary conditions are largely determined by those in the United States via the linked exchange rate system. Thus, the decline in U.S. interest rates in 1990–93 occurred at a time when Hong Kong's economy was in an expansionary phase of the business cycle and experiencing tight labor market conditions and accelerating inflation, so that interest rates became negative in real terms. In such an environment, consumption expanded strongly and households shifted their asset portfolios from financial savings toward properties and stocks, fueling asset price inflation. The occasional lack of synchrony between monetary conditions and the business cycle is, however, an acceptable tradeoff in view of the much larger benefits of the link as a confidence-enhancing anchor for financial policies, and given that factor markets in Hong Kong historically have adjusted rapidly to changing cyclical conditions. In the above case, for example, pressures to reduce costs and restore competitiveness increased substantially in many Hong Kong industries by early 1994. As a result, wages and asset prices began to decline in mid-1994. The concurrent increase in U.S. interest rates helped speed up these adjustments.

III   Adjustment in the Mid-1990s

Hong Kong's economy has shown a high degree of resilience over the past few years. The asset markets consolidated during 1994–95 and subsequently recovered in 1996, while the external sector responded to swings in real exchange rates and a slowdown in regional trade. Factor markets adjusted flexibly to changing economic circumstances and thus created macroeconomic conditions conducive to the smooth transfer of sovereignty. Against the background of these adjustments, Hong Kong's economy continued to grow at a reasonably rapid rate. This section analyzes the key developments in asset markets, the labor market, product markets, and the external sector that characterized this successful adjustment episode. The description focuses on the role played by relative prices, interest rates, and the real exchange rate in conditioning the behavior of households and firms during this period.

Why Adjustment Was Needed

The adjustment in the mid-1990s came on the heels of a boom in domestic demand, reexports, and asset markets that began in mid-1990 and peaked during the first quarter of 1994. This boom was largely unexpected at the beginning of the decade. At that time, the outlook for the Hong Kong economy was thought to be bleak, given the large-scale emigration of skilled workers and professionals, and uncertainties about the future course of economic reforms in China following the events of 1989. Despite these factors, however, economic activity revived in 1991, supported by a substantial boost to confidence from the Sino-British agreement reached in July on the building of a large new international airport in Hong Kong. As Hong Kong's exports picked up and investments in China strengthened, growth in private consumption and activity in asset markets accelerated.

The expansion quickly ran into a labor market constraint, however. Owing to demographic trends, a tightening of restrictions on the admission of unskilled workers from China, and increased emigra-

tion, the labor force generally recorded negative growth over 1989–92. In addition, the labor force participation rate declined, partly reflecting increased opportunities for tertiary education. To cope with the resulting labor shortage, the government introduced several labor importation schemes in the early 1990s. Nevertheless, labor market conditions remained tight through early 1994, exerting strong upward pressure on wages and, hence, prices, especially in the nontradable service sectors.

As noted in Section II, these developments coincided with cuts in U.S. interest rates, which had added to pressures in consumer demand and asset markets during the early 1990s. In addition, global fund managers rerated the Hong Kong stock market in mid-1993, leading to a surge in institutional buying, while the demand for property strengthened. By early 1994, these pressures had built to such a degree that they began seriously to affect competitiveness of Hong Kong's services industries.

Consolidation in Asset Markets

After peaking in January 1994, stock prices fell by 40 percent by January 1995 (Figure 6). The decline in stock prices was part of a global phenomenon triggered by the tightening of U.S. monetary policy in early 1994.[8] However, the correction in a large measure also reflected concerns about the impact of China's economic stabilization plan, which led many overseas investors to pull out from the Hong Kong stock market, while large Chinese enterprises suddenly short of liquidity began to sell off their Hong Kong assets. Closer to Hong Kong, there were concerns about the profit outlook of its property companies, which account for a large share of the stock market capitalization.

---

[8]IMF staff estimates suggest that movements in real interest rates in Hong Kong have a significant negative effect on real equity prices both in the short and long runs (see Chapter V in IMF (1996)).

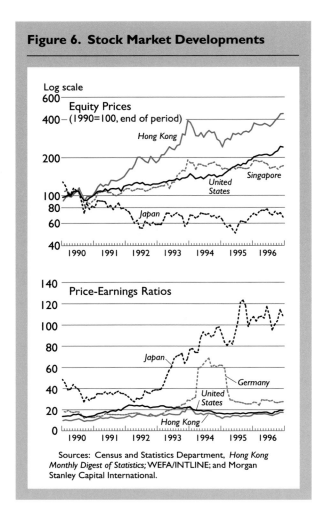

Figure 6. Stock Market Developments

Sources: Census and Statistics Department, *Hong Kong Monthly Digest of Statistics*; WEFA/INTLINE; and Morgan Stanley Capital International.

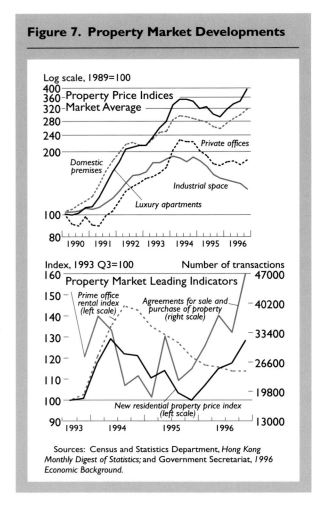

Figure 7. Property Market Developments

Sources: Census and Statistics Department, *Hong Kong Monthly Digest of Statistics*; and Government Secretariat, *1996 Economic Background.*

The property market began to consolidate about four months later, after peaking in April 1994. During the first quarter of 1994 alone, apartment prices rose by 33 percent on average, and 60 percent in the case of luxury apartments (Figure 7). Although the rally in property prices was not surprising given the prevailing demand and supply conditions—the underlying demand for properties from end-users, including overseas companies, was very strong, and the supply of new apartments and prime office space had declined over the previous two years—speculation was rampant and there were growing concerns about a property bubble. In response, the government took measures to curb speculation and increase the supply of land and public housing.[9] These measures, together with rising interest rates, led to a shift in market sentiment. During the second half of 1994

residential property prices began to decline and prices of office property leveled off. By the end of 1995, residential property prices fell by 20 percent, and prices of office property by 25 percent on average from their peak levels recorded in early 1994. The decline in property prices quickly spilled over into private residential construction and the real estate developers' margins—which on average account for over 10 percent of GDP—and began to affect overall growth.

Adjustment in Product and Factor Markets

Product and factor markets adjusted more slowly than the asset markets. Private consumption slowed gradually during the second half of 1994 and stayed flat during 1995 in response to rising real interest rates and falling wages (Figure 8). On the supply side, manufacturing firms maintained competitive-

---

[9]The measures were announced in April 1994 and adopted in June 1994; see Section IV.

Figure 8. Developments in GDP

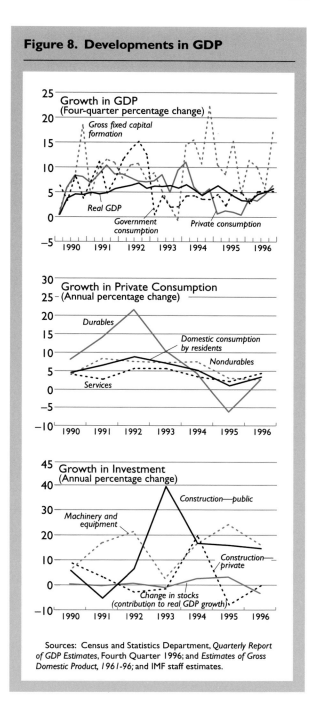

Sources: Census and Statistics Department, *Quarterly Report of GDP Estimates,* Fourth Quarter 1996; and *Estimates of Gross Domestic Product, 1961–96;* and IMF staff estimates.

ness in the face of rising costs during 1994–95 by accelerating relocation of their operations to low-cost production bases in southern China. Service firms, for which such options were more limited, initially responded to rising labor and property costs by trying to restrain price increases and temporarily absorb higher costs. These adjustments led to continued growth in business but falling profit margins.

During 1994–95, many service firms therefore stepped up investment in labor-saving capital equipment, the price of which was growing more slowly relative to wages, and began to reduce employment. Some overseas companies relocated offices to Singapore and Shanghai, as rents for prime office space in Hong Kong were among the highest in the world at the height of the boom in mid-1994 (about US$120 per square meter per month), raising concerns about Hong Kong's competitiveness. The cumulative effect of these adjustments was soon felt at the macroeconomic level.

- Imports of capital goods surged at double-digit growth rates during 1994–95 and—along with massive imports of raw materials and equipment for the new airport—were a major factor behind the sharp deterioration in the merchandise trade deficit from 3¼ percent of GDP in 1993, to 14 percent of GDP in 1995 (Figure 9).
- In the labor market, growth in employment slowed significantly in 1995 (Figure 10). In addition, labor supply was rising strongly from early 1994 through 1995, reflecting a substantial return of professionals who had earlier emigrated (Box 2). As a result, real wages were pushed down by over 3 percent between March 1994 and September 1995.
- The fall in real incomes and the swing in real interest rates (from about –2 percent at the end of 1993 to 2½ percent in 1996) slowed dramatically the growth rate of private consumption (see Appendix I).[10] As a result, the contribution of private consumption to real GDP growth fell from an average of 4½ percent per year over mid-1991 to mid-1994, to just ½ percent during 1995.

The unemployment rate peaked during the third quarter of 1995 at 3¾ percent—a level not recorded since the bursting of the asset bubble in the early 1980s. The fall in demand for low-skilled service jobs and the skill mismatches between the unemployed and job vacancies were interpreted by some observers as a structural phenomenon, leading to calls on the government to reexamine its noninterventionist labor market policies (see Section IV). Job uncertainty suddenly became a major issue for workers and professionals used to changing jobs every two years or so. Consumer confidence was profoundly affected. The volume of retail sales fell consistently for 12 months beginning with February 1995. Private consumption expendi-

---

[10]Real interest rates are measured as the Best Lending Rate less the realized (12-month) rate of CPI(A) inflation. Consumer price index (A), the most commonly used measure of inflation in Hong Kong, is based on the expenditure patterns of about 50 percent of households.

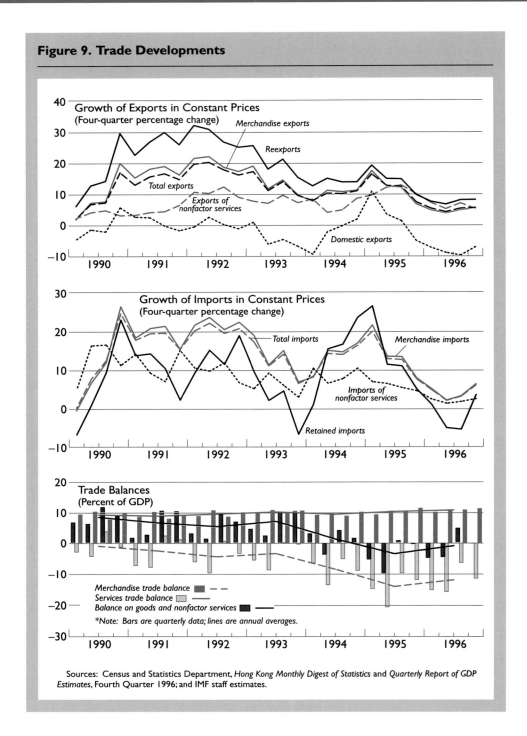

Figure 9. Trade Developments

Growth of Exports in Constant Prices
(Four-quarter percentage change)
Merchandise exports
Reexports
Total exports
Exports of nonfactor services
Domestic exports

Growth of Imports in Constant Prices
(Four-quarter percentage change)
Total imports
Merchandise imports
Imports of nonfactor services
Retained imports

Trade Balances
(Percent of GDP)
Merchandise trade balance
Services trade balance
Balance on goods and nonfactor services
*Note: Bars are quarterly data; lines are annual averages.

Sources: Census and Statistics Department, *Hong Kong Monthly Digest of Statistics* and *Quarterly Report of GDP Estimates*, Fourth Quarter 1996; and IMF staff estimates.

ture on durables was hit particularly hard, dropping by over 6 percent in 1995. This marked a major change in consumer sentiment compared with the early 1990s, when spending on durables grew at double-digit rates. An aggravating factor was the up-tick in inflation during 1995, which—although mainly due to external factors (the uptrend in world commodity prices, a weaker U.S. dollar, and relatively high inflation in China)—further depressed consumption.

Reflecting these developments, real GDP growth decelerated steadily from over 6 percent in 1993 to 3½ percent at the bottom of the cycle in the first quarter of 1996. Over this period, GDP growth was

Figure 10. Labor Market Developments

Sources: Census and Statistics Department, *Hong Kong Monthly Digest of Statistics.*

sustained by public infrastructure investment (especially in the new airport), private sector investment in machinery and equipment, and inventory accumulation, most of which was accounted for by inputs into public infrastructure projects. Growth in government consumption also accelerated in 1995–96 as the size of the civil service increased moderately following the reductions in the early 1990s and as expenditure on social programs increased in the

FY1995 and FY1996 budgets. The Airport Core Program is estimated to have contributed about 0.4 percentage points to growth of real GDP in 1995, and about 0.8 percentage points in 1996 according to official estimates. In addition, merchandise exports performed relatively well during 1994–95, and exports of services were robust throughout the mid-1990s.

Analysis of the overall balance of payments is constrained by lack of data on factor incomes and capital transactions; however, the decline in the trade balance for goods and nonfactor services—which, as noted above, was largely due to the acceleration in import growth for industry retooling and infrastructure construction—is likely to have been partly offset by increases in net factor income.

Recovery

In late 1995 and early 1996, there was a prevailing mood of pessimism and widespread concern about the possibility of a vicious circle emanating from Hong Kong's "feel-bad factor." There were, however, fundamentally healthy adjustments taking place in the real sector and asset markets. The extensive substitution of capital for labor, declining property prices, and the steep drop in real wages significantly relieved cost pressures in Hong Kong's service industries and helped restore their competitiveness.

As in the case of the downturn, the recovery began in the stock market. After bottoming out in January 1995, stock prices gained over a third in value by the end of 1995, as overseas investors returned to the market attracted by the low price/earnings ratios of Hong Kong stocks and improved macroeconomic conditions in China. During 1996, reflecting a global trend, stock prices continued to recover robustly and the Hang Seng Index began to set new records.

The office property market bottomed out in late 1995, when rents for prime office space became once again competitive with office rents in Singapore. In the residential property market, market sentiment shifted in early 1996, when the outlook for the labor market brightened and Hong Kong banks, following the reduction in U.S. interest rates, reduced their lending rates amidst intensifying competition in the mortgage market.[11] In response, the

[11]The average markup for mortgage rates declined from the previously customary level of 175 basis points above the Best Lending Rate to 50–75 basis points in February 1996. This decline helped to offset the impact of higher real interest rates, which rose in 1996 owing to declining inflation.

Box 2. Labor Supply in the Mid-1990s

Because of stable population growth, fluctuations in Hong Kong's labor supply traditionally are determined by migration flows. In 1995, when labor supply surged by 2½ percent, there was a sharp increase in the balance of arrivals and departures, resulting from a decline in emigration (from 61,600 persons in 1994 to 43,100 persons in 1995), and an increase in immigration (from 140,400 persons in 1994 to 156,100 persons in 1995). Almost two-thirds of the increase in immigration in recent years (close to 100,000 persons in 1995) is estimated to have been accounted for by returning Hong Kong residents and foreign professional workers. The other main groups of immigrants were Chinese citizens (28 percent of the total in 1995), and foreign domestic helpers (10 percent).[1]

The economic slowdown in 1995 did not affect the demand for labor in different segments of the labor market equally. The job market for professional workers in the services industries remained buoyant, so that returning Hong Kong residents and foreign professionals generally had few problems finding employment. However, the number of lower-end service jobs, especially in retail trade, restaurants, and entertainment, was reduced significantly, thus affecting the low-skilled workers released from the manufacturing sector and the Chinese immigrants who competed for such jobs.

[1]The daily quota for immigration from China was increased from 75 to 105 in January 1994, and further to 150 immigrants in July 1995. The recent Chinese immigrants were for the most part reuniting their families in Hong Kong. The immigration of domestic helpers peaked at about 20,000 in 1994, but declined by almost a quarter in 1995 (Siu (1996)).

Population and Employment

	Population Increase	Natural Increase	Net Migration	Labor Force Increase	Employment Increase
1993	110,400	41,000	69,400	64,100	62,500
	(1.9)	(0.7)	(1.0)	(2.3)	(2.3)
1994	121,300	42,500	78,800	72,600	72,700
	(2.0)	(0.7)	(1.3)	(2.5)	(2.6)
1995	150,700	37,700	113,000	71,700	32,300
	(2.5)	(0.6)	(1.9)	(2.4)	(1.1)

Source: Data provided by the Hong Kong authorities. Figures are based on results of the 1996 by-census.
Note: Numbers in parentheses represent annual percentage change.

residential property market staged a strong rebound, with apartment prices rising by 32 percent on average by end-1996. In late 1996, the market revived to such an extent that speculative activities once again became apparent, and the government, along with property developers, took measures in early 1997 to limit the price increases, which were especially pronounced at the luxury end of the market (see Section IV).

In the labor market, employment growth resumed at a brisk pace in early 1996, as the decline in real wages raised the demand for labor. Employment grew particularly strongly in the construction sector, but also revived in retail trade, personal services, and tourism, suggesting the onset of a broader-

based economic recovery led by domestic demand. At the same time, the labor force grew at a slower pace, and the labor force participation rate edged lower, as the more moderate wage growth reduced the incentive for part-time job seekers to join the workforce. Consumer confidence gradually strengthened and the volume of retail sales turned positive during the first quarter of 1996. Following robust employment growth during the second half of 1996 (at close to 4 percent, year-on-year), the unemployment rate slipped back to 2.6 percent, close to its long-run average. Meanwhile, real wages grew by 1.2 percent over the second half of 1996 (year-on-year), providing a boost to private consumption.

Figure 11. Price Developments

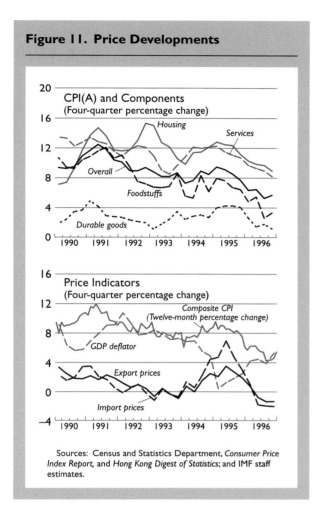

CPI(A) and Components
(Four-quarter percentage change)

Price Indicators
(Four-quarter percentage change)

Sources: Census and Statistics Department, *Consumer Price Index Report,* and *Hong Kong Digest of Statistics;* and IMF staff estimates.

In addition to private consumption, private construction also resumed growth at a relatively brisk pace in 1996. The completion of major works on the airport project freed up construction capacity for other infrastructure projects, while residential construction responded to the rally in the property market. Exports also strengthened during the second half of 1996 as external demand in China and overseas markets revived.

Inflationary pressures began to recede in the second half of 1995, when the Hong Kong dollar, along with the U.S. dollar, strengthened in nominal effective terms, the labor market slackened, and rents eased (Figure 11). This trend continued into early 1996, when weaker levels of demand were experienced throughout the economy. The rate of CPI(A) inflation for 1996 as a whole was 6 percent, compared with 8¾ percent in 1995. Lower inflation in China, resulting from successful implementation of macroeconomic adjustment measures and a rela-

tively good harvest, helped to alleviate pressure from food prices, usually the most dynamic component of Hong Kong's CPI. In addition, retained imports prices fell by 3 percent in 1996, compared with an increase of 7 percent in 1995.

External Sector and the Real Exchange Rate

While the asset markets were adjusting to rising interest rates, and factor and product markets to changes in relative prices of capital and labor, the external sector was responding to large swings in the real exchange rate of the Hong Kong dollar. From early 1994 to mid-1995, following the depreciation of the U.S. dollar against other major currencies, the Hong Kong dollar gradually depreciated by 9 percent in real effective terms. In addition, external demand—unlike domestic demand—strengthened during this period. As a result, total exports responded robustly: total merchandise exports grew by 11 percent per year during 1994–95, and even domestic exports revived noticeably in 1995 for the first time since 1988 (Figure 9 and Box 3).

From mid-1995 to end-1996, however, reflecting the strengthening of the U.S. dollar, the real effective exchange rate of the Hong Kong dollar appreciated by 13½ percent. This reversal in the real exchange rate trend coincided with a weakening of external demand. Exports declined in 1996 throughout much of Asia, including China. As Hong Kong's own export performance in a large measure depends—through reexports and outprocessing activities on the mainland—on China's exports, the impact on Hong Kong's external sector was almost immediate: growth in reexports was halved to 7½ percent for the year as a whole, while domestic exports fell by over 8 percent. Meanwhile, imports also slowed significantly in 1996, reflecting an adjustment to the large inventory buildup in 1995, tapering off of import demand for airport construction, and a deceleration in reexport trade. As a result, the balance on goods and nonfactor services improved by 2½ percent of GDP during 1996 to a deficit of 1 percent of GDP.

Conclusion

The adjustment experience of the mid-1990s confirmed that markets in Hong Kong respond flexibly and quickly to changes in relative prices and demand and supply conditions. The decline in real wages and property prices and the upgrading

Box 3. Determinants of the Trade Balance

Hong Kong's external trade developments have been largely determined by domestic and external demand and relative price factors (i.e., the real exchange rate). Estimates of the export supply function indicate that a 1 percent increase in the relative price of Hong Kong's exports leads to a ½ percent fall in export volume, while a 1 percent rise in foreign demand generates a 0.9 percent increase in exports.[1] With regard to import demand, the estimates indicate that a 1 percent rise in the relative price of imports leads to a fall in imports by 0.45 percent, while a 1 percent rise in domestic demand implies a 1.05 percent increase in import volume.[2] These estimates support the view that imports were buoyed in the early 1990s by rising real incomes, negative real interest rates, and an ambitious program of public infrastructure development. On the other hand, swings in relative prices and external demand explain the relative strength of exports in 1995 and their disappointing performance in 1996.

The impact of the real exchange rate, foreign activity, and domestic demand on the trade balance was also estimated using the following single equation model:[3]

$$TBY_t = 0.50 \ TBY_{t-1} - 0.23 \log (RER_{t-1}) +$$
$$(2.47) \qquad (-2.28)$$

$$0.15 \log (IMW_t) - 0.16 \log (DD_t) + 2.51,$$
$$(1.54) \qquad (-1.32) \qquad (2.01)$$

$$\overline{R}^2 = 0.73, \ SEE = 0.03, \ DW = 1.32,$$

where: TBY = net exports of goods and nonfactor services (expressed as a ratio to GDP)

RER = CPI-based real effective exchange rate of the Hong Kong dollar

IMW = weighted average of partner countries' import volumes using Hong Kong's export weights

DD = total real domestic demand.

The estimated parameters indicate that a 1 percent appreciation in the real effective exchange rate of the Hong Kong dollar leads to a fall in the external balance of about 0.23 percent of GDP in the short run (with a 1 year lag), and about 0.46 percent of GDP in the long run. The estimated impact of foreign and domestic demand on the external balance is almost equal in size: in the short run, a 1 percent rise in the import volumes of trading partners raises the external balance by 0.15 percent of GDP, whereas a 1 percent rise in domestic demand lowers the external balance by 0.16 percent of GDP.

Simulations based on a simple macroeconometric model suggest that, for the external position to stabilize under the assumption of domestic demand converging to the growth rate of potential output, real exchange rate appreciation would need to slow to the long-run average of around 2 percent per year over time. Under the linked exchange rate, this would require that inflation decline to a 4½–5 percent annual rate. While this rate of inflation would still exceed that in trading partners' countries, currently projected at about 3 percent, Hong Kong's external competitiveness would not deteriorate provided that, relative to partner countries, Hong Kong's tradable industries maintain the high long-term productivity differential with respect to nontradable industries (see Section V).

---

[1]See Appendix I. Exports were defined to include domestic exports, net reexports (i.e., reexports less nonretained imports), and exports of services.

[2]Imports were defined to include retained imports and imports of services.

[3]Estimates were made using the OLS on the annual data from 1979 to 1996.

---

of office and production technology enabled firms to reduce excessive costs and maintain competitiveness. Labor productivity thus grew by over 3 percent in 1995 and 1996 and profits recovered quickly. These developments created favorable conditions for lower domestic inflation and resumption of growth in the runup to the transfer of sovereignty.

IV   Macroeconomic Policy Framework

Since its settlement as an economic entity in 1842, the basic approach of the Hong Kong government has been to foster trade, industry, and commerce, and to leave legitimate business to operate at a profit without government interference. In line with this view, the government has adopted a policy of "positive noninterventionism" as a cornerstone of its involvement in the economy. This policy holds that the primary role of government is to provide the necessary infrastructure and a stable legal and administrative framework conducive to growth and development. A former Financial Secretary explained it (Haddon-Cave (1982)).

> Positive non-interventionism involves taking the view that it is normally futile and damaging to the growth of an economy, particularly of an externally oriented economy, for a government to attempt to plan the allocation of resources available to the private sector and to frustrate the operation of market forces, no matter how uncomfortable may be their short term consequences. The implications of the adjective 'positive' are important: when faced with an interventionist proposal, the Hong Kong Government does not simply respond that such a proposal must, by definition, be incorrect. . . . in all cases, decisions are made positively, and not by default, and only after the immediate benefits and costs are weighed against the medium and longer term implications of the interventionist acts proposed (including the inevitable difficulties of unwinding them).

In adhering to this view, the government has maintained over time a coherent set of fiscal, monetary, and regulatory policies that has helped preserve the predominance of the private sector and the flexibility of the cost-price structure. Fiscal policy has traditionally followed a prudent approach, aimed at maintaining a small government and fostering a flexible and competitive private sector. Budgets have been kept broadly neutral and have not been used to moderate cyclical swings. This prudent approach was also followed in the budget for FY1997/98, which straddles the transition to Chinese sovereignty.

Since 1983, the primary objective of monetary and exchange rate policies has been to maintain the exchange rate link with the U.S. dollar. The government has been of the view that any costs incurred through the loss of an independent monetary policy were far outweighed by the confidence and stability engendered by the linked exchange rate, which acted as an anchor for other policies. In addition, it has been argued that the flexibility of factor prices and the ability of Hong Kong firms to adjust quickly to changing circumstances gave the economy a resilience that would be weakened if the exchange rate link were abandoned. In this context, the authorities are according high priority to maintaining a banking supervision system and developing the financial regulatory framework in line with international standards appropriate for a major financial center.

In the labor market, the government has sought to ensure that labor market flexibility, supplemented with employee retraining and job matching schemes, enables the unemployed to return to work quickly. Social welfare policies have been targeted at those who are not expected to work—children, the elderly, the sick, and the disabled—and only to a limited extent at the unemployed. In the property market, land market, and provision of basic infrastructure, government intervention has come mainly through a large public housing program and provision of transportation facilities. Hong Kong has traditionally practiced free trade and open competition in domestic markets.

Fiscal Policy

In line with the basic noninterventionist approach, fiscal policy in Hong Kong has been guided by four broad principles: to maintain a simple and stable tax system with low tax rates, to keep current spending increases in line with GDP growth, to provide funding for key infrastructure projects, and to maintain an adequate level of fiscal reserves for dealing with contingencies. While the government has generally projected balanced budgets, its prudent revenue projections and frequent capital underspending have tended to result in surpluses—budget deficits were recorded in just ten years since 1947. This has enabled the government to build up substantial fiscal reserves, which have played a key role in supporting confidence and stability.

Budgetary Performance

Over FY1984–96, Hong Kong has established an outstanding record of budgetary performance. The budget was in deficit only once—in FY1995—and the annual budget surplus on average amounted to almost 2 percent of GDP (Figure 12).[12] On average, the government collected about 17¾ percent of GDP a year in revenue and incurred about 15¾ percent of GDP a year in expenditure over this period. Hong Kong's fiscal reserves had accumulated to 13½ percent of GDP at the end of FY1996.

Budgetary outcomes over this period were characterized by occasional sizable discrepancies between actual budget outcomes and projections in initial budgets, which resulted in some fiscal years in unexpected and substantial budget surpluses (up to 4 percent of GDP). Total revenue was typically higher than projected, and total expenditure was lower, with most of the variations occurring in capital revenue and expenditure (Table 4).

The discrepancy in revenue estimates largely reflects a cautious assessment of volatile sources of revenue—stamp duties on asset transactions and land sales revenue—in initial budgets. As such revenue is closely related to the turnover in the stock and property markets, it tends to overshoot the consistently conservative budget projections by a wide margin when the markets are very active.[13] The underestimates of capital spending largely resulted from project delays; forecasts of the time needed to start public works contracts have been overly optimistic in the past.[14] Owing to improvements in planning procedures for public works projects, capital underspending has been reduced since 1994.

Budgets in Hong Kong are not formulated to have a specific cyclical impact—this approach stands at the center of the rules-based fiscal policy framework. Nevertheless, it is revealing to analyze the macroeconomic impact of actual fiscal policy outcomes and to assess the fiscal outcomes implied by the original budgets. The former provides an ex post view of aggregate effects of fiscal policy, while the

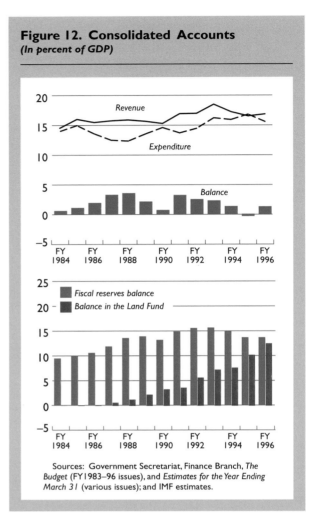

Figure 12. Consolidated Accounts
(In percent of GDP)

Sources: Government Secretariat, Finance Branch, *The Budget* (FY1983–96 issues), and *Estimates for the Year Ending March 31* (various issues); and IMF estimates.

latter indicates what macroeconomic effects the budgets were expected to have—and the policymakers were prepared to contend with—at the time the budgets were formulated.

To assess the macroeconomic impact of fiscal policy outcomes, the fiscal impulse of the actual budgetary outcome is derived (Box 4) and then considered against the cyclical position of the economy. The budgetary outcomes did not have a major expansionary or contractionary effect. When considered against the cyclical position of the economy, the effects have generally been either countercyclical or neutral over the past two business cycles (Figure 13).[15] In particular, the moder-

---

[12]The small deficit in FY1995 (¼ percent of GDP) resulted from peak spending (3 percent of GDP) on the huge airport project.

[13]For example, more than half of the budget surplus in FY1993 resulted from buoyant stamp duty revenue, which was 80 percent higher than budgeted.

[14]This was especially the case for public works projects outside the Airport Core Program in FY1990–92.

[15]The determinants of the cyclical position of the economy that were considered included the level and growth rate of actual GDP relative to potential GDP, and indicators of tightness (or slack) in the labor and property markets.

Table 4. Discrepancy Between Actual, Preliminary, and Projected Budgetary Outcomes, FY1984–95

(In percent)

	Deviation of Actual Outcome from Initial Budget	Deviation of Actual Outcome from Preliminary Estimate
Total revenue	6.9	1.3
Current	5.8	1.1
Capital	15.8	2.9
Total expenditure	−3.9	−2.2
Current	−1.4	−1.1
Capital	−8.8	−5.1

Source: IMF staff calculations.

ate fiscal expansion of FY1995–96 was counter-cyclical, as real GDP growth slowed over this period and positive fiscal impulses helped to stimulate the economy.

To assess the effects the original budgets were expected to have, projections contained in initial budgets are compared with preliminary budget estimates for the preceding fiscal year, both of which are released at the same time. From 1984 to 1989, policymakers generally expected the original budgets to have a slightly contractionary effect, which was appropriate ex ante given that the economy was expected to grow rapidly in initial budgets during this period (Figure 13). Since 1990, the original budgets were expected to have an expansionary effect (except in FY1991). As the economy was expected to grow at a strong pace and inflation was expected to accelerate in initial budgets during the early 1990s, it seems that policymakers were prepared to contend with the expected stimulative effects of the budgets.

In FY1995 and FY1996, the budgets were also expected to be slightly expansionary. As private consumption and asset markets were expected to consolidate (in FY1995) or recover at a moderate pace (in FY1996), this was expected to provide some stimulus to the recovery. It should be emphasized, however, that providing a stimulus for purely countercyclical purposes was not the main objective, but rather the expected consequence of fiscal policy. As discussed below, the underlying reason for the fiscal expansion in the 1990s was the need to develop Hong Kong's transportation infrastructure and respond to demographic changes by providing adequate funding for social programs.

Box 4. Fiscal Impulse

The fiscal impulse measures the size of the initial stimulus to aggregate demand arising from discretionary and other changes in fiscal policy after eliminating the cyclical component of the change in the budget balance. A positive (negative) sign indicates that fiscal policy has become expansionary (contractionary) relative to the previous year. The estimates of the fiscal impulse presented in this paper are based on actual budget outcomes adjusted for government equity investments and revenue from land sales. These items are excluded because they represent an exchange of assets between the public and private sectors and therefore should not have a significant impact on aggregate demand. Since both equity investments and land revenue at times accounted for a large proportion of government expenditure and revenue in Hong Kong, the adjusted fiscal impulse sometimes provides a different characterization of fiscal policy outcomes than does a more conventional measure such as the change in the budget balance. The estimated fiscal impulse and the budget balance over FY1984–96 (in percent of GDP) were as follows.

	1984	1986	1988	1990
Fiscal impulse	1.2	−1.2	−0.8	−0.8
Budget balance[1]	0.5	1.9	4.1	0.7

	1992	1993	1994	1995	1996
Fiscal impulse	−0.5	0.2	−0.3	0.7	0.4
Budget balance[1]	2.5	2.3	1.3	−0.3	1.3

[1]Proceeds of government bond issues (principal repayment) are excluded from revenue (expenditure).

Fiscal outcomes generally had a slightly contractionary effect in the second half of the 1980s and the early 1990s, as well as in FY1994. The effect was slightly expansionary in FY1993 and FY1995–96. It should be noted that, in FY1996, the budget balance swung from a small deficit at the end of FY1995 to a moderate surplus—a change that normally would be associated with fiscal contraction. However, as the surplus partly resulted from a decrease in equity investments and an increase in land revenue, both of which are excluded from the impulse measure, the estimated fiscal impulse was (slightly) expansionary.

FY1997 Budget

The budget for FY1997 is unique in straddling the transfer to Chinese sovereignty. As the imperative for fiscal policy in the year of the transition was to main-

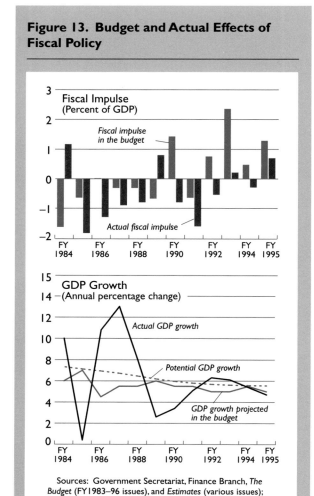

Figure 13. Budget and Actual Effects of Fiscal Policy

Sources: Government Secretariat, Finance Branch, *The Budget* (FY1983–96 issues), and *Estimates* (various issues); Census and Statistics Department, *Hong Kong Annual Digest of Statistics*, and *Estimates of Gross Domestic Product, 1961–96;* and IMF saff estimates.

tain stability, the FY1997 budget continued the prudent fiscal policies described above. No major changes in either expenditure or taxation policies were proposed. Despite the projected increase in the budget surplus, the macroeconomic impact of the budget remained broadly neutral, as much of the increase was expected to come from higher land revenue.

The overall budget surplus for FY1997 is forecast at HK$27 billion (2 percent of GDP) (Table 5). Taking into account new spending initiatives, total government expenditure is projected to increase by 11 percent over the previous year, of which current expenditure is expected to increase by 12¾ percent (5½ percent in real terms), and capital expenditure by 7½ percent (½ percent in real terms). The low increase for capital spending reflects the winding down of financial commitments for the airport proj-

ect.[16] Although, on the revenue side, total receipts are projected to increase by 16 percent over FY1996, this is mainly due to accounting and other changes to the treatment of land revenue after the transfer of sovereignty (Box 5). Fiscal reserves accounting in FY1997 is also complicated by the transfer of a special Land Fund to the government of the Hong Kong Special Administrative Region on July 1, 1997.

The Medium Range Fiscal Forecast prepared in conjunction with the FY1997 budget projects budgetary surpluses of 1–1½ percent of GDP per year over FY1998–2000 (Table 6). However, the medium-range forecast omits a substantial contribution that may be needed for high-priority projects under the Railway Development Strategy. This contribution is estimated at up to HK$50 billion, compared with total surpluses of HK$59 billion during FY1998–2000. The medium-range forecast did not cover this item because the precise amount and the timing of the investments were not yet determined, although it is expected that the government of the Hong Kong Special Administrative Region would need to contribute this sum between 1998 and 2001.

Tax Policy

The basic approach of the Hong Kong government with regard to taxation has been to derive revenue from a limited number of sources and to maintain low tax rates with a flat profile. The structure of taxation has remained basically unaltered since 1947. Despite the small number of taxes and their elementary structure, Hong Kong's tax system has, over the years, generated sufficient revenue to meet budgetary commitments and maintain a healthy growth of fiscal reserves. The revenue system has worked well because of the sustained growth of GDP, low administrative and compliance costs associated with the simple tax structure, and appropriate incentives that the low and stable tax rates have provided for domestic and foreign enterprise and investment. In particular, the income tax system has favored quick turnover of capital and reinvestment of retained profits and has obviated the pressure for special tax incentives.

Income taxes, comprising a salaries tax and a profits tax, are the main source of revenue, accounting for 43 percent of total revenue (7 percent of GDP) in FY1995. Hong Kong has arguably the simplest income tax and the lowest tax rate of any industrial economy. Income taxes are limited to income derived from sources within Hong Kong, with

---

[16]Excluding equity injections, which would fall from HK$9.4 billion in FY1996 to HK$0.8 billion in FY1997, capital spending is projected to increase by 17½ percent (9¼ percent in real terms) in FY1997.

Table 5. Consolidated Government Account[1]

	FY1993	FY1994	FY1995	FY1996 Budget	FY1996 Rev. est.	FY1997 Budget
(In billions of Hong Kong dollars)						
General Revenue Account						
Revenue	143.9	151.1	153.2	162.6	168.0	177.8
Expenditure	98.5	108.2	123.3	142.1	141.5	164.4
Current	93.2	106.0	120.3	137.9	137.1	154.4
Capital	5.3	2.1	3.0	4.2	4.2	10.0
Transfers to Funds	22.5	39.1	32.5	15.0	13.4	4.3
Consolidated Account Funds[2]						
Revenue[3]	22.7	23.9	26.8	33.1	34.3	56.9
Capital expenditure[4]	47.7	53.6	59.8	52.0	45.7	43.7
Total Consolidated Account						
Revenue	166.6	175.0	180.0	195.7	202.3	234.7
Current	139.8	147.1	150.9	159.3	165.2	172.1
Capital	26.8	27.9	29.1	36.4	37.1	62.6
Expenditure	146.2	161.8	183.1	194.1	187.2	208.0
Current	93.2	106.0	120.3	137.9	137.1	154.4
Capital	53.0	55.7	62.8	56.2	50.1	53.7
Net borrowing	−1.2	−2.4	...	...	...	...
Balance	20.4	13.2	−3.1	1.6	15.1	26.7
Fiscal reserves balance[5]	140.2	151.0	147.9	150.2	163.0	359.3
(In percent of GDP)						
Total Consolidated Account						
Revenue	18.6	17.3	16.6	15.5	16.9	17.3
Current	15.6	14.9	13.9	12.6	13.8	13.1
Capital	3.0	2.4	2.7	2.9	3.1	4.6
Expenditure	16.3	16.0	16.9	15.3	15.6	15.3
Current	10.4	10.5	11.1	10.9	11.5	11.4
Capital	5.9	5.5	5.8	4.4	4.2	4.0
Balance	2.3	1.3	−0.3	0.1	1.3	2.0
Fiscal reserves balance[5]	15.6	14.9	13.6	11.9	13.6	26.5
(Percentage change)						
Total Consolidated Account						
Revenue	25.5	5.0	2.9	8.7	12.4	16.1
Current	17.2	5.2	2.6	5.6	9.5	4.2
Capital	98.5	4.1	4.3	25.1	27.5	68.7
Expenditure	29.0	10.6	13.2	6.0	2.2	11.1
Current	14.2	13.7	13.5	14.6	14.0	12.6
Capital	67.2	5.3	12.5	−10.5	−20.2	7.2
Fiscal reserves balance[5]	15.9	7.7	−2.1	1.6	10.2	120.4

Sources: Data provided by the Government Secretariat, Finance Branch; and IMF staff projections.

[1]Fiscal year begins April 1.

[2]Consists of the Capital Works Reserve Fund; Capital Investment Fund and Loan Fund beginning FY1990; Disaster Relief Fund beginning FY1993; and Civil Service Reserve Fund beginning FY1994.

[3]Includes revenue from land sales.

[4]Includes direct financing of airport-related projects as well as government equity injections into the Airport Authority and the Mass Transit Railway Corporation.

[5]As of end-fiscal year. Fiscal reserves at the end of FY1997 include the projected HK$170 billion balance in the Land Fund, which will revert to the Hong Kong Special Administrative Region on July 1, 1997.

Box 5. The Land Fund and Fiscal Reserves

The Land Fund of the Hong Kong Special Administrative Region is a special trust fund set up under the terms of the Joint Declaration and managed on behalf of the future government of the Region, in which half of all proceeds from land sales have been deposited since 1986. (The other half of land revenue has been credited to a capital account of the Budget and has financed capital projects.) On July 1, 1997, the Land Fund reverted to the government of the Special Administrative Region; its assets were projected to stand at HK$164 billion (12 percent of GDP) as of that date.

Fiscal reserves arise from budgetary surpluses accumulated over the years. They are deposited with the Hong Kong Monetary Authority's Exchange Fund, which manages them along with other assets that serve as backing for the Hong Kong currency, and pays the government interest realized by investing the reserves. At March 31, 1997, fiscal reserves were estimated to stand at HK$163 billion (13½ percent of the 1996 GDP).

Future arrangements for the management of the Land Fund were clarified in May 1997, when the Chief Executive-Designate of the Hong Kong Special Administrative Region, Mr. Tung Chee-Hwa, nominated the Financial Secretary to manage the assets of the Land Fund as part of fiscal reserves. Initially, the Land Fund would be managed by the Hong Kong Monetary Authority under Financial Secretary's direction as a separate portfolio from the Exchange Fund. The Land Fund has been operating under a set of investment criteria that differs from that of the Exchange Fund and hence embodies a more diversified portfolio.

The transfer of sovereignty will also mark an important change in accounting arrangements for land revenue. The government of the Region will start receiving full proceeds from land sales as of July 1, 1997, and will collect rents equivalent to 3 percent of the rateable value from the extension of leases in the New Territories and New Kowloon. The latter measure alone is expected to generate additional revenue of about HK$5 billion per year (2 percent of total revenue). As a result, fiscal reserves are projected to jump by HK$196 billion (13 percent of GDP) to HK$359 billion (26½ percent of the 1997 GDP) at March 31, 1998, representing about two years' worth of current expenditure. IMF staff estimates of the contribution of various factors to this increase in reserves are tabulated below:

	(In billions of Hong Kong dollars)	(In percent of GDP)
Land Fund at March 31, 1998	169.6	12.6
Land Fund at July 1, 1997	163.5	12.1
Interest from July 1, 1997– March 31, 1998	6.1	0.5
Fiscal surplus at March 31, 1998	26.7	2.0
Of which:		
New Territories leases	3.2	0.2
Full proceeds of land sales[1]	11.0	0.8
Total increase in fiscal reserves	196.3	14.6
Total fiscal reserves at March 31, 1998	359.3	26.6

[1]Represents the share of land revenue from July 1, 1997 which, under the arrangements applying before that date, would have been paid to the Land Fund.

---

no tax levied on capital gains, dividends, or interest income.[17] The salaries tax payable is based on a sliding scale that progresses from 2 percent to 20 percent of income after the deduction of allowances.[18] However, the total amount payable is subject to a limit of 15 percent of total income, the so-called standard rate. The current allowances are generous, so that almost half of the workforce is not subject to any income tax at all.[19] The profits of corporations are taxed at a rate of 16½ percent.

About 30 percent of total fiscal revenue in recent years was directly related to land and property.[20] A large part resulted from land sales under Hong Kong's peculiar system of land tenure. However, the income from land sales has been a rather unstable source of revenue, reflecting the difficulty of plan-

---

[17]Interest income from domestic sources received by licensed banks and corporations carrying on business in Hong Kong is subject to the profits tax.

[18]The tax rates of 2 percent, 8 percent, and 14 percent are applicable to different segments of the first HK$30,000 of net income, and the 20 percent rate to the remaining net income.

[19]The allowance is HK$100,000 for a single person and HK$200,000 for a married couple. There are several additional allowances, for example, for children and dependent parents, grandparents, and siblings.

[20]This revenue includes property taxes, the profits tax on property-related businesses, stamp duty on property assignments and leases, and premiums from land sales.

Table 6. Medium-Range Fiscal Forecast[1]

	FY1996 Estimate	FY1997 Budget	FY1998	FY1999	FY2000
			Official projection		
			(In billions of Hong Kong dollars)		
Revenue	202.3	234.7	252.2	280.1	317.4
General Revenue Account	168.0	177.8	200.5	224.8	257.7
Consolidated Account Funds	34.3	56.9	51.7	55.3	59.7
Of which: Capital Works Reserve Fund[2]	29.0	49.4	40.0	46.9	49.4
Expenditure	187.2	208.0	228.9	261.7	300.2
General Revenue Account[3]	141.5	164.4	181.5	206.5	235.5
Consolidated Account Funds	45.7	43.6	47.4	55.2	64.7
Of which: Capital Works Reserve Fund[4]	30.4	35.7	40.8	48.0	54.9
Capital Investment Fund[5]	9.4	0.8	0.9	1.0	1.1
Surplus	15.1	26.7	23.3	18.4	17.2
Fiscal reserves balance[6]	163.0	359.3	382.6	401.0	418.2
Balance in the Land Fund of the HKSAR[7]	...	163.5	...	...	...
			(In percent of GDP)		
Revenue	16.9	17.3	16.4	16.1	16.1
Of which: Land sales[8]	2.2	2.4	2.4	2.4	2.3
Expenditure	15.7	15.3	14.9	15.0	15.2
Surplus	1.3	2.0	1.5	1.1	0.9
Fiscal reserves balance[6]	13.6	26.5	24.9	23.0	21.2
Balance in the Land Fund of the HKSAR[7]	...	12.1	...	...	...
Adjusted fiscal impulse[8]	0.4	0.0	0.0	0.7	0.3

Sources: *The 1997/98 Budget;* and IMF staff estimates.

[1]Fiscal year begins April 1.

[2]Includes mainly revenue from land sales. From July 1, 1997, onward, land revenues that previously accrued to the Land Fund will be included in the budget of the Hong Kong Special Administrative Region.

[3]The FY1997 figure includes the proposed HK$5 billion injection in the Mandatory Provident Fund.

[4]Includes financing of airport-related projects.

[5]Includes government equity investments into the Airport Authority and Mass Transit Railway Corporation.

[6]As of end-fiscal year. Fiscal reserves at the end of FY1997 include the projected HK$170 billion balance in the Land Fund (including the projected interest earnings between July 1, 1997, and March 31, 1998), which will revert to the Hong Kong Special Administrative Region on July 1, 1997.

[7]Balance shown is as of July 1, 1997.

[8]Staff estimates. It is assumed that land revenue accounts for 90 percent of the projected revenue of the Capital Works Reserve Fund.

ning an even release of land over the years and the sometimes large increases in land prices. Another important revenue source in this category has been the stamp duty on property transfers and stock market transactions. Although the stamp duty—like the land revenue—complicates financial planning because of the volatility of the underlying tax base, it has useful automatic stabilizer properties: during asset market booms, stamp duty revenue soars, generally producing a budget surplus and dampening a boom. Hong Kong also has standard property taxes ("rates"), which are adjusted every three years to take account of the effects of inflation on property values.

By virtue of its status as a free port, Hong Kong has no international trade taxes. Domestic taxes on goods and services have been few and applicable only to nonessential items. Proposals for introduction of a broad-based sales tax have been repeatedly rejected on grounds that such a tax was not needed for revenue purposes. Another unusual feature—at least from a developed country perspective—is the high yield of motor vehicle taxes (1½ percent of total revenue). The use of this tax base can be justified in Hong Kong on both environmental and distributional grounds.

Nontax revenue features prominently in Hong Kong's tax structure. One reason for the relatively high yield of nontax revenue has been the government's firm adherence to the principle of full cost recovery in setting user fees and charges.

Data for the period 1981–95 indicate that the revenue system is quite buoyant: a 1 percent increase in GDP raised tax revenue by 1.1 percent, and capital revenue by 1.6 percent.[21] It is interesting to note that buoyancy for the income tax is quite high—1.1 percent for a 1 percent increase in GDP. In other words, frequent increases in tax allowances and the granting of other tax concessions have been more than compensated for by the broadening of the tax base brought about by rapid increases in individual income.

Expenditure Policy

The basic approach of the Hong Kong government with regard to expenditure policy has been to provide a relatively narrow range of public goods for which government supply is deemed efficient, while keeping spending increases in line with the growth rate of nominal GDP.

There have been several shifts in the structure of public expenditure since 1984, reflecting shifts in spending priorities and demographic factors. In particular, spending on social welfare, health, housing, and the environment has grown rapidly (Figure 14), while infrastructure spending has been boosted mainly by the implementation of the Airport Core Program. Relatively less spending was directed at security and community and external affairs.

In comparison with OECD countries, public spending in terms of GDP is fairly low in Hong Kong (Figure 15). Most notable is the absence of high spending on social security and defense. The cost of social security is low because pension funds are for the most part in the private domain. With regard to defense spending, under the 1988 Defense Costs Agreement, the Hong Kong government covers 65 percent of the recurrent cost of defense services provided by the United Kingdom as well as all capital costs. However, the amount involved (about 0.1 percent of GDP in recent years) is negligible compared with the cost of defense in most other countries. Public expenditure on administration, education, and health also is fairly low, while spending on housing, community affairs, and economic services (such as transportation) is comparable to that in the OECD countries. Except for defense costs, Hong Kong's level and pattern of public expenditure are similar to those of Singapore.

Figure 14. Expenditure Developments
(Percent of GDP)

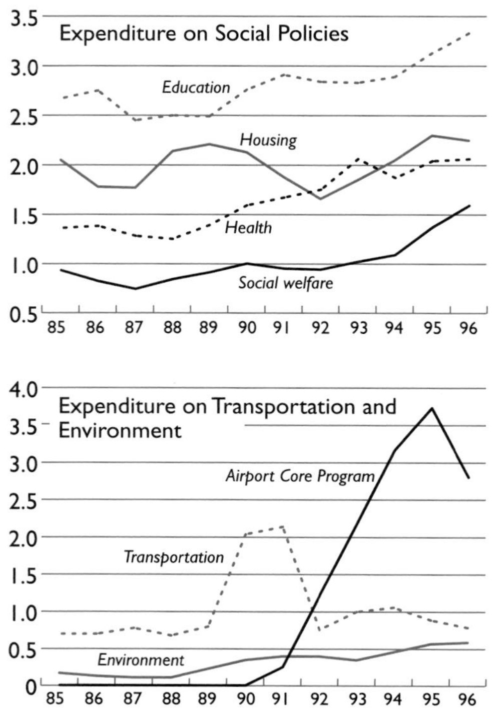

Sources: Data provided by the Government Secretariat, Finance Branch; and Census and Statistics Department, *Annual Digest of Statistics* (various issues).

Transportation Infrastructure

The rapid increase in regional and overseas air and sea transport involving Hong Kong and the expansion of cross-border trade with China have put considerable pressure on the physical infrastructure in the territory. In addition, domestic rush-hour congestion problems have increased because of the continuing geographic separation of work and residential areas. In particular, the rapidly growing services sectors tend to be concentrated in the central business district on Hong Kong Island, despite the availability of less expensive locations. In response to these developments, public expenditure on expanding and upgrading transportation infrastructure has increased markedly, by 16 percent a year on average from 1985 to 1995.

The Airport Core Program (ACP) is the largest public infrastructure program in Hong Kong and one of the largest in the world. The Program includes a large new airport on the Chek Lap Kok island and nine related projects providing urban infrastructure

---

[21]For detailed estimates, see Chapter III in IMF (1997a).

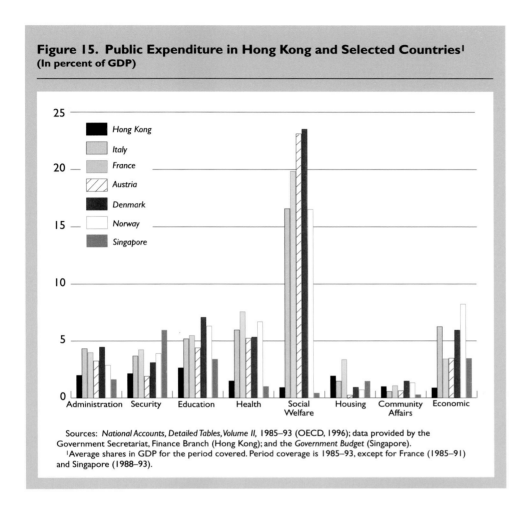

Figure 15. Public Expenditure in Hong Kong and Selected Countries[1]
(In percent of GDP)

Sources: *National Accounts, Detailed Tables, Volume II*, 1985–93 (OECD, 1996); data provided by the Government Secretariat, Finance Branch (Hong Kong); and the *Government Budget* (Singapore).

[1]Average shares in GDP for the period covered. Period coverage is 1985–93, except for France (1985–91) and Singapore (1988–93).

services to the airport.[22] The total cost of the program, which is to be completed in 1998, is now projected at the equivalent of about 15 percent of GDP (Box 6).

Work on the Airport Core Program has progressed on schedule and, by the end of 1996, was about 75 percent complete. The airport is scheduled to open in April 1998. The Airport Railway, which will connect the new airport to the main terminal on Hong Kong Island in 23 minutes, is expected to open by June 1998. According to the current plans, the site of the existing Kai Tak airport will, after the airport's closure in 1998, mainly be used for housing, roads, commercial development, and open space.

Other important infrastructure projects in the transportation sector include the expansion of Hong Kong's container handling capacity. The Sino-British Land Commission allocated land for the provision of a ninth container terminal, to be constructed by private sector developers. The terminal is scheduled to be completed in the coming five years. The government is also planning to seek private sector bids for the construction of two additional container terminals on northeast Lantau Island in the early 2000s. Separately, the government has awarded a tender to a private sector operator to design, build, and operate a river trade terminal in northwest New Territories to cater to the fast-growing river trade with China. The project is planned for completion by the end of 1999.

Planning is under way for new road and railway facilities connecting China, the urban areas in the New Territories, and the Central Business District. In particular, the government has recently decided to proceed with the implementation of the Western Corridor Railway by phases. The first phase of the project, comprising a passenger line connecting the northwestern parts of the New Territories with the existing network, would be completed by the end of

---

[22]These projects include: railway and highway links between the airport, Kowloon, and Hong Kong Island; a new town for 20,000 people near the airport; two large suspension bridges; a third harbor tunnel; and two major land reclamation projects.

Box 6. Cost of the Airport Core Program

The projected total costs of the Airport Core Program have been revised downward several times: in 1994 from HK$163.7 billion to HK$158.2 billion, and at the end of 1996 to HK$154.4 billion. The financing is distributed between public and private sources as follows:

	Budget			
	Direct	Equity	Private	Total
	(In billions of Hong Kong dollars)			
Airport-related projects	48.9	...	...	48.9
Airport	...	36.6	26.4	65.0
Airport Railway	...	23.7	10.3	35.0
Western Harbor crossing	...	...	6.5	6.5
Total	48.9	60.3	43.2	154.4

Seven airport-related projects are directly funded by the government through the Capital Works Reserve Fund at HK$48.9 billion. The airport and the airport-railway are developed and will be operated by statutory bodies—the Airport Authority and Mass Transit Railway Corporation, respectively. These two bodies will receive a total of HK$60.3 billion in equity injections from the government through the Capital Investment Fund, and will issue debt to meet their remaining financing requirements. Some airport facilities will be managed not by the Airport Authority, but by private tenants contributing HK$15.4 billion in franchises to the project's financing. Finally, the Western Harbor Crossing is a fully privately financed project. The projected spending profile of the Airport Core Program is as follows:

Fiscal year	Billions of Hong Kong dollars	Percent of total cost	Percent of GDP
1991	1.7	1.1	0.3
1992	9.5	6.2	1.2
1993	19.6	12.7	2.2
1994	31.9	20.7	3.2
1995	40.5	26.2	3.7
1996	33.5	21.7	2.8
1997	17.8	11.5	1.4
Total	154.4	100.0	14.8

2003, at an estimated cost of HK$50 billion. The government has also decided to extend the existing Mass Transit Railway in the east of the New Territories, at an estimated cost of HK$25 billion.

The Airport Core Program and the other transportation infrastructure projects are likely to have sizable spinoff effects on private sector investment, as new sites will become attractive locations for business and residential use. In addition, as the overall size of government investment is reduced with the completion of the huge airport, there will be less crowding out of private sector investment through the use of specialized labor and other scarce construction inputs.

Linked Exchange Rate System

Hong Kong's monetary system and exchange rate regime, known as the linked exchange rate system, was established in October 1983 against the background of a severe currency crisis. The Hong Kong dollar, then on a floating regime, depreciated by almost a third against the U.S. dollar between mid-1981 and the autumn of 1983, when concerns about Hong Kong's future degenerated into a confidence crisis. The linked rate system is a variant of a conventional currency board, the Exchange Fund, which operated in Hong Kong between 1935 and 1972 (Box 7). Under this system, monetary policy has a simple and transparent objective to maintain a stable exchange rate between the Hong Kong and U.S. dollars. Currency stability has been maintained in the face of considerable political uncertainties and a massive structural change that took place in the economy since 1983. By preserving confidence in the Hong Kong dollar and making the exchange rate a credible and transparent benchmark, the linked rate system has acted as an anchor for other macroeconomic policies and facilitated real adjustments in the private sector. The link has also played a crucial role in maintaining confidence and stability in the runup to the transfer of sovereignty.

This section describes the main characteristics of the linked rate system, provides examples of the use of monetary instruments developed over the years, analyzes movements in interest rates and exchange rates under the system, and reviews recent institutional and market infrastructure developments in the area of monetary policy.

Note-Issuing Mechanism

Under the linked exchange rate system, bank notes are issued and redeemed against U.S. dollars at a fixed exchange rate of HK$7.80 per US$1 (the "linked rate"). The government has authorized three private commercial banks ("note-issuing banks") to issue currency notes in Hong Kong. They are the Hongkong and Shanghai Banking Corporation Limited, the Standard Chartered Bank, and the Bank of China. The bank notes issued bear the name of, and

Box 7. Evolution of the Hong Kong Monetary System

From 1845 to 1935, Hong Kong was on the international silver standard.[1] Banknotes issued by various private commercial banks became the dominant customary means of payment, despite their lack of legal tender status. In 1895, the Bank Notes Issue Ordinance restricted the issue of banknotes to the Hongkong and Shanghai Banking Corporation and the Chartered Bank of India, Australia, and China (now the Standard Chartered Bank). As China went off the silver standard in November 1935, Hong Kong followed suit.

Under the Exchange Fund Ordinance of 1935, an Exchange Fund was set up, to which note-issuing banks were required to submit their silver holdings in exchange for Certificates of Indebtedness, which have since then served as legal backing for all bank notes. New bank notes issued by the note-issuing banks between December 1935 and June 1972 had a 100 percent sterling cover, and Hong Kong dollars could be exchanged into sterling at a fixed exchange rate. This monetary system, known as the sterling exchange standard, operated as a classical currency board.

In July 1972, following the United Kingdom's decision to float the pound sterling, the Hong Kong government linked the Hong Kong dollar with the U.S. dollar at the rate of HK$5.65 to US$1, with provision for a 2¼ percent fluctuation either way. However, the note-issuing mechanism was changed. The note-issuing banks were no longer required to pay foreign currency to the Exchange Fund when issuing additional Hong Kong dollar banknotes. Instead, the backing could be provided in Hong Kong dollars, which were used by the Exchange Fund to acquire foreign currency assets equivalent to the nominal value of the note issue at the current exchange rates.

After a global speculative attack on the U.S. dollar in November 1974, the Hong Kong government found it impossible to maintain the existing parity, and allowed the Hong Kong dollar to float. To administer the Exchange Fund and handle other central banking functions not yet assumed by the note-issuing banks, the government created a separate Monetary Affairs Branch in 1976.

In a separate move, the government transferred the fiscal reserve balances to the Exchange Fund, which has thus become the sole repository of the government's financial assets, including the foreign exchange reserve backing for the note issue and fiscal reserves.

The note-issuing mechanism that was introduced in July 1972 remained unchanged, so that any increase in the note issue was reflected in an increase in the Exchange Fund's Hong Kong dollar balances at the note-issuing banks. Although the authorities mostly used such balances to purchase foreign exchange assets, there was no formal obligation on them to do so. Monetary policy had thus become potentially discretionary. However, the authorities had no mechanisms for actually exercising discretionary monetary control. At the same time, the banking sector was unrestricted in creating currency, subject to prudential and commercial considerations. Hong Kong thus entered a period devoid of an effective anchor for monetary policy.

As the Hong Kong dollar was a strong currency at that time, floating in effect meant revaluation. Overall, the first two years of the floating rate regime worked relatively well. After mid-1977, however, the performance of the floating rate regime began to deteriorate. The growth of money supply and bank credit accelerated sharply, and the exchange rate of the Hong Kong dollar depreciated persistently, pushing inflation to the double-digit range during 1979–83. The depreciation of the Hong Kong dollar was aggravated by the confidence crisis engendered by China's announcement in the summer of 1982 that it intended to regain sovereignty over the whole Hong Kong area, and the subsequent protracted negotiations between China and the United Kingdom on the future of Hong Kong.

The crisis peaked on September 24, 1983, when the exchange rate fell to an all-time low of HK$9.60 to US$1 (from HK$5.91 per US$1 in July 1982), panic buying of staples and imported goods broke out, and some banks temporarily suspended payment as a large number of customers tried to switch their deposits to U.S. dollar cash (see Jao (1990)).

To address the crisis, the Hong Kong government unveiled a two-point program for currency stabilization on October 15, 1983. The first measure was the requirement that the note-issuing banks pay U.S. dollars to the Exchange Fund as full cover for banknotes issued, at a fixed rate of HK$7.80 to US$1.

The second measure was the abolition of the 10 percent withholding tax on interest income from Hong Kong dollar deposits held with financial institutions, which removed the tax advantage from holding foreign currency deposits. These two measures effectively stabilized the Hong Kong dollar and laid the foundation for the linked exchange rate system.

---

[1]This box draws on Jao (1990 and 1994), Latter (1994), and Nugée (1995).

are the liabilities of, the note-issuing banks. The Hong Kong Monetary Authority issues only coins.

To issue Hong Kong dollar banknotes, the three note-issuing banks are required to deliver to the Exchange Fund an amount in U.S. dollars that is equivalent to the local currency issued at the linked rate as backing for their Hong Kong dollar note issues. The Exchange Fund, in turn, issues to each note-issuing bank non-interest-bearing Certificates of Indebtedness denominated in Hong Kong dollars, which serve as legal backing for the note issue. Other banks may acquire local currency notes from the note-issuing banks against Hong Kong dollar deposits for Hong Kong dollar value. To redeem U.S. dollars from the Exchange Fund, the note-issuing banks are required to deliver Certificates of Indebtedness to the Exchange Fund and withdraw local banknotes from circulation at the linked exchange rate.

Currency supply is determined entirely by demand considerations under this note-issuing mechanism— the monetary authority has virtually no control over the amount of currency in circulation. At the end of 1996, banknote circulation in Hong Kong was about HK$83 billion and coin circulation was about HK$4 billion. With Hong Kong's foreign reserves standing at close to US$64 billion (over HK$490 billion), Hong Kong dollar currency circulation was backed almost six times by foreign currency assets.

Exchange Rate of the Hong Kong Dollar

As noted above, transactions conducted for note-issuing purposes between the Exchange Fund and the note-issuing banks are carried out at the linked exchange rate of HK$7.80 per US$1. For all other transactions, the exchange rate of the Hong Kong dollar is set in the exchange market at freely negotiated rates. In particular, foreign exchange transactions between the public and banks (including the note-issuing banks), as well as all interbank transactions involving foreign exchange, are conducted at the market-determined exchange rate.

The market exchange rate has, of course, remained very close to the linked rate (Figure 16, top panel). Indeed, since mid-1991, the market rate has been on the "strong side of the link," that is, slightly appreciated—typically less than 1 percent—relative to the linked rate. This development arose from a number of factors, including persistent, strong capital inflows, which reflect Hong Kong's growing role in financial intermediation in the region, and the sound fundamentals of Hong Kong's own economy. In support of the linked rate system, the authorities have accumulated substantial international reserves (Box 8) and given priority to improving prudential supervision of the banking system.

Monetary Management

When the linked exchange rate system was set up in 1983, the clearing and payment system was operated by the Hongkong and Shanghai Bank. This bank could at the time adjust the net clearing balance of the banking system on its own and thus offset any impact on interbank liquidity—and, hence, the exchange rate—of the monetary authorities' transactions with the banking system. This implied that the monetary authorities did

Figure 16. Exchange Rate Developments

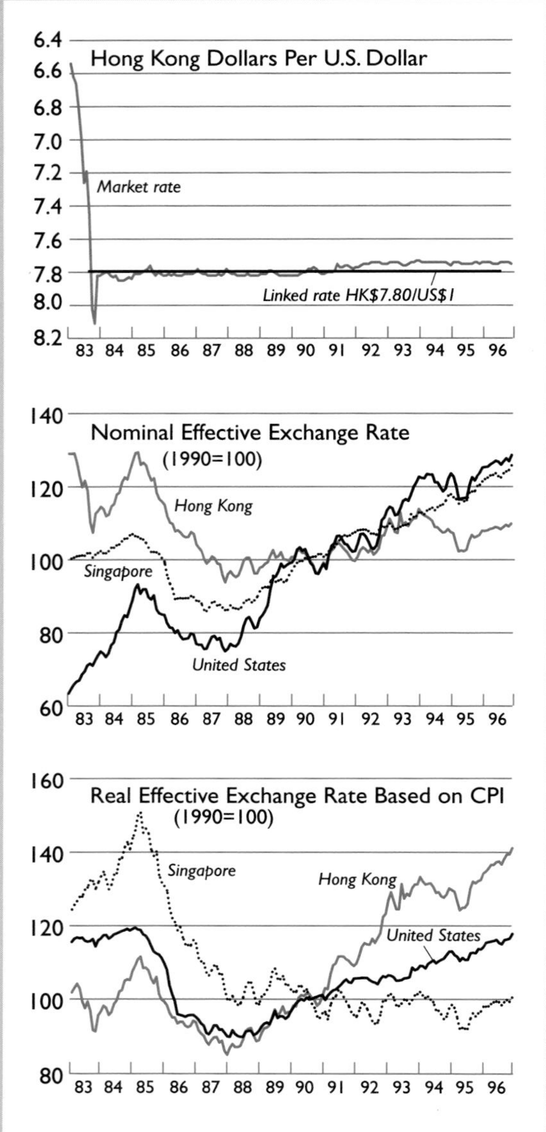

Sources: IMF staff estimates; and WEFAS/UKFT.

not have control over interbank liquidity.[23] To address this problem, in July 1988 the Accounting Arrangements between the Exchange Fund and the Hongkong

---

[23]To illustrate this point, suppose the Hong Kong dollar is weakening from the linked rate and the Exchange Fund wants to tighten interbank liquidity to raise interbank interest rates. To this end, the Exchange Fund would borrow from the interbank market and the Hongkong and Shanghai Bank would debit the clearing account of the bank that lent to the Exchange Fund. At the same

Box 8. Foreign Exchange Reserves

Hong Kong's international reserves have accumulated rapidly since 1983 owing to strong external sector performance and prudent fiscal policies. When the linked exchange rate system was introduced, foreign assets of the Exchange Fund stood at about US$6 billion; 13 years later, after growing by over 20 percent annually, the reserves reached US$63 billion (see tabulation below). A major part of foreign reserves (about 30 percent) is the counterpart of the fiscal reserves, which had accumulated steadily over the years, reflecting large budgetary surpluses. The foreign reserves are sufficient to cover more than ten months of retained imports of goods and, at close to US$10,000 per capita, are among the highest in the world.

	1983	1988	1990	1993	1996
Foreign currency assets of the Exchange Fund (end of period; in billions of U.S. dollars)[1]	5.9	16.3	24.7	43.0	63.3
Growth over the preceding subperiod (average annual percentage change)	...	23.1	23.2	20.4	13.7
In months of retained imports	4.4	6.0	7.9	10.0	10.7
In months of total merchandise imports	3.1	3.0	3.6	3.7	3.8
Per capita foreign reserves (in U.S. dollars)	1,000	2,870	4,320	7,170	9,940

Sources: Hong Kong Monetary Authority, *Monthly Statistical Bulletin*; Census and Statistics Department, *Hong Kong Monthly Digest of Statistics*; and IMF staff estimates.

[1]Converted into U.S. dollars at the linked exchange rate of HK$7.80 per US$1.

and Shanghai Bank were established, under which the bank was required to adjust its net clearing balance with the rest of the banking system so that it was equal to "the Balance," which the bank in turn held with the Exchange Fund. Policymakers could thus affect interbank liquidity by varying the amount of the Balance, initially through lending and borrowing of Hong Kong dollars or sale and purchase of foreign currencies in the interbank market, and later through open market operations and the transfer of funds between the Treasury and the Exchange Fund. When the Exchange Fund would reduce the level of the Balance, it would tighten liquidity of the banking system, and vice versa.[24] The changes in interbank liquidity, in turn, would influence interbank interest rates and ultimately the market exchange rate of the Hong Kong dollar.

Unlike the quantity of banknotes in circulation, which adjusts to demand, with the Accounting Arrangements the level of interbank liquidity came under direct control of the Exchange Fund. From the beginning, however, the power to control interbank liquidity has been used with restraint. For example, the authorities would inject additional liquidity into the system in the days before large new share offerings in the stock exchange to relieve the tightness arising from the sharp increase in the volume and value of interbank payments.

Since the introduction of the Accounting Arrangements, the exchange rate has been considerably smoother, and overnight interest rates in general have also been less volatile (Table 7).

Major innovations in monetary management in the post-1988 period include the introduction of the Liquidity Adjustment Facility (Hong Kong's version of a discount window) in 1992,[25] a revised mode of money

---

time, some other customer of the Hongkong Bank may have purchased U.S. dollars, and the Hongkong Bank may have credited the clearing account of the bank that sold the U.S. dollars with an equivalent amount of Hong Kong dollars. The level of interbank liquidity prevailing before the Exchange Fund intervention would thus be restored.

[24]If the net clearing balance was greater than the Balance (i.e., if the Hongkong and Shanghai Bank had overlent to the rest of the banking system), the Exchange Fund charged a penal interest on the bank in respect of the excess amount. If the net clearing balance was less than the Balance, the bank would in effect forgo interest income on interbank liquidity that was available to it but had not been on-lent.

---

[25]The Liquidity Adjustment Facility, introduced in June 1992, enables banks to make late adjustments to their liquidity positions through a Sale and Repurchase Agreement of government debt with the Monetary Authority. The facility is only open during the final hour of the working day. The spread between the Liquidity Adjustment Facility offer and bid rates, which are linked to the U.S. Federal Funds Target Rate, is currently 2 percentage points.

Table 7. Financial Indicators, Pre- and Post-Accounting Arrangements

(In basis points, daily data)

	January 1984–June 1988	October 1988–September 1996
Average absolute change in:		
Hong Kong dollar/U.S. dollar (in percent)	0.04	0.02
Overnight HIBOR	141	26
Overnight U.S. Federal Funds Rate	25	22
Three-month HIBOR	21	7
Average absolute difference between:		
Overnight HIBOR and LIBOR	291	62
Three-month HIBOR and LIBOR	154	32

Source: Data provided by the Hong Kong Monetary Authority.

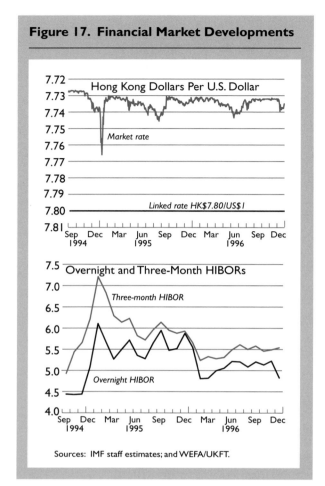

Figure 17. Financial Market Developments

Sources: IMF staff estimates; and WEFA/UKFT.

market operations in 1994,[26] and the introduction of a Real Time Gross Settlement system in 1996. The introduction of these instruments of monetary management led to a further (small) reduction in exchange rate and interest rate volatility. Such interest rate smoothing is limited to the very short term because of the high degree of capital mobility in Hong Kong and the absence of any exchange controls. More important, interest rate smoothing is a secondary objective to the primary goal of defending the exchange rate.

When pressures on the exchange rate become evident, the power to influence the supply of base money may be used to magnify rather than attenuate the impact of the reserves outflow on the monetary base and thereby raise interest rates. A recent example of such action—and the most important test of the linked exchange rate system to date—took place in January 1995. Following the Mexican peso crisis, during the second week of January 1995 the Hong Kong dollar came under speculative attack. The Hong Kong dollar depreciated from HK$7.7375 per U.S. dollar at the beginning of 1995 to a low of HK$7.7725 per U.S. dollar on January 12 (Figure 17). In response to sell-

ing pressures, the Monetary Authority tightened interbank liquidity and intervened directly in the foreign exchange market.[27] Banks, concerned that the Monetary Authority would also raise bid and offer rates on its discount window, began actively to bid for funds on the interbank market. The overnight Hong Kong interbank offered rate (HIBOR) surged to an intraday high of 12 percent—rising by almost 5 percentage points in one day—and closed the day some 2½ percentage points higher. During the following days, as interbank liquidity was kept tight and HIBOR remained at an elevated level, the exchange rate began to recover quickly, rising to HK$7.734 per U.S. dollar on January 20. The prompt squeeze of interbank liquidity by the Monetary Authority successfully halted the speculative attack and, reflecting the prompt

---

[26]Before mid-March 1994, the Monetary Authority varied the Balance only infrequently (30 changes in five years), making any adjustment in the Balance a high-profile event and leading at times to considerable volatility in overnight interest rates. The Monetary Authority now targets short-term interbank interest rates instead of the level of interbank liquidity, injecting or withdrawing liquidity so as to prevent excessive volatility in overnight interest rates.

[27]The Balance fell to HK$ –4.6 billion at midday on January 12. Technically, the banking system was net debtor to the Monetary Authority at the time and had to place Hong Kong dollar assets in its clearing balances to square its position vis-à-vis the monetary authorities.

demonstration of the Monetary Authority's ability to defend the link, there have been no speculative pressures since then.

Market Infrastructure and Institutional Developments

On April 1, 1993, the Hong Kong Monetary Authority was established against the background of the growing importance of Hong Kong as an international financial center and the recognition that monetary stability, the soundness and integrity of the financial system, and the efficiency of the financial infrastructure are closely interrelated and should be coordinated in a single body. The Monetary Authority was formed by merging the Office of the Exchange Fund with the Office of the Commissioner of Banking. The Monetary Authority has, in recent years, sought to boost Hong Kong's role as a major international financial center by upgrading financial market infrastructure, promoting the development of the Hong Kong dollar debt market, and expanding the scope of its own international activities.

Real Time Gross Settlement System

Monetary operations conducted by the Hong Kong Monetary Authority have further evolved with introduction in December 1996 of a Real Time Gross Settlement system. Under this system, the clearing account held by the Hongkong and Shanghai Bank with the Exchange Fund was replaced with 182 clearing balances, one for each licensed bank. The Monetary Authority directly operates each of the clearing balances and has become, in effect, the underwriter for interbank settlement transactions.

Clearing transactions under this system are settled continuously on a gross basis, compared with settlement on a net basis on the morning of the business day following the transaction under the old system. While the Real Time Gross Settlement system does not allow overdrafts, banks requiring intraday liquidity may sell their holdings of Exchange Fund paper, or enter into repurchase agreements with the Monetary Authority for such paper. Such intraday repurchases using Exchange Fund paper are interest-free. Liquidity shortfalls at the end of the day must be met by borrowing funds from the Liquidity Adjustment Facility at the offer rate. To help banks to meet their bulk clearing obligations at specified time of the day, the Monetary Authority introduced a Liquidity Adjustment Window that accepts all private sector paper eligible under the Liquidity Adjustment Facility in exchange for liquidity at the Facility's offer rate.

The Real Time Gross Settlement system is expected to enhance the robustness of the linked exchange rate system. In the past, the Hongkong and Shanghai Bank often found it difficult to project the amount of clearing transactions of the entire banking system, particularly large deposits and withdrawals that took place close to the end of the business day. As a result, the Hongkong and Shanghai Bank was unable to ensure that the net clearing balance was always equal to the Balance and, consequently, liquidity management operations by the Monetary Authority were often not fully and immediately reflected in the net clearing balance of the banking system. Under the new system, liquidity operations—managed through open market operations and foreign exchange transactions with banks—would become more direct and effective, since each bank would have to ensure that its own clearing balance with the Monetary Authority was sufficient to cover its settlements, plus all transactions it had engaged in with the Monetary Authority.

The Real Time Gross Settlement system also is expected to reduce liquidity and solvency risks—since clearing transactions are settled continuously, banks experiencing a shortage of funds will be detected immediately. Under the old system, such liquidity or solvency problems would not have been discovered until the following business day.

Interest Rate Deregulation

In 1981, after a period of intense competition among banks, the Hong Kong Association of Banks reached an agreement on Interest Rate Rules, under which the Association, after consultation with the monetary authorities, determined maximum interest rates paid by licensed banks on Hong Kong dollar deposits of less than HK$500,000 and of maturity less than 15 months. In addition, the Interest Rate Rules prohibited the payment of interest on current or checking accounts. Before interest rates were liberalized, the Rules affected almost one half of all deposits. While defended on the grounds that they promoted stability in the banking system in Hong Kong's potentially volatile financial environment by enabling banks to build substantial reserves against external and internal shocks, the Rules were criticized by Consumer Council and foreign banks. The Consumer Council (1994) complained that the Rules enabled large local banks to earn monopoly rents by virtue of their extensive branch networks. Foreign banks, particularly those that did not enjoy large branch networks and were forced to borrow funds at a premium from local banks or engage in currency swaps, argued that the Rules simply boosted profits of the major local banks.

In response to these criticisms and in view of the growth of swap deposits, a plan to deregulate the payment of interest on time deposits was approved in 1994 (HKMA (1994)).[28] Demand and savings deposits affected by the Interest Rate Rules, which comprised the bulk of affected deposits, were not part of the deregulation plan. Restrictions on time deposits were removed in stages between October 1994 and October 1995, when the Monetary Authority lifted the ceilings on interest rates of time deposits of exactly seven days. Further deregulation would not be considered until after 1997, as concerns were expressed about the effect of increased liberalization on the stability of the banking system.

As interest rates were liberalized, deregulated Hong Kong dollar time deposits grew sharply. This mainly reflected a shift in funds from swap deposits. By mid-1996, deposit movements had stabilized and the growth of deregulated time deposits had slowed to 10 percent. Spreads between Hong Kong and U.S. time deposit rates returned to the levels prevailing prior to the interest rate liberalization.

Hong Kong Dollar Debt Market

Compared with the large stock market, Hong Kong's domestic debt market is relatively undeveloped. At the end of 1995, bonds outstanding issued by Hong Kong private issuers represented only 12 percent of GDP, while the stock market capitalization was more than double the size of GDP. Historically, the development of the Hong Kong dollar debt market has been constrained by the lack of benchmark risk-free government securities, the absence of a bond rating, and the dominance of banks in the financial sector relative to securities firms (World Bank (1995)). However, the bond market began to grow rapidly in recent years, in large part owing to the authorities' efforts.

In 1990, the Exchange Fund Bills program was launched to facilitate open market operations and develop the domestic debt market. In 1993, the program was extended to Exchange Fund Notes with maturities longer than one year. The proceeds of the bills and notes are not used to fund government spending. Instead, these proceeds are invested by the Monetary Authority, which also took over the government Bond Program in March 1993.

The gradual lengthening of the maturity of the Exchange Fund bills and notes has provided a bench-

mark for the issuance of debt instruments of longer maturities. The first issue of 5-year notes was launched in 1994, and 10-year notes were launched in 1996. New issues of Exchange Fund notes have been favorably received by the market, and investor confidence for the notes that straddle the 1997 handover date appears to be high. The average accepted yield of the first issue of the 10-year notes launched in October 1996 was 90 basis points above corresponding U.S. treasury bills. The yield spread has since fallen to around 50 basis points.

A very active primary and secondary market has developed in Exchange Fund bills and notes. As the value of bills and notes outstanding has grown from HK$8 billion at the end of 1993 to HK$92 billion in March 1997, the average daily trading volume has risen steadily to almost one-fifth of total bills and notes outstanding in 1996. The Monetary Authority has taken measures to boost the liquidity of the debt market by extending the eligibility of repurchase securities under the Liquidity Adjustment Facility to Mass Transit Railway Corporation and Airport Authority debt instruments, as well as to certain other privately issued Hong Kong dollar bonds.

Regarding the private debt market, the Stock Exchange of Hong Kong has been successful in attracting new bond listings from overseas corporations, supranational organizations, and sovereign issuers whose bonds trade on a regional or global basis. However, debt securities and warrants together account for less than 1 percent of the market capitalization of the Stock Exchange. In 1995, HK$60 million was raised through private debt issues, compared with HK$7.6 billion raised in the Stock Exchange through initial public offerings of equity.

Hong Kong Mortgage Corporation

The growth of the Hong Kong dollar debt market has been hindered by the absence of a broad range of debt instruments, including mortgage-backed securities. The development of a market in mortgage-backed securities, in turn, has been constrained by the lack of standardization in mortgage loans, which has prevented the pooling of such loans into marketable instruments that could be easily analyzed by prospective investors. Moreover, it was difficult for any single bank to launch a securities issue of sufficient size to form a market for mortgage-backed securities.

In light of these constraints, the authorities approved in July 1996 the establishment of the Hong Kong Mortgage Corporation, with a capital base of HK$1 billion. The operations of the Mortgage Corporation are expected to commence in the fourth quarter of 1997. The intention is for the Mortgage Corporation to intermediate between mortgage loan

---

[28]Foreign currency swap deposits are fixed time deposits where the depositor purchases foreign currency on the spot market and places it on deposit with banks, entering at the same time into an agreement with the bank to sell the foreign currency forward at the time of maturity. The development of swap deposits for retail customers significantly reduced the negative impact of the Interest Rate Rules—as well as consumer price inflation—on nominal deposit rates.

originators and investors by purchasing mortgage loans for its own portfolio and funding these purchases through the issue of unsecured debt securities.[29] Once it becomes more established, the Mortgage Corporation will also package the mortgage loans from its own portfolio (or from banks) into mortgage-backed securities, guaranteeing the timely payment of principal and interest on these securities. By helping to reduce the maturity mismatch in the structure of commercial banks' assets and liabilities, the Mortgage Corporation is expected to contribute to overall banking stability.[30] While almost all mortgages are at floating rates—and thus there is little interest rate risk—the maturity mismatch can result in substantial liquidity and funding risks. To reduce such risks, the Mortgage Corporation would help the banks to unload the mortgage loans as and when needed. Similarly, it would help the banks to reduce the risk of high concentration of mortgage lending in their loan portfolios.[31]

The Hong Kong Mortgage Corporation will initially be owned by the government, but will operate on commercial principles and will eventually be turned over to the private sector.

International Activities of the Hong Kong Monetary Authority

The Monetary Authority has played an active role in promoting regional and international monetary cooperation. Following the Mexican financial crisis, the central banks of Hong Kong, Australia, Indonesia, Malaysia, and Thailand signed, in 1995, a series of bilateral repurchase agreements. Under these agreements, a central bank could borrow amounts reported to be up to US$500 million on a one-week basis from another central bank in the region against the security of U.S. treasury bonds in order to boost its U.S. dollar liquidity in times of market stress. In 1996 and early 1997, the Hong Kong Monetary Authority also signed similar bilateral agreements with the central banks of China, Japan, the Philippines, Korea, New Zealand, and Singapore.

Reflecting the international financial community's recognition of the arrangements for two mu-

tually independent monetary authorities after the transfer of sovereignty, both the People's Bank of China and the Hong Kong Monetary Authority joined the Bank for International Settlements (BIS) in 1997. The Hong Kong Monetary Authority will also participate in the IMF's New Arrangements to Borrow.

Financial System and Regulatory Framework

With about 500 banks and representative offices of foreign banks present in Hong Kong, the financial sector makes a significant and rising contribution to the economy in terms of employment, payroll, value added, and foreign exchange earnings. Accordingly, the authorities have given increasing prominence to the prudential supervision of banks and development of the financial regulatory framework in line with international standards. In response to episodes of instability in the financial sector, a concerted effort to strengthen the regulatory framework was begun in the late 1980s. Hong Kong's financial sector now meets major international prudential standards, such as those of the Basle Committee and the International Organization of Securities Commissions.

Bank Soundness

Overall, Hong Kong banks are profitable and well capitalized. During the first half of the 1990s, the Hongkong and Shanghai Bank and its subsidiary Hang Seng Bank were often among the most profitable banks in the world. Many other Hong Kong banks also reported posttax returns on equity approaching 20 percent during this period, compared with rates of return of about 15 percent for banks in industrial countries. In 1996, posttax profits of local banks increased by about 13 percent.

Banks' capital bases have strengthened since the early 1990s. The average risk-weighted capital adequacy ratio for the entire banking sector rose from 13 percent in 1991 to 17.8 percent in 1996, well above the international minimum standard of 8 percent.

In 1995, when the property market was severely depressed, only 1.7 percent of loans made by all banks in Hong Kong were classified as nonperforming (the share was 2.8 percent for local banks). In 1996, the proportion of nonperforming loans increased as many foreign banks were affected by the decline in offshore lending. Bad debt charges more than doubled in 1996 to 0.18 percent from 0.08 percent in 1995. Nevertheless, these levels remain relatively low by international standards.

---

[29]The Mortgage Corporation would thus earn the spread between the mortgage yield (given by the Best Lending Rate plus a customary margin of about 175 basis points) and funding costs (the Mortgage Corporation's debt would be issued at a floating HIBOR).

[30]On average, mortgage loans in Hong Kong have a contractual life of 15 years, while funding consists mainly of customer deposits and interbank borrowing with a maturity of less than three months.

[31]Presently, mortgage loans account for about 22 percent of loans for use in Hong Kong.

The reasons underlying the high profitability of Hong Kong banks have been the subject of some debate.[32] In this context, an important question has been whether the caps on interest on time deposits, as well as demand and savings deposits, contributed to bank profitability in Hong Kong. The available evidence suggests that, although banks in Hong Kong have enjoyed a higher interest rate spread relative to their counterparts abroad, the net interest income of Hong Kong banks is not high by international standards.[33] Rather, operating expenses and provisions for bad loans and other losses are substantially lower for Hong Kong banks, resulting in a higher return on assets. The low operating expenses reflect the fact that banks in Hong Kong are relatively efficient, despite increases in the costs of doing business in recent years.

The impact of property price fluctuations on the financial sector has been a perennial concern in view of the concentration of bank lending to the property sector. As of the end of 1996, residential mortgages represented a quarter of loans for use in Hong Kong. If loans for building, construction, and property development and investment are included, then the share of property-related lending in total loans for use in Hong Kong rises to 46 percent; however, the share of property-related lending in total loans is much lower (19 percent). The historical record indicates that the rate of mortgage loan default is very low by industrial country standards. One reason is that more than half of property-related loans are to end-users, who have traditionally serviced mortgage loans diligently. Banks have also voluntarily adopted conservative loan-to-value ratios for mortgage lending—70 percent on average, and 50 percent for luxury properties—giving them a cushion against property price declines (the effective loan-to-value ratio is on average about 55 percent). Also, banks have traditionally avoided loans at fixed interest rates. As a result, the sharp decline in property values experienced over 1994–95 did not have a significant impact on banks' balance sheets.

As for the property developers, they have generally followed conservative financial policies and avoided high gearing. These policies have been acknowledged by international rating agencies, which have assigned the debt of some major property companies a rating equivalent to that of Exchange Fund Notes.

Owing to the large share of loans to the property sector, there is a mismatch between the maturity structures of banks' assets and liabilities. Although interest rates on the bulk of assets and liabilities reprice relatively quickly—for the banking sector as a whole, 75–80 percent of interest-bearing assets and liabilities reprice within three months—the Monetary Authority has supported the establishment of a mortgage corporation that would, inter alia, standardize the procedures for banks to sell their mortgage loans in the secondary market.

Banking Supervision

The strong performance of Hong Kong's banking sector in recent years belies its volatile past (Box 9). Banking crises occurred in 1982–86, and to a lesser extent in 1991, when the worldwide collapse of the Bank of Commerce and Credit International led to the closure of BCCI (HK) and bank runs on some of the other local banks. However, a major source of potential banking sector instability—regulatory weakness—has been addressed through a series of regulatory and supervisory measures taken since the mid-1980s.

With the establishment of the Hong Kong Monetary Authority in 1993, the powers and duties of the Office of the Commissioner of Banking to develop standards and regulations, supervise banks, and oversee the stability and the development of the banking system as a whole were vested in the Monetary Authority. The Monetary Authority has adopted as one of its cornerstones the policy of ensuring the safety and stability of the banking system. In its approach, it aims to balance the need to preserve the general stability of the banking system with the provision of sufficient incentives for banks to operate efficiently.

Banks in Hong Kong are monitored on a continuous basis using a variety of techniques with the goal of detecting any problem at an early stage. At the core of the Monetary Authority's approach is the on-site examination of individual financial institutions. About one-half of the Monetary Authority staff are bank examiners. Banks are examined, on average, once every two years, with banks based in OECD countries examined once every two to three years, and banks based in developing countries once every 18 months. Bank examinations are supplemented with off-site reviews, prudential meetings, and analyses by external auditors. The Monetary Authority also maintains direct communications with home regulators of foreign banks in Hong Kong. In supervising banks with international operations, it follows international practice as embodied in the principles of the revised

---

[32]See Chapter VI in IMF (1996) for an overview.

[33]The ratio of net interest income to total assets of Hong Kong banks has, in recent years, exceeded that of Japanese banks, but has been somewhat below that of German banks and considerably below that of banks in the United States. One should note that international differences in net interest income as a proportion of total assets reflect not only differences in interest rate spreads but also differences in the maturity and repricing structures of assets.

Box 9. Banking Crisis of the Early 1980s

Hong Kong's most serious recent banking crisis evolved over 1982–86.[1] The crisis affected a wide range of banks and was caused by, among other factors, ineffective prudential supervision. A general crisis of confidence and macroeconomic instability contributed to banking instability. As a result of the crisis, the authorities have adopted strengthening of prudential supervision and improving bank soundness as top priorities for monetary policy.

The crisis began with a run in September 1982 on Hang Lung Bank, then suspected of high-risk exposure. Quick support actions by other leading banks temporarily suppressed the incipient bank run. In November 1982, following the disclosure of financial difficulties of two large property firms (Eda Investment and Carrian Holdings), several deposit-taking companies found themselves on the brink of insolvency. To avert a crisis, the Hongkong and Shanghai Bank issued a statement pledging its support for "soundly-based and well-managed" deposit-taking companies. However, by early 1983 seven of these companies had failed, causing heavy losses to their depositors. These failures created a mounting sense of apprehension about the soundness of the banking system.

On "Black Saturday," September 24, 1983, when the Hong Kong dollar plunged to a record low of HK$9.60 per US$1, rumors also spread quickly about the difficulties of certain banks. In response, the government announced that it was considering a currency stabilization plan, which a few weeks later led to the creation of the linked exchange rate system. In addition, the government took over Hang Lung Bank, which was unable to meet its obligations, and organized with the Hongkong and Shanghai Bank a joint rescue package for the Sun Hung Kai Bank.

For a while, these actions helped restore confidence. But in mid-1985, the Overseas Trust Bank, then Hong Kong's fourth largest domestically incorporated bank, declared insolvency. The Hong Kong government took over the bank by using an estimated HK$2 billion from the Exchange Fund. Despite this rescue action, several other banks suspected of imprudence once more became the targets of deposit withdrawal.

Three main causes of the banking crisis were identified (see Jao (1992)). First, the owners or managers of individual banks or deposit-taking companies were guilty of various forms of imprudence, mismanagement, malpractice, or even criminal offences. Second, the banking regulatory framework was inadequate and enforcement of prudential regulations was lax. Third, adverse changes in the general environment, including political shocks and the worldwide economic downturn, affected the viability of financial institutions and public confidence in them.

With regard to regulatory deficiencies, the Banking Ordinance at the time had a number of loopholes. The liquidity ratio could be manipulated easily, there were no capital ratio provisions to cushion losses and defaults, and there was no control over insider transactions. The enforcement of the Banking Ordinance was relatively lax. Finally, the inability of the authorities to control growth of money and credit during the floating-rate regime of 1974–83 contributed to macroeconomic overheating and deterioration in the quality of bank management.

The most lasting consequence of the crisis has been a radical overhauling of the whole system of prudential supervision, which began in 1985. In 1986, a revised Banking Ordinance was passed with the following features:

• The separate ordinances for licensed banks and deposit-taking companies were consolidated.

• A minimum capital-to-risk-assets ratio of 5 percent was introduced for all Hong Kong banks and deposit-taking companies. The Banking Commissioner was empowered to increase the ratio for particular institutions to 8 percent in the case of banks and 10 percent in the case of the deposit-taking institutions.

• A minimum liquidity ratio of 25 percent against qualifying liabilities was introduced for all banks and deposit-taking companies.

• The powers of the Banking Commissioner were widened, and he was also empowered to appoint a second auditor for banks and deposit-taking companies, and to call a tripartite meeting between the Banking Commission, the auditors, and the institution concerned.

---

[1]This box draws on Jao (1992), pp. 58–61.

Concordat issued by the Basle Committee. In addition, the Minimum Standards of the Basle Committee have been incorporated into the authorization criteria for overseas applicants for banking licences.

In recent years, bank disclosure requirements have been enhanced in order to encourage market participants to influence banks' commercial decisions more directly. In 1994, banks were for the first time required to publish information on transfers to inner reserves and, in 1995, to disclose the level of these reserves. The 1996 disclosure package covered such areas as cash flow statements and market risk expo-

sure. It is expected that in due course regulators would increasingly focus on evaluating banks' risk management systems.

Box 10 summarizes the key features of Hong Kong's banking regulatory framework.

Regulatory Framework for the Securities Market

The stock market crash of October 1987 brought to light serious flaws in both the regulation and operation of Hong Kong's securities markets. In re-

---

Box 10. Summary of Banking Regulations

Exchange controls

None.

Types of financial institutions

Licensed banks, restricted license banks, and deposit-taking companies are authorized banking institutions. "Nonauthorized institutions" are representative offices of overseas banks, insurance companies, mutual funds, securities brokers, finance companies. Nonauthorized institutions are subject to a number of different regulatory frameworks.

Structure

Licensed banks are akin to retail or "high-street" banks; restricted license banks are specialized in merchant banking services, whereas deposit-taking companies are mainly engaged in business such as trade finance and personal loans. Restricted license banks and deposit-taking companies are restricted according to the types of deposits they can accept, rather than the types of activities they can engage in.

Entry/ownership requirements

1. Domestic entities applying to become licensed banks: entity must not be a subsidiary of a local or overseas bank already licensed in Hong Kong, and must have been an authorized institution for 10 years, with deposits not less than HK$3 billion and assets not less than HK$4 billion. The Hong Kong Monetary Authority exercises control over shareholding issues, and over banks' controllers and executives.

2. Foreign entities: An overseas bank must obtain the Monetary Authority's approval, and have assets in excess of US$16 billion, and reciprocity in the bank's home country must be available to Hong Kong banks.

Reserve requirements

None.

Capital adequacy

1. BIS standards applied to domestic licensed banks (the minimum 8 percent ratio may be increased for any particular institution, up to 12 percent for licensed banks and 16 percent for a restricted license bank or a deposit-taking company).

2. Quarterly capital adequacy ratio reporting system.

Liquidity

1. A 25 percent minimum liquidity ratio in each calendar month.

2. Monthly liquidity ratios reporting system.

Deposit insurance

None. A small depositors' prior claim scheme on the liquidation of a bank was adopted by the Legislative Council in 1995.

Interest rate controls

The Interest Rate Rules, which set maximum rates paid on certain Hong Kong dollar deposits, were removed on all time deposits with a maturity of seven days or more. Interest cannot be paid on current (that is, checking) deposits.

Lending restrictions

1. Loans to one borrower limit: 25 percent of capital base.

2. Sectoral exposure limits: Moral suasion used to urge prudence in real estate lending, in particular with regard to loan-value ratios for mortgage lending. Banks may not hold real estate of an aggregate value exceeding 25 percent of their capital base (exceptions are the bank's own premises and land for which the bank is mortgagee).

3. Country exposure limits: Guidelines on provisioning, based on the Bank of England matrix, exist. There are controls on exposure to foreign banks.

4. Aggregate value of unsecured specified liabilities to connected parties: 10 percent of authorized institution's capital base.

5. Security market exposure: An authorized institution may not hold shares to an aggregate value exceeding 25 percent of capital base. Underwriting permitted if the commitment is disposed of in seven working days.

6. Exchange rate risk: Industry guideline issued to banks. Overnight open position agreed with authorized institution. Monthly reporting of foreign exchange position.

Reporting

Liquidity return is submitted on a monthly basis. In addition to the returns mentioned in this box, there are other returns that authorized institutions need to submit on a monthly, quarterly, and semiannual basis.

Prudential supervision

Approximately annual to biannual on-site examinations to check bank records and management practices, particularly asset quality. Off-site annual reviews of bank statistics, followed by prudential interviews with senior management of banks. Auditing of banks' systems for compiling prudential returns and ensuring compliance with certain banking regulations. Tripartite meeting would also be held with management of banks and external auditors.

Public disclosure

Audited annual financial statements are required under the Companies Ordinance, which apply to locally incorporated authorized institutions regardless of whether they are incorporated under the Ordinance. Disclosure of inner reserves required for all authorized institutions. Banks incorporated outside Hong Kong, subject to auditing and accounting requirements of their home country, can apply for an exemption to these requirements. Audited annual financial statements (inner reserves not allowed). "Reports of Condition and Income" are available to the public. Financial disclosure is applied to all authorized institutions.

sponse to these flaws, the Securities and Futures Commission was established in 1989, with responsibility for supervising the stock and futures exchanges, regulating other financial intermediaries, enforcing codes of conduct, and recommending securities market legislation. The Stock Exchange of Hong Kong and the Hong Kong Futures Exchange were reorganized, and the Securities and Futures Commission has increased market transparency and efficiency, and strengthened investor protection, surveillance, and investigative work. Hong Kong's securities markets have adopted international regulatory standards.

In establishing a framework for H share listings for Chinese enterprises, the Securities and Futures Commission, the Stock Exchange of Hong Kong, and the Chinese authorities recognized that a sound regulatory framework was critical. In this context, H share companies were required to meet all the listing and reporting standards that apply to Hong Kong listings. Efforts were also coordinated between the Chinese and Hong Kong authorities to curtail backdoor listings, the practice whereby Chinese enterprises entered the Hong Kong stock market by purchasing listed Hong Kong companies and used them as shell companies to raise equity finance in Hong Kong.

Other recent regulatory developments include the introduction of Codes of Conduct for futures and securities dealers by the Futures Exchange and the Securities and Futures Commission, and new disclosure requirements for all listed companies, which require companies to report on directors' and managers' salaries, liquidity and capital resources, material changes in operational items, investments, and prospective merger negotiations. In addition, a new Securities and Futures Bill, to be introduced in 1997, will consolidate existing legislation on the regulation of the securities and futures market, and will streamline the regulatory framework.

Factor Markets and Social Policies

The Hong Kong government has generally refrained from direct intervention in factor markets, focusing instead on measures to facilitate market-based adjustments. In the labor market, the government has been involved mainly through its role in social policies, which has expanded rapidly in recent years, but nevertheless remains relatively small by international standards. In the property market, the main intervention has come through the large public housing program and, to a lesser extent, as a by-product of the government's title to ownership of all land in the territory.

Labor Market Policies

During the past decade, the main labor market issue has been labor shortage rather than unemployment. To address this issue, in 1989 the government put in place a General Labor Importation Scheme, under which no more than 25,000 low- and semi-skilled workers (about 1 percent of the labor force) were allowed to work in Hong Kong at any one time.[34] In 1992, a special labor importation scheme was approved to meet the temporary surge in demand for construction workers on the airport project. Labor imports of up to 17,000 workers were allowed under this program. A new pilot program to recruit about 1,000 Chinese professionals began in 1994 in order to meet the excess demand for labor in the financial sector.

The sharp and somewhat unexpected rise in unemployment during 1995 led to calls for the government to reexamine its noninterventionist labor market policies. Unemployment was concentrated in the restaurant and retail sectors, which traditionally have absorbed a part of the low-skilled workforce released from manufacturing. As employment in manufacturing continued to contract at a double digit rate in 1995, the weakening of the demand for low-skilled service jobs was interpreted by many observers as a structural phenomenon. In addition, the skill mismatches between the unemployed and job vacancies had increased and prolonged the job search process, contributing to an increase in unemployment.

The continuing strength in overall employment suggested, however, that the impact of demand-side factors was limited. The government therefore focused on the microeconomic aspects of the problem. The Employees Retraining Scheme, introduced in 1992 to provide vocational training to workers displaced from the manufacturing sector, was expanded to teach new skills (such as computing), and a separate Job Matching Program was introduced in order to fill the large number of vacancies.[35] Under the program, more than 10,000 workers (75 percent of participants in the program) found jobs between April 1995 and December 1996. In addition, as public concern about the unemployment problem initially centered around imported labor, the government tightened the General Labor Importation Scheme by cutting the quota on imported labor to

---

[34]The workers were recruited mainly from China under two-year nonrenewable contracts and received a minimum allowable wage (equal to the median wage in a given sector), accommodation, and other benefits. Expatriate professionals and domestic helpers have not been subject to quotas under the General Labor Importation Scheme.

[35]In the third quarter of 1995, there were 50,700 job vacancies and 113,400 unemployed.

2,000 workers. In the event, the decline in real wages brought about by these adjustments led to increased demand for labor and easing of unemployment pressures in 1996.

Social Policies

Over the past ten years, social services, comprising health, education, and social welfare, have been the fastest growing category of government spending. The growth in social spending partly reflected secular trends, such as the structural shift to a services economy, which required the workforce to obtain new skills, and demographic changes, such as increased immigration and the aging of the population. However, at about 8½ percent of GDP in FY1995 (including the budgetary cost of the public housing program), the level of social spending is still low in comparison with the OECD countries, and accounted for slightly less than half of total public expenditure:

	In billions of Hong Kong dollars	In percent of GDP	In percent of public expenditure
Education	33.6	3.1	17.6
Health care	24.3	2.2	12.7
Social welfare	14.1	1.3	7.4
Public housing	19.1	1.8	10.0
Total	91.1	8.4	47.7

Social Welfare

Social welfare in Hong Kong comprises social security and other targeted programs aimed at supporting vulnerable groups and those who are not expected to work, for example, children or the disabled. For the working population, as discussed above, the government has sought to ensure that labor market flexibility, combined with the schemes for employee retraining and job matching, enable the unemployed to return to work quickly. In comparison with the OECD countries, Hong Kong does not have an extensive social safety net—total public expenditure on social security only reached 1 percent of GDP in FY1995. The following programs constitute Hong Kong's social safety net.

• The *Comprehensive Social Security Assistance* scheme raises income to a minimum level for eligible persons in five categories: the elderly, the disabled, children, the sick, and able-bodied adults. Able-bodied adults, with certain exceptions, have to register for job placement in order to qualify. The scheme includes a means test and requires residence in Hong Kong for at least one year. The Comprehensive Social Security Assistance scheme covered

about 130,000 cases at the end of 1995 at a cost of HK$4.2 billion.[36] The number of its recipients grew by 14 percent a year over 1991–95.

• The *Social Security Allowance* (SSA) scheme provides modest flat rate allowances for the elderly and severely disabled who do not qualify for the Comprehensive Social Security Assistance. Eligibility for the old-age allowance requires Hong Kong residency for at least five years prior to receiving assistance under the scheme. Except for those aged between 65 and 69, the scheme does not include a means test. At the end of 1995, the Social Security Assistance scheme covered almost half a million people at a cost of HK$3.6 billion. The program grew by 2 percent a year since 1990.

• There are also three other schemes, for victims of crime and law enforcement acts, traffic accidents, and natural or other disasters, who are not means-tested.

The welfare schemes are funded entirely from government's current revenue. Grants and loans for capital projects with a welfare content are provided out of the Lotteries Fund. Apart from schemes providing financial assistance, the government and nongovernmental organizations run welfare programs to help families, children, the disabled, and the elderly.

Pension System and Care for the Elderly

The aging of the population has increased assistance for the elderly in recent years. The number of people aged 65 and above increased from an estimated 390,000 in 1984 (7 percent of total population) to 630,000 by mid-1996 (10 percent) and is projected to increase to about 1 million by 2016 (13 percent). Public spending on health and welfare services for the elderly increased by 55 percent in real terms from FY1992 to FY1996, reaching about HK$12 billion in FY1996.

Care for the elderly is provided through income-support schemes (discussed above), government and private pension schemes, and residential care institutions. The coverage of these schemes is as follows.

• About half a million elderly people received old-age allowances under the Social Security Assistance and Comprehensive Social Security Assistance schemes in mid-1996.

• The government operates three retirement schemes: a pay-as-you-go pension scheme for about 180,000 civil servants (6 percent of the employed), a

---

[36]As of April 1996, the average monthly payments, which include standard rates (for adults expected to work but currently without a job, these rates were set at HK$1,615) and various types of special grants, amounted to HK$2,400, and for a household with four members to HK$10,270; medical service was available free of charge. By comparison, in March 1996 the average monthly salary amounted to about HK$9,800.

similar scheme for those employed in the judiciary, and a fully funded provident fund scheme for about 50,000 teachers.

• About 15,000 private pension schemes cover about 830,000 employees in the private sector (about 29 percent of the employed). During FY1995, total value of assets of some 8,800 retirement schemes registered with the Office of the Registrar of Occupational Retirement Schemes amounted to about HK$84 billion, while the total annual contributions to these schemes amounted to about HK$18 billion, three-fourths of which were funded by employers.

• The government provides residential care for about 15,000 elderly who can no longer be cared for at home and funds community support services for the elderly.

Under the present system, the government encourages the establishment of voluntary retirement protection schemes and monitors and regulates them under the Occupational Retirement Schemes Ordinance. However, the possibility of introducing some form of compulsory retirement benefit scheme has been discussed in Hong Kong for many years. In December 1993, the government tabled a proposal for a pay-as-you-go old-age pension scheme, which would have provided a fixed monthly benefit to every eligible resident aged 65 and over. The scheme was to be financed by a levy of 3 percent on assessable income, to be split equally between the employees and employers, while the government proposed to make a HK$10 billion (1¼ percent of GDP) one-time contribution. The key benefit of the scheme, according to the original proposal, was that it would have provided immediate benefits upon implementation to all eligible elderly residents, including low-income employees, homemakers, and retirees. The proposal gave rise to a number of concerns, including the lack of relationship between the contribution and benefit rates and the risks of creating a large unfunded liability for the future government. After public consultation in early 1995, the old-age pension scheme proposal was withdrawn due to lack of public support.

In March 1995, the government unveiled a new pension proposal—the privately managed Mandatory Provident Fund scheme—that would cover about 2 million employees (Box 11). It has been proposed that existing private pension schemes could continue to operate if they met some minimum requirements, including providing employees with a choice of staying with or joining existing occupational retirement schemes or opting for Mandatory Provident Fund coverage. The government has elaborated various aspects of the Mandatory Provident Fund with consultants, the financial industry, and representatives of the employers and employees during 1996, and has presented to the Legislative Council the draft subsidiary legislation in the second quarter of 1997. If approved, the Fund could start operation in 1998.

Property Market and Land Policy

Public Housing Program

Hong Kong's government operates an extensive public housing program, which covers almost half the population (about 3.1 million people). The program was started in 1954 in response to an acute housing crisis that developed after World War II. The program received a major boost in 1972, when the government revealed a long-term plan calling for an acceleration of public housing construction to provide accommodation for 1.8 million people over 10 years. In the early 1980s, public housing policy shifted from massive production to a more quality-oriented approach. Housing production in the public sector nevertheless continued to exceed that in the private sector:

	1995	1996	1995–2001
Public rental units	14,559	18,560	141,000
Subsidized housing units	22,023	18,968	175,000
Units under the Home Ownership Scheme[1]	21,141	...	151,000
Units for "sandwich class" families	882	...	24,000
Subsidized loans for private purchase	...	...	16,000
Private housing units	20,351	...	195,000
Total	56,933	...	520,000

[1]Including the Private Sector Participation Scheme, which is complementary to the Home Ownership Scheme but uses private sector resources. Under this scheme, 66,000 apartments had been built by March 1996, and a further 62,000 are planned for the period up to March 2001.

Total housing stock of 2 million units as of mid-1996 included 700,000 public rental units and about 220,000 subsidized housing units.

The main areas of the public housing program are public rental housing, subsidized home ownership schemes, financial assistance for home buyers, and facilitation of private housing production.

• The Home Ownership Scheme was introduced in 1978 to build new public housing units for sale to qualified applicants at about half the market price. It has since become the largest public housing scheme. Households with an income below HK$26,000 and public housing tenants (for whom there is no income limit) are eligible for this scheme. The subsidy mainly comes in the form of land granted by the government to the Housing Authority and the Housing Society. In addition, favorable mortgage terms are available under the scheme.

• The Sandwich Class Housing Scheme targets families with monthly income of HK$26,000–50,000.

Box 11. Mandatory Provident Fund Scheme Proposal

The main elements of the proposed Mandatory Provident Fund scheme are as follows.[1]

- **Coverage:** All employees and self-employed between the age of 18 and 65 are covered, except civil servants, judicial officers, and teachers covered by statutory pension schemes, and domestic employees and persons who entered Hong Kong to work for a limited period or who already have a home country scheme.

- **Contributions:** For monthly incomes of HK$4,000–20,000, both the employee and employer have to contribute 5 percent of the employee's income each. If the monthly income exceeds HK$20,000, the employee and employer have to contribute up to the first HK$20,000 of the monthly salary; for the portion of salary above this amount contributions are not mandatory. An employee with monthly income below HK$4,000 is not required, but may elect to contribute; the employer must, however, contribute 5 percent of the employee's income.

- **Vesting and preservation of benefits:** All contributions to the Fund must be fully and immediately vested with the employee's account. All benefits derived from the Fund must be preserved until the employee reaches the age of 65, or retires between the ages of 60 and 65.

- **Portability of benefits:** The accrued benefits of an employee can be transferred to another scheme when an employee changes an employment, or left with the trustee of the scheme maintained by the previous employer.

- **Mandatory Provident Fund Schemes Authority** will administer and regulate the system. The Authority will also approve trustees, regulate their operations, and make rules and guidelines for administration and regulation of the system.

- **Trustees** are responsible for all aspects of a scheme and must comply with regulations and duties imposed by the Authority. Trustees may be corporate or individuals; overseas trustees and master trusts can be established if they meet certain requirements.

- A **compensation fund** will be established to compensate employees for losses due to fraud or misfeasance. Losses due to poor investment will not be compensated. The government intends to contribute HK$300 million as seed money toward the compensation fund.

The authorities estimated the size of annual contributions to the Mandatory Provident Fund at about 4 percent of GDP. Assuming a 3 percent real rate of return and a 40-year contribution period, benefits under the Fund are projected at about 50 percent of the average wage. The Fund is not expected to affect the gross flow of saving significantly because it would mainly rechannel saving from personal to organized funds. Given the requirement to invest 30 percent of the funds in Hong Kong dollar assets, the scheme could help accelerate the development of the Hong Kong dollar debt market, although currently pension funds already allocate a comparable share of their portfolio to such assets.

---

[1]Hewitt Associates and GML Consulting (1995).

These families have too high an income to qualify for public housing, but cannot afford mortgages for private housing. This scheme is also based on the granting of land to the Housing Authority on concessional terms, and it provides for mortgages at a 2 percent interest rate.

- Financial assistance under the Home Purchase Loan Scheme consists of interest-free loans or a monthly subsidy to low- and middle-income families. The income limits are the same as those for the Home Ownership Scheme.

The demand for housing has increased over the past few years, and future demand may surpass the current production targets for the period up to 2001.[37]

The most important agency involved in the implementation of the public housing program is the Housing Authority, a quasi-autonomous nongovernmental organization with 15,000 employees. The practice of granting land outright for public housing projects has resulted in a large implicit subsidy that is not transparently classified as social spending in the fiscal accounts. The total market value of land granted to the Housing Authority and the Housing Society during FY1991–95 was HK$126 billion (up to 3½ percent of GDP a year). The value of all land granted to the Housing Authority alone was HK$142 billion (valued at historical cost) at the end of FY1995.

A number of concerns about the allocative efficiency and equity aspects of the program have been expressed over the years.[38] In particular, there have been concerns about long waiting periods for public housing (about 6½ years on average), while many current occupants had sufficient means to move to private housing. The government estimated that in

---

[37]See Government Secretariat Housing Branch (1996).

[38]See, for example, Chau (1992) and Fu (1995).

1995 at least 13 percent of families living in public housing owned other property.[39] In 1996, the Housing Authority decided to strengthen the means tests for tenants and applicants, so that those with means above prescribed levels will be required to pay market rents. In January 1997, the government also proposed to raise public housing rents to 15–18½ percent of household income from the current average of 9 percent. These measures are aimed at increasing the home ownership rate from 52 percent to 60 percent of the households by the year 2001.

Private Residential Property Market

The government has only rarely intervened in the private residential market, generally leaving the property cycle to run its course. In recent years, however, prompted by signs of widespread speculation, the government intervened twice to cool the escalating property prices—in early 1994 and again in early 1997 (Box 12). Many of these measures were aimed at the forward sales of apartments, which have spontaneously developed during the early 1990s in response to persistent housing shortage. This market innovation had allowed the developers to act as wholesalers, that is, to unload their stock to speculators (or end-users), who then served as retail distributors for developers. It has been argued that restrictions on forward sales would raise both the risks of property development (by eliminating an important leading indicator for private developers), and the overall costs of property development (by forcing developers to hold on to their stock until final sale), thereby reducing the incentives for developers to acquire developable land. However, while the speculators may have played a useful market role, their activities were regarded as having generally amplified price fluctuations. In the event, the measures restricting the presale of uncompleted apartments taken in 1994 proved effective, as the share of speculative sales in total sales stood at about 10 percent in November 1995, compared with over 20 percent in early 1994.[40]

Land Policy

As land in Hong Kong is owned by the Hong Kong government, the land market is essentially a market for land leases, most of which are transferable. The leases for newly released land are generally allocated to the highest bidder at public auctions.[41] As each lease term requires a large lump-sum premium and a small annual rent, the premium attached to any given land lease approximates the land value. In view of these special characteristics of the land market in Hong Kong and the steady increase in property prices in recent years, a key issue has been whether the policy of auctioning off land to the highest bidder has negatively affected the supply of property and amplified the secular rise in prices. Several factors suggest that this has generally not been the case.

• In the residential market, the historical correlation between land supply and net private housing supply is relatively weak, even allowing for a lag of 2–3 years between the land sales and housing completions. However, the negative correlation between land sales and housing prices (with about a year's lag) is relatively strong.[42]

• Since 1984, land releases have been subject to an annual limit of 50 hectares agreed to in the Sino-British Joint Declaration (see Section VI). Under agreements negotiated in the Sino-British Land Commission, this limit has been consistently breached, especially with respect to land for housing development, suggesting that the pressure on the government has been to increase rather than withhold the supply of land.

• The bulk of land for commercial development has traditionally been supplied through redevelopment of old sites. Evidence suggests that the incentive to acquire land for redevelopment (from both the government and private owners) and the speed of redevelopment depend primarily on the market response in the forward sales market, which is generally driven by market sentiment about the macroeconomic outlook.

• While land sales are a major source of revenue for the government, the Hong Kong government share of this revenue is earmarked for capital works projects.

• Rather than depressing the supply of property, the restrictive land policy may have actually encouraged the production of housing units in the short run because the anticipated higher future rents have been capitalized into higher current housing prices (Peng and Wheaton (1994)). In the long run, the main effect of the current land policy seems to have been to promote substitution of capital for land by encouraging the construction of high-rise apartment buildings and raising the density of development.

Despite the downturn in the property market, prices achieved in land auctions during 1994–96 were generally higher than expected. As property companies typically acquire land long before developing the sites in order to build up strategic "land

---

[41]The reservation price for a given site is based on the market price prevailing one week before the auction.

[39]An income test and a property ownership test are applied at the time of allocation of apartments. After ten years of tenancy, and every two years thereafter, occupants have to declare their income.

[40]Speculative property transactions are defined as those effected within two years of the last purchase of an apartment.

[42]See Peng and Wheaton (1994). Their data cover 1965–90.

Box 12. Government Measures for the Residential Property Market

Following the sharp escalation in property prices and the intensification of property speculation in 1993 and early 1994, the government took the unusual step of intervening directly in the property market in March and June of 1994. A government task force identified a number of factors underlying the rapid price increases (Planning, Environment, and Lands Branch (1994)).

The demand-side factors included the exceptionally high population growth since 1990 (over 2 percent per year), the decline in household size, a growing number of expatriate professionals working in Hong Kong, the rising affluence of the population, negative real interest rates, and strong inflows of capital.

The main supply-side factor was the small net increase in the housing stock (about 3 percent per year between 1990 and 1993). The task force concluded that there was no reason to be concerned about the overall stability of the residential property market, but measures were needed to address concerns about social stability and Hong Kong's competitiveness. The measures announced by the government were, therefore, directed at curbing speculation and increasing the supply of land and housing:

- Changes in town planning rules, including rezoning of land for commercial purposes
- Increasing the supply of new sites and facilitating redevelopment of existing sites
- Speeding up the processing of new land grants, land exchanges, and lease modifications

- Involving the private sector in the supply of infrastructure for major private sector projects
- Increasing housing and land supply, including a plan to increase the overall supply of apartments built on new land by 45,000 units by 2001
- Measures to dampen speculative activities, including

 (1) Lowering the quota for private (insider) sales of uncompleted apartments;

 (2) Restricting forward sales of apartments to not more than nine months before the anticipated date of assignment to buyers; and

 (3) Increasing the initial deposit and the penalty for default of purchase to 10 percent of the purchase price.

In March 1997, following the strong runup in residential property prices in the second half of 1996 and early 1997, the government passed additional measures.

- The presale period was extended from 12 months to 15 months before the estimated date of completion of the development.
- Property developers were required to put all apartments for presale onto the market within six months of the date of consent given, and to increase the proportion of apartments for presale.
- It was agreed to release 587 hectares of land for housing development (327 hectares for public housing and 260 hectares for private housing) by the year 2002.

---

banks," the intensive bidding in land auctions indicated their confidence in the longer-term outlook for the Hong Kong economy.

Trade and Competition Policies

Trade Policy

Free trade is one of the founding principles of Hong Kong as an economic entity. Long before the worldwide process of trade liberalization began and the multilateral trading system was established, Hong Kong had been practicing free and open trade with no tariffs, no trade restrictions, and no unilateral trade policy instruments to protect domestic industries or promote exports. The commitment to this principle has derived from the simple reality that Hong Kong has a small domestic market, limited usable land, and no natural resources other than its deep-water harbor. Against this background, Hong Kong's economy has benefited enormously from the world trade liberalization and, in particular, the opening up of China to foreign trade and investment. China's anticipated accession to the World Trade Organization (WTO) would bring to Hong Kong

enhanced access to China's vast market and the resulting increase in trade between China and other countries, a large part of which would continue to be conducted through Hong Kong.

The Hong Kong Special Administrative Region will possess full autonomy in the conduct of its external economic relations with separate membership in the WTO, the Asian Development Bank, and the Asia-Pacific Economic Cooperation (APEC) forum, among others.

Import and Export System

Hong Kong is a duty-free port and does not levy any tariffs on imports. Apart from import quota control on rice and certain ozone-depleting substances, Hong Kong does not maintain any quantitative restrictions. Import licensing requirements are kept to a minimum and either stem from obligations under international agreements, or are applied for reasons of health, safety, or access to high-technology products, or for environmental reasons. Uniform excise taxes are imposed for revenue-raising purposes on imports and domestic production of tobacco, cosmetics, alcohol, and some hydrocarbon oils.[43] A sub-stantial tax (40–60 percent published retail price) also is imposed on the initial registration of motor vehicles, which are all imported, to raise revenue and contain vehicle growth. Voluntary export restraint arrangements and marketing arrangements do not exist, either at the government or the industry level. Government procurement policies treat all local and overseas suppliers on an equal footing. Export controls apply only in the textiles and clothing sectors, required by commitments under the Multi-Fiber Arrangement.[44] The Hong Kong government does not provide subsidies, tax exemptions, or other financial incentives to assist the promotion of exports from Hong Kong.[45] Finally, there is no foreign exchange control in Hong Kong. Movement of funds into and out of Hong Kong is completely free and the Hong Kong dollar is freely convertible.

Trade Policy Objectives and Issues

Consistent with its belief in free trade, the Hong Kong government strongly supports the multilateral trading system and does not participate in any preferential trading arrangements. To the extent that Hong Kong participates in such arrangements, however, the objectives of trade policy are to safeguard Hong Kong's rights and fulfill its obligations under relevant agreements and to maintain and improve access for Hong Kong exports (GATT (1994)).

Hong Kong played an active role in the Uruguay Round of multilateral trade negotiations and was one of the founding members of the WTO.[46] At the first WTO Ministerial Conference in Singapore in December 1996, Hong Kong proposed a broad-based review of WTO rules to assess their interaction with globalization and investment and competition policy. Hong Kong has also participated in services negotiations in several areas, and supported China's accession to the WTO. On the regional trade front, Hong Kong has actively participated in the APEC forum since becoming a member in 1991. Hong Kong has taken the position that trade and invest-

ment liberalization within APEC should be consistent with the multilateral trading system.

While the full impact of the phaseout of quantitative restrictions under the Agreement on Textiles and Clothing, which replaced the Multi-Fiber Arrangement, has yet to be felt, Hong Kong's textiles and clothing sectors have already adjusted to structural changes over the past decade by shifting to production of high value-added items such as fashion clothes, relocating labor-intensive production processes to China and other low-cost economies, and setting up production facilities in the United States and Europe to gain better access to these markets. Hong Kong has thus increasingly become a control and support center for production bases in foreign countries.

In recent years, the trade policy issues of greatest importance for Hong Kong have been market access for Hong Kong exports and trade relations between the United States and China. In regard to market access, several countries have taken antidumping measures against Hong Kong exporters. Although there have been no legal rulings against Hong Kong on charges of dumping, the accusations often inflicted considerable economic damage during the protracted period prior to the resolution of legal proceedings. The government has therefore pressed, in the context of the Uruguay Round, for strengthening the WTO rules on the settling of antidumping disputes.

With regard to U.S.-China trade relations, the main issue for Hong Kong has been the annually recurring renewal of China's Most Favored Nation trading status. According to official estimates, a withdrawal of China's favored status would reduce Hong Kong's reexports to the United States by up to 45 percent. As various trade-related services would also be affected, this could result in losses of up to 60,000 jobs in Hong Kong, and a reduction in the annual growth rate of real GDP of between 2 and 2¾ percentage points.[47] There would be further losses in income and jobs for Hong Kong if China were to cut back on its imports from the United States, and if there was a consequent weakening of investment in China by Hong Kong and foreign companies. In view of the magnitude of this impact, the Hong Kong authorities have actively advocated the renewal of China's Most Favored Nation status before the U.S. authorities.

Competition Policy

Owing to Hong Kong's openness, firms in the traded goods and services sectors are subject to strong competition from abroad. In the nontraded goods and services sectors, the degree of competition also is generally high, as restrictions on entry exist only in a few industries. However, there has been increased attention paid

---

[43]For a detailed description, see GATT (1994).

[44]Under this arrangement, Hong Kong currently maintains bilateral agreements with Canada, the European Union, Norway, and the United States.

[45]The promotional activities of the Hong Kong Trade Development Council, an independent statutory body subvented by the government, are restricted to market research, dissemination of business information, and organizing trade fairs, exhibitions, and trade missions.

[46] Hong Kong acquired contracting party status in the GATT in 1986, following a declaration by the British government that Hong Kong was a separate customs territory possessing full autonomy in the conduct of its external relations and of other matters provided for in the GATT; previously it had participated in the GATT as a member of the U.K. delegation.

[47]Hong Kong Government Press Release, April 18, 1997.

to competition policy in the nontraded sector with the realization that a fair and open competition in this sector is an essential element in Hong Kong's efforts to maintain its status as an international business center.

Questions concerning the degree of competition are largely limited to those few markets where, owing to scale economies or specific entry restrictions, only a limited number of firms are active. Important examples are property development, telecommunications, public utilities, broadcasting, and supermarkets. Also, licensing requirements in the legal, accounting, and medical professions, while serving a legitimate cause, have the effect of reducing entry and competition. Because many nontraded services are used as inputs for traded goods and services, elevated costs resulting from a lack of domestic competition can affect Hong Kong's pattern of comparative advantage as well as its attractiveness to foreign capital and labor.

Hong Kong has no comprehensive competition policy based on laws against collusive agreements, the abuse of market power, or mergers and acquisitions that create a dominant market position. Instead, for certain activities with a recognized oligopoly, the government controls private firms' behavior under clearly defined schemes of control, which list strict performance criteria and prescribe a specific formula on the basis of which agreed profits can be generated. Such regimes exist for power utilities, telecommunications, and public transportation. The gambling sector is a regulated monopoly, run by the Hong Kong Jockey Club. For other sectors, the government follows a case-by-case approach in determining the need for controls on anticompetitive behavior.

Responding to a call by the governor to work toward the development of a comprehensive competition policy, the Consumer Council has examined the degree of competition in domestic sectors in a series of studies since 1992.[48] The studies covered banking (in particular, the issue of caps on interest rates on time deposits, discussed above), domestic gas supply, broadcasting, telecommunications, private residential property, and supermarket industries. In 1996, in a general study of Hong Kong's competition policy, the Consumer Council argued that transparency and effectiveness of the regulatory framework could be enhanced, and recommended the adoption of a comprehensive competition law, with a competition authority to investigate breaches of the law (Consumer Council (1996d)).

The degree of competition in domestic sectors also was examined in a recent study commissioned by a private group, the Vision 2047 Foundation (Enright and others (1997)). The nontraded sectors, by and large,

scored good marks in this study for quality and—when compared with other countries in the region—the price of services provided. However, the study also found scope for greater efficiency and more competition in a number of important areas, including in the self-regulated legal and accounting professions, where the lack of competition has led to relatively high costs and charges. The study also concluded that, while Hong Kong has the potential to become a significant supplier of medical and educational services to the region, this opportunity has not been exploited. High barriers to entry into local medical practice and a virtual government monopoly in both sectors were considered to have contributed to the loss of such potential.

Sectoral Competition Issues

The market for residential property development is dominated by a small number of firms. According to the Consumer Council (1996c), between 1991 and 1994, one firm supplied 25 percent of the housing units, 55 percent came from four developers, and seven suppliers supplied 70 percent of new private housing. Since 1981 no new firm has been able to secure a market share larger than 5 percent, indicating a low degree of contestability. The Consumer Council noted a number of de facto barriers to entry, including large resources needed to enter the sector, high finance costs for entrants owing to the lack of a track record, and entrants' weak bargaining power in hiring professionals and contractors. The Council also noted that prolonged apartment vacancies, downward price rigidity, and the release of apartments in batches rather than on a continuous basis may indicate oligopolistic behavior within the sector. Enright and others (1997) concluded, however, that concentration had not made the domestic property developers inefficient, since they successfully sold their services outside Hong Kong. According to this study, the high property costs in Hong Kong should primarily be attributed to the scarcity of land and the government's ability to influence land supply, rather than developers' oligopolistic behavior.

Hong Kong's two privately owned electricity suppliers are subject to both profit and price controls. Their tariffs depend on a user's level of consumption, but there are no sector-specific concessions. The terms of these schemes of control rewarded the companies for capital investment. Enright and others (1997) found that this had led to the creation of one of the highest quality power supply infrastructures in the world, that, while not among the most expensive in Asia, was arguably more expensive than it should be, given the low overhead costs of delivering such services in Hong Kong's geographically compact territory.

In the gas supply market, the sole piped-gas supplier, Hong Kong & China Gas, has not been subject

---

[48]The Consumer Council, established in 1974, is a statutory body charged with protecting and promoting the interests of consumers of goods, services, and immovable property. The chairman and members of the council are all appointed by the governor.

Box 13. Regulation of the Telecommunications Industry

The regulatory framework governing Hong Kong's telecommunications sector currently adopts an open market approach. Except for certain international circuits and services, competitive conditions exist in local telephony (four carriers), radio paging (with over 30 licenses and more than 1 million subscribers), cellular phone services (four operators, with more than 1.3 million subscribers), and a wide variety of other communications services.

By far the largest operator, the Hong Kong Telecom Group comprises three entities operating telecommunications services. Hong Kong Telephone Company holds one of the four local telephone network licenses. Hong Kong Telecom CSL provides liberalized telecommunications services. Hong Kong Telecom International holds an exclusive licence, expiring in 2006, for certain international circuits and services.[1] The separation into three entities, with their own accounting requirements, is intended to ensure transparency and prevent cross-subsidization between regulated and nonregulated areas. Hong Kong Telephone Company is subject to a system of price caps, limiting annual price increases to the increase in the CPI less 4 percent. Hong Kong Telecom International must comply with a tariff ceiling on its international calls. Both arrangements were intended to induce the companies to share productivity gains with consumers. All other segments of the industry are free of price or profit controls.

---

[1]Private companies may operate their own international circuits for intracorporate traffic by certain specified means.

In the area of local fixed telephone services, residential users are charged a flat-rate monthly tariff for unlimited local calls. The government allowed three new companies into the market in July 1995 when Hong Kong Telephone Company's monopoly franchise expired. Net proceeds from international calls are shared between Hong Kong Telecom International and local providers in compensation for delivering basic access. At the beginning of 1996, Hong Kong Telephone Company still accounted for 99 percent of basic telephone calls. Official estimates have put the consumer savings from the opening of local telephony at about HK$1.7 billion over 1995–2005.

In the area of international telecommunications, Hong Kong Telecom International was granted in 1981 a 25-year exclusive licence to provide certain external circuits and services. The Consumer Council (1996b) recommended that the Telecommunications Authority of Hong Kong monitor the accounting rates negotiated by the Hong Kong Telecom International with its counterparts in foreign countries. The government agreed to this recommendation, and proposed in the Telecommunication (Amendment) Bill that adequate power be conferred on the Telecommunications Authority to influence the implementation of the international accounting rate system in Hong Kong so that public interest is not hurt.

The government has reviewed the Telecommunications Ordinance and published in March 1997 a consultation document setting out a series of legislative amendments to update the regulatory framework for the industry.

---

to price regulation or operated under franchise, since it is deemed to have to compete with electric power companies and suppliers of bottled liquefied petroleum. The Consumer Council (1995) argued that these policies helped Hong Kong & China Gas earn high profits to the detriment of its customers, and recommended that it be regulated proactively by imposing profit or price controls in the public interest. The Consumer Council also proposed the introduction of a "common carrier" system to eliminate the entry barrier into gas supply transmission and distribution networks. The government, while viewing the rate of return earned by the Hong Kong & China Gas as being in line with those of electric power companies, has engaged a consultant to conduct a study on the feasibility of the common carrier system.

Water is supplied by a government department to all commercial users at a flat rate set to recover full productions costs plus a return on assets; the tariffs are determined by the Executive Council.

Hong Kong's two railway operators, the Kowloon Canton Railway Corporation and the Mass Transit Railway Corporation, are publicly owned and their Board members appointed by the governor. Under existing legislation, both corporations are free to determine their fares. Though the Governor in Council is empowered to give directions to ensure the public interest, this has never occurred. The increase in fares over the past ten years has been in line with inflation.

Bus and ferry services are provided mainly by franchised operators. Their fares are determined by the Executive Council and their services monitored by the Legislative Council. The largest bus operator, Kowloon Motor Bus, has been subject to a profit control scheme specifying maximum annual profits. The companies face competition from other modes of transport, including public light buses and the railways. In the latest survey of household expenditure, transportation expenses were found to constitute a relatively high proportion—around 7 percent—of average household expenditure.

Owing to rapid pace of technological progress, the regulatory framework for the telecommunications industry has undergone significant changes in recent years (Box 13).

V Competitiveness in Services and Manufacturing

Throughout its history, Hong Kong has been a highly competitive and open economy. In domestic markets as well as international commerce and finance, the government has followed noninterventionist policies, leaving legitimate business to operate without much interference. Given the level playing field at home and the small size and openness of the economy, Hong Kong entrepreneurs have been forced to compete against each other and those abroad in order to sustain and improve their business. In this environment, Hong Kong has established a record of robust growth, resiliency to shocks, and factor market flexibility.

Recently, however, rising costs of labor and property, and the emergence of competition from regional centers such as Singapore, Shanghai, and Kuala Lumpur have raised concerns about Hong Kong's long-run competitiveness. These concerns have been heightened by uncertainties associated with the transfer of sovereignty. There have been calls for the government to consider policy measures to maintain Hong Kong's competitiveness. In August 1995, the Hong Kong Monetary Authority issued a strategy paper on steps to maintain and enhance the status of Hong Kong as an international financial center (HKMA (1995), Yam (1995)). In his budget speeches in 1996 and 1997, the Financial Secretary further raised the profile of this issue by releasing, along with the annual budget, special addenda on services promotion (Government Secretariat (1996 and 1997)). Public debate on the role of government in business—in particular, on the merits of providing support to declining manufacturing industries—intensified in the run-up to the transfer of sovereignty, with reference frequently being made to Singapore's industrial policy. A key question is how the government can offer the policies and programs necessary to support Hong Kong's continued success as a major international services center, while ensuring that these policies and programs are "business friendly" and leave the economic decision making and risk taking to the private sector.

Given the government's noninterventionist approach in industrial policy matters, suggestions for policy actions to maintain competitiveness have been highly controversial. Part of the problem has been that it was difficult to assess whether the services sector had a competitiveness problem in the first place. Data on value added by sector in constant prices are not available, and there were no systematic attempts to construct such data from various indicators of real activity or price deflators. Another aspect of the problem is a perception in some quarters that retrenchment in manufacturing—which has maintained competitiveness by relocating labor-intensive production to China and moving up the value-added scale—has gone too far, and that Hong Kong could not survive without producing manufactured goods.

To further discussion of these issues, this chapter constructs estimates of competitiveness in Hong Kong's manufacturing and services industries for the period 1982–94. The estimates are derived from highly disaggregated production-based GDP data in current prices using a variety of price deflators constructed from the data on exports and imports of services, components of the consumer price index, or other relevant price data (property rentals, real estate developers' margins, prices of retained imports). The use of such deflators provides the first comprehensive estimates of real growth in Hong Kong's services industries and makes it possible to compare the performance of manufacturing and services industries, as well as tradable and nontradable sectors in the Hong Kong economy. The estimates should be regarded as tentative and policy implications need to be interpreted with caution. However, while the approach used here remains approximate, the characterization of longer-term developments that it provides conforms well with the stylized facts on recent developments in Hong Kong's services industries.

The following conclusions emerge from the analysis.

• Real output expanded rapidly in most services industries since the early 1980s. The highest growth rates—on average, at double-digit levels—were recorded in wholesale trade, import/export trade, transportation, communications, financing and insurance, and business services.

• Growth of labor productivity was strong, not only in manufacturing, but also in many services industries (wholesale and retail trade, communications, financing, insurance).

• Growth in manufacturing and services industries peaked in the mid-1980s, reflecting strong expansion in external trade. Since the mid-1980s, services industries continued to expand, but manufacturing began to contract, as relative prices and wages shifted in favor of the services sector. This suggests that there was a shift in comparative advantage toward the services around 1988.

• In the early 1990s, many services industries experienced a decline in competitiveness, as labor shortages and property price inflation pushed up wages, rents, and other costs. In response, many services industries upgraded technology and lowered the intake of new workers. These adjustments restored their competitiveness in the mid-1990s.

• Labor and other resources moved flexibly across industries in response to relative price changes and relative wage differentials. Taking manufacturing as a benchmark, industries whose prices and wages increased most rapidly relative to manufacturing were generally the ones that recorded the highest growth rates of real output and employment.

• Growth paths of real output, labor productivity, and output prices have differed markedly between tradable and nontradable industries. Manufacturing and tradable services expanded, on average, twice as fast as nontradable services (about 10 percent per year over 1983–94), and experienced output price increases were half those in nontradable industries. As employment growth was generally much slower in tradable industries, labor productivity growth in tradable industries was, on average, about 8 percentage points a year higher than in nontradable industries.

• The productivity differential between tradable and nontradable industries was considerably higher than the Hong Kong/U.S. inflation differential, which on average amounted to 4¼ percentage points a year over 1983–94. In a model where consumer price inflation depends on the prices of tradables and nontradables, and wages are equalized across sectors, the large productivity differential between Hong Kong's tradable and nontradable industries can explain almost the entire differential in inflation between Hong Kong and the United States.

• The productivity differential between tradable and nontradable industries in Hong Kong was much higher than that in its trading partners. This suggests that the long-run appreciation of the real exchange rate of the Hong Kong dollar was consistent with movements in the equilibrium real exchange rate. With the nominal exchange rate fixed under Hong Kong's linked exchange rate system, and the real exchange rate exhibiting trend real appreciation, higher inflation in Hong Kong was essentially an equilibrating factor.

• Given that markets have done their basic job in allocating resources, the government's policy of not intervening has been appropriate. Looking ahead, it will be important to maintain this noninterventionist approach and avoid measures that might impede the resource movements or reduce the flexibility of factor markets.

Methodology

The main issues analyzed in this paper are developments in real growth, labor productivity, and profitability in Hong Kong's manufacturing and services industries between 1982 and 1994; the intersectoral resource allocation; and comparative performance of tradable and nontradable industries. The performance of industries in Hong Kong is not compared with those abroad.

To obtain estimates of real growth for a given sector, nominal value added for the sector is deflated by an index of sectoral output price or sectoral input costs.[49] For most tradable industries, the deflator used is an index of the international price of goods or services.[50] For industries producing nontraded goods and services, nominal value added is deflated by an index of domestic output price or domestic input cost. Because of the prevalence of cost-plus pricing in nontraded sectors, either method provides a good estimate of real value added.

Changes in labor productivity are measured as changes in real value added per worker (data on person-hours are not available). Given that most services industries are not capital-intensive, and given the high degree of labor mobility, differences in labor productivity growth should be broadly indicative of the trends in overall efficiency of services industries.

The concept of competitiveness of a sector used in this paper refers to the degree to which, given current domestic factor prices and current international product prices, domestic products (or services) can be marketed profitably. Short-term changes in prof-

---

[49]See Appendix II for a description of deflators used.

[50]The use of such deflators provides a good estimate of the changes in gross output at constant prices, but not necessarily value added at constant prices, since changes in (international) output prices of a sector do not necessarily correspond to changes in (domestic) input costs of that sector. However, as labor is the most important input in services industries, and as wages are generally equalized through labor mobility, the use of output price deflators should not systematically underestimate (or overestimate) growth of real value added in different sectors.

itability are assessed by looking at indicators of price incentives for sectoral resource shifts, such as gross operating surplus and changes in relative output prices and unit labor costs. A sector that is more competitive will, ceteris paribus, grow faster. This will be reflected in faster growth of gross operating surplus, and higher increases in relative output prices and relative wages, which are necessary in order to attract more resources into the rapidly growing sector.

Comparative advantage refers to the pattern of competitiveness of various industries obtained using the long-term product prices and long-term domestic factor costs. Long-term changes in profitability are assessed using long-term averages of these variables.

The following model of structural adjustment is implicitly postulated in this approach. Assume a common technology for all industries, with labor as the dominant input. Changes in the costs of capital and land then affect all industries roughly equally. Labor mobility between sectors is high, leading to equalization of wages for similar types of labor. However, labor is not mobile internationally. Then, if labor productivity in one sector increases, labor demand in that sector will increase. In the short run, this demand signal will lead to economy-wide wage increases rather than an immediate shift in production, as other sectors will try to keep their workers. Sectors where productivity increases do not adjust to higher wages experience a decline in competitiveness over time. If there is a shift in comparative advantage—for example, the relative output price of a sector declines to such to an extent that a decline in wages that is feasible given labor mobility is not sufficient to restore competitiveness—then that sector will experience a permanent decline in output and labor will stay in other sectors. Competitiveness could then be restored only through a change in technology that permanently increases labor productivity.

Manufacturing

According to the conventional view on Hong Kong's economic development described in Section II, the development of manufacturing in southern China since the early 1980s put downward pressure on prices in industries in which Hong Kong until then enjoyed a comparative advantage. Manufacturing competitiveness gradually declined, and Hong Kong firms started to relocate their labor-intensive operations to southern China. The decline in employment since the mid-1980s and the upgrading of skills in industries that remained in Hong Kong (to supervisory and technical func-

tions, product design and marketing) led to strong productivity increases.

As explained in Appendix II, it is not trivial to verify this view on the evolution of manufacturing on the basis of existing data. Estimates based on the index of industrial production suggest that real growth in manufacturing averaged 5¼ percent per year, and manufacturing prices rose by 2 percent per year over 1983–94 (Table 8). Although a double-digit rate of productivity growth was maintained throughout the period considered, the data clearly indicate a structural break in the sources of labor productivity growth around 1988, that is, before the relocation of manufacturing operations to southern China began on a massive scale. After 1988, nominal wages started to grow at double-digit rates and layoffs accelerated. However, real output declined by much less than employment, suggesting that there has been a significant increase in the use of labor-saving technology. As discussed below, this suggests that, beginning around 1988, there was a shift in comparative advantage toward the services sector. This shift prevented wages in manufacturing from decreasing in line with output prices, and forced the large-scale restructuring that has essentially continued to this day.

Services Industries

The trade and tourism sector has traditionally been the largest service industry in Hong Kong and, reflecting Hong Kong's entrepôt role, historically one of the most dynamic parts of the economy. In 1994, the sector contributed 26 percent of GDP and employed 35 percent of total workforce. Almost two-thirds of output in trade and tourism is generated by import/export trade, which has absorbed the largest number of workers released from manufacturing since the mid-1980s.[51]

All trade and tourism industries recorded high real growth rates over 1983–94, with the sector as a whole expanding by close to 12 percent per year since 1983 (Table 9). There has been considerable fluctuation in real growth over the years, reflecting real exchange rate movements and changes in domestic demand conditions. Labor productivity in the sector as a whole grew on average by 5½ percent per year between 1983 and 1994, slightly faster than in overall economy, but less than half the average growth rate of manufacturing productivity (Table 10). Because of the relatively faster growth of wages

---

[51]A detailed breakdown of output, employment, and wages by industry is available in Chapter III in IMF (1997b).

Table 8. Basic Indicators for Manufacturing
(Annual percentage changes)

	1983	1984	1985	1986	1987	1988	1989	1990	1991	1992	1993	1994	Average 1983–94
Real output[1]	13.0	16.7	–4.4	14.9	16.0	6.0	0.8	–0.8	0.8	1.6	–0.8	0.0	5.3
Implicit price deflator[1]	7.5	8.1	0.8	3.5	4.1	5.2	6.0	3.1	–1.9	1.0	–6.5	–5.6	2.1
Employment	–0.6	3.5	–4.4	0.7	1.2	–3.0	–4.9	–8.3	–10.2	–12.5	–12.2	–13.9	–5.4
Nominal wages	7.5	8.7	6.4	5.7	9.0	8.7	11.5	12.2	11.0	9.5	10.6	8.8	9.1
Real wages	–2.9	0.4	2.5	3.9	3.8	2.0	2.9	2.5	–1.1	0.2	2.8	1.3	1.5
Labor productivity	13.7	12.7	–0.0	14.1	14.6	9.3	6.0	8.1	12.3	16.1	12.9	16.2	11.3
Unit labor costs	–5.4	–3.5	6.4	–7.4	–4.9	–0.6	5.1	3.8	–1.2	–5.7	–2.0	–6.3	–1.8
Memorandum items:													
Real growth rate derived from:[2]													
Index of value added at constant prices	14.7	17.5	–3.0	16.3	15.8	7.2	3.7	0.1	–4.7	0.4	–8.3	–7.8	4.3
Deflator for domestic exports	10.5	11.9	–3.3	16.6	17.1	9.1	3.9	1.0	–2.9	1.5	–7.0	–7.4	4.3
Implicit price deflator derived from:[2]													
Index of value added at constant prices	5.9	7.4	–0.7	2.3	4.3	4.1	3.0	2.1	3.7	2.2	1.2	2.3	3.2
Deflator for domestic exports	9.9	12.7	–0.4	2.0	3.1	2.2	2.8	1.3	1.8	1.1	–0.2	1.9	3.2

Sources: Census and Statistics Department, *Hong Kong Monthly Digest of Statistics* (various issues), and *Estimates of Gross Domestic Product, 1961 to 1996*; and IMF staff estimates.

[1]Derived from the index of industrial production.

[2]Derived from the index of manufacturing value added at constant prices.

in this sector, unit labor costs in trade and tourism increased faster than in overall economy.

As Hong Kong specialized in trade intermediation for much of its history, transportation industry has traditionally been well developed in the territory. In recent years, a sophisticated communications industry has developed in support of Hong Kong's growing prominence as an international business center.

Real growth rates in this sector varied considerably across industries (Table 11). Like in other sectors, there was marked fluctuation in activity levels over time: in 1986–88, growth in several transportation subsectors took off explosively, reflecting acceleration in external trade and, most likely, the expansion of capacity (especially in air transportation). Labor productivity growth in communications industry was very high, making a worker in this industry 18 times more productive in 1994 than in 1982 (Table 12). Productivity growth in air transportation was extremely volatile, reflecting the lumpy nature of investment. Average unit labor costs grew by close to 5 percent per year over 1983–94, slightly faster than in overall economy. The results for individual subsectors have to be interpreted with caution, because a breakdown of the wage index by industry is not available for this sector.

Financing, insurance, real estate, and business services traditionally are the second largest services sector in Hong Kong. These four industries on average contributed one-fifth of GDP and employed 9 percent of total workforce over 1982–94. Within the sector, real estate services generated slightly less than half of value added, and financing about one-third, most of which was contributed by banks.

Nonbanks outperformed other industries in this sector by a huge margin; however, real (as well as nominal) output of nonbanks was extremely volatile (Table 13). These large amplitudes reflect the underlying volatility of the Hong Kong stock market, which is under much stronger influence of changing expectations than other services industries. Real output growth in banking and business services averaged about 10 percent per year, while in real estate services it averaged only 1 percent per year. By contrast, prices of real estate services increased on average by 17 percent per year—double the rate of inflation—reflecting the strong upward trend in property prices.

Growth of labor productivity in general reflected the record of real growth in this sector (Table 14). However, in business services, labor productivity

Table 9. Real Output and Deflators in Trade and Tourism
(Annual percentage changes)

	1983	1984	1985	1986	1987	1988	1989	1990	1991	1992	1993	1994	Average 1983–94
Real output													
Total	2.7	21.6	5.7	9.3	28.2	16.6	8.9	4.6	10.1	11.8	13.2	9.1	11.8
Wholesale	−7.7	14.0	11.6	1.5	27.5	5.5	14.0	21.7	2.7	6.0	18.0	−1.3	9.5
Retail	−12.4	19.2	5.9	0.9	22.3	15.2	4.7	−4.9	12.3	9.7	1.4	10.7	7.1
Import/export	9.3	29.3	3.6	12.4	34.4	20.8	9.7	9.8	14.5	13.6	17.8	11.5	15.5
Restaurants	9.1	8.1	8.1	10.3	20.0	8.0	10.4	−8.9	−5.1	5.6	−0.2	−0.2	5.4
Hotels	1.2	15.9	11.0	14.1	14.3	15.5	4.3	−5.7	0.1	16.6	10.2	2.3	8.3
Deflators													
Total	9.7	10.8	−1.2	4.2	5.5	5.5	4.3	7.8	5.4	4.5	3.9	1.8	5.2
Wholesale	12.8	9.8	−5.2	6.9	5.0	4.5	0.1	7.3	3.5	2.2	2.3	0.7	4.2
Retail	9.4	8.2	0.6	3.5	6.2	7.5	6.1	6.5	6.3	5.1	5.4	5.8	5.9
Import/export	11.9	11.3	−2.5	4.2	4.2	3.3	1.6	6.7	4.1	3.4	3.2	−0.1	4.3
Restaurants	8.6	7.1	3.1	2.9	5.2	9.7	15.5	14.8	12.5	2.5	5.7	4.8	7.7
Hotels	13.4	12.7	4.5	6.6	10.4	10.1	7.0	6.5	5.7	7.3	6.9	8.9	8.3

Sources: Census and Statistics Department, *Annual Digest of Statistics* (various issues), and *Estimates of Gross Domestic Product, 1961 to 1996*; and IMF staff estimates.

growth was stagnant, while in real estate services it was negative. Interestingly, growth of labor productivity in this industry was positive only in those years when the property market turned down (for example, 1983–85, 1990, and 1994). In periods of rising property prices—which came to be considered "normal" for this industry—there were apparently not many incentives to raise labor productivity. Only banks and insurance companies kept unit labor costs increases below the rate of inflation.

Most community, personal, and social services are public and nontraded goods, provided by nontrading bodies of the government or small private establishments. Real output in this sector grew on average by

Table 10. Productivity and Unit Labor Costs in Trade and Tourism
(Annual percentage changes)

	1983	1984	1985	1986	1987	1988	1989	1990	1991	1992	1993	1994	Average 1983–94
Labor productivity													
Total	−1.6	15.3	−0.6	5.3	21.6	7.4	1.9	−3.1	2.0	8.4	8.3	−0.3	5.4
Wholesale	−12.4	12.6	12.1	3.8	24.8	−0.3	9.1	13.4	−4.8	3.6	19.3	−1.7	6.6
Retail	−14.5	19.3	2.6	2.2	20.7	9.1	1.5	−9.7	7.9	9.3	2.2	7.3	4.8
Import/export	4.4	13.2	−12.7	0.8	19.9	4.5	−1.4	−1.1	2.5	8.2	5.4	−5.6	3.2
Restaurants	2.7	2.2	8.0	8.6	17.6	5.7	7.1	−14.7	−10.5	3.2	1.5	−2.1	2.4
Hotels	−1.3	13.5	6.3	5.3	7.5	6.2	−9.1	−7.8	−4.4	10.4	8.1	3.4	3.2
Unit labor costs													
Total	10.0	−2.5	9.0	4.9	−5.3	8.2	10.9	19.7	8.8	3.5	2.8	5.4	6.3
Wholesale	28.2	−3.1	−3.7	4.5	−9.7	12.8	−1.1	0.6	14.4	10.4	−5.9	9.2	4.7
Retail	24.9	−5.9	6.8	9.1	−0.4	10.9	13.5	29.2	3.6	3.8	7.5	−9.1	7.8
Import/export	7.2	5.0	24.2	10.9	−4.3	10.1	13.2	19.5	7.6	4.1	5.5	11.9	9.6
Restaurants	1.6	3.6	−3.9	−2.4	−7.1	5.0	6.2	27.6	23.7	3.8	6.1	8.3	6.1
Hotels	9.5	−0.8	2.0	5.0	1.0	6.9	25.8	25.4	17.1	0.6	5.4	6.3	8.7

Sources: Census and Statistics Department, *Annual Digest of Statistics* (various issues), and *Estimates of Gross Domestic Product, 1961 to 1996*; and IMF staff estimates.

Table 11. Real Output and Deflators in Transportation, Storage, and Communications
(Annual percentage changes)

	1983	1984	1985	1986	1987	1988	1989	1990	1991	1992	1993	1994	Average 1983–94
Real output													
Total	11.8	5.7	5.5	15.5	28.6	20.9	2.5	14.2	7.4	14.8	11.6	11.6	12.5
Transportation	10.0	4.4	4.1	13.7	28.3	19.6	–2.5	11.7	2.6	11.6	8.1	10.3	10.2
Land	2.5	1.4	5.7	8.3	13.6	8.5	0.6	11.9	–0.8	13.4	7.8	5.3	6.5
Passenger	1.2	5.7	5.0	7.1	11.2	3.0	3.6	1.8	0.2	9.5	2.0	9.2	5.0
Freight	6.6	–10.9	8.0	12.4	21.2	24.1	–6.4	38.2	–2.8	21.1	18.1	–0.8	10.7
Water	13.6	14.4	0.9	6.8	23.7	16.1	–2.9	11.9	11.5	9.2	15.4	7.6	10.7
Air	10.6	10.4	3.7	16.5	16.3	16.9	3.4	9.2	3.6	13.2	14.7	9.8	10.7
Services	25.5	5.2	16.6	25.5	11.3	20.4	–0.7	24.7	–3.1	23.4	13.9	9.9	14.4
Government	–11.1	–8.7	9.6	5.5	12.2	8.9	11.0	9.8	0.4	0.4	–0.9	4.8	3.5
Storage	32.4	2.2	–15.0	23.0	7.9	–12.3	4.3	–1.7	4.9	1.6	–16.0	–2.2	2.4
Communications	23.3	23.8	30.8	27.2	37.5	38.5	30.7	27.0	25.7	25.7	22.9	15.4	27.4
Deflators													
Total	4.9	5.9	3.6	0.8	3.3	4.0	8.6	5.2	5.8	2.2	0.0	3.2	4.0
Transportation	8.6	7.2	2.6	2.3	6.7	5.9	11.7	7.5	8.5	4.0	2.4	5.2	6.1
Land (passenger), government	12.0	10.3	5.6	3.9	7.2	5.4	12.1	13.7	12.4	7.2	7.8	8.9	8.9
Water, land (freight), services	5.4	5.5	1.1	1.1	6.1	5.9	11.7	5.2	7.1	3.0	0.7	4.0	4.7
Air	10.6	10.4	3.7	16.5	16.3	16.9	3.4	9.2	3.6	13.2	14.7	9.8	10.7
Storage	–17.6	0.0	4.8	6.8	17.0	40.0	29.9	5.0	3.8	7.3	10.3	3.1	9.2
Communications	–10.5	–8.1	–7.2	–8.9	–13.3	–12.0	–9.2	–3.7	–2.1	–2.7	–5.5	–1.9	–7.1

Sources: Census and Statistics Department, *Annual Digest of Statistics* (various issues), and *Estimates of Gross Domestic Product, 1961 to 1996*; and IMF staff estimates.

4½ percent per year over 1983–94, about half the growth rate in other services industries (Table 15). Growth was fairly stable and, unlike in most other sectors, positive over the entire period considered. As employment expanded at roughly the same rate as real output, labor productivity growth was stagnant. Unit labor costs rose at double-digit rates over the period, reflecting rapid growth in wages. These results are not surprising in view of the severe labor shortages experienced in the early 1990s and given that compensation of employees constitutes a much larger share of value added than in other service sectors.

Profitability and Intersectoral Resource Allocation

The data used to derive real growth estimates for different sectors can also be used to answer some more basic questions. To what extent have the observed movements in resources responded to profitability, relative price changes, and relative wage differences among industries? And to what extent have tradable industries, which are exposed to international competition, performed better than nontradable industries, which are subject only to domestic competitive pressures?

Profitability in Services

The sectoral pattern of profitability is very similar to the pattern of real output and labor productivity growth (Table 16). Between 1986 and 1988, profitability improved markedly in most industries. After 1988, however, profitability in manufacturing decelerated sharply, while in services it continued to grow rapidly after a temporary setback in 1989. Over the long term, rapid increases in profitability were recorded in transportation and trade and tourism. The relatively low growth rate of profitability in financing, real estate, and business services is mostly due to the large weight of the real estate services and the fact that property price inflation was very high, so the operating surplus in constant prices grew relatively slowly for the sector as a whole. Community, social, and personal services, which include many nonprofit activities, turned out to be the least profitable sector. Unit labor costs generally moved in line with changes in gross operating surplus in

Table 12. Productivity and Unit Labor Costs in Transportation, Storage, and Communications

(Annual percentage changes)

	1983	1984	1985	1986	1987	1988	1989	1990	1991	1992	1993	1994	Average 1983–94
Labor productivity													
Total	9.0	1.6	3.5	12.4	21.6	11.4	−6.9	8.2	5.4	6.6	4.4	5.0	6.9
Transportation	7.3	−0.4	2.2	9.2	20.4	9.0	−11.5	6.1	−0.6	5.0	0.9	3.8	4.3
Land	−13.0	−4.2	1.7	5.4	11.7	8.2	0.7	7.0	−2.1	6.6	2.0	−3.4	1.7
Water	6.1	6.2	−1.9	3.8	19.2	1.5	−14.3	6.1	13.1	−0.9	3.4	4.2	3.9
Air	34.9	−5.6	−12.5	32.5	80.8	20.0	−21.1	−4.1	−12.4	−5.4	−9.8	17.4	9.6
Services	10.8	−6.9	18.2	10.6	−2.2	3.2	−6.9	14.2	−5.8	12.1	2.9	0.6	4.2
Storage	41.2	4.2	−15.2	22.7	7.7	−12.5	4.0	−1.9	4.6	−7.7	−21.1	−6.8	1.6
Communications	20.2	20.6	27.5	29.1	31.7	30.8	16.6	18.2	29.3	11.5	16.4	5.6	21.5
Unit labor costs													
Total	2.0	8.9	6.3	−3.4	−10.7	−1.7	23.9	5.8	8.5	5.1	6.9	5.4	4.8
Transportation	3.6	11.2	7.7	−0.6	−9.9	0.4	30.3	7.9	15.1	6.7	10.6	6.7	7.5
Land	27.8	15.6	8.2	3.0	−2.9	1.2	14.5	7.0	16.9	5.2	9.5	14.5	10.0
Water	4.8	4.3	12.2	4.6	−8.9	7.8	34.6	8.0	1.2	13.1	8.0	6.2	8.0
Air	−17.6	17.3	25.8	−18.0	−40.0	−8.7	46.2	19.3	30.6	18.4	23.8	−5.8	7.6
Services	0.3	18.9	−6.9	−1.8	11.0	6.0	23.8	0.3	21.5	0.0	8.6	10.0	7.6
Storage	−21.2	6.2	29.8	−11.5	0.8	25.1	10.9	16.7	9.4	21.5	41.5	18.7	12.3
Communications	−7.5	−8.2	−13.7	−15.9	−17.6	−16.3	−1.1	−3.1	−11.5	0.6	−4.0	4.8	−7.8

Sources: Census and Statistics Department, *Annual Digest of Statistics* (various issues), and *Estimates of Gross Domestic Product, 1961 to 1996*; and IMF staff estimates.

constant prices (Table 16). Thus, when unit labor costs declined across the economy in 1987, gross operating surplus rose sharply, while the reverse happened in 1989.

These results support the view described in Section III that the advantages enjoyed in the late 1980s and early 1990s by the firms providing services related to trade and investment in China were gradu-

Table 13. Real Output and Deflators in Financing, Insurance, Real Estate, and Business Services

(Annual percentage changes)

	1983	1984	1985	1986	1987	1988	1989	1990	1991	1992	1993	1994	Average 1983–94
Real output													
Total	3.0	5.4	7.4	6.9	2.4	5.5	2.0	8.4	14.6	3.3	3.3	7.1	5.8
Financing	−5.2	1.9	−1.5	25.4	21.4	3.6	2.2	3.0	42.2	18.1	11.9	0.6	10.3
Banks	−2.8	−6.8	−2.3	8.9	27.2	13.5	−0.2	14.5	35.7	9.7	7.7	4.7	9.1
Nonbanks	−22.8	84.1	2.2	101.0	6.9	−25.6	12.7	−42.8	94.1	64.5	27.3	−12.3	24.1
Business services	8.6	6.2	19.2	19.7	21.9	24.6	−5.3	−0.7	8.0	6.7	2.6	11.0	10.2
Real estate services	5.8	7.2	8.4	−3.2	−13.5	−1.5	4.5	17.5	−0.2	−12.5	−9.9	12.0	1.2
Insurance	7.7	−0.2	18.4	7.3	22.7	19.2	11.3	−3.0	10.3	13.8	28.1	23.8	13.3
Deflators													
Total	−16.2	−0.1	1.3	15.5	27.5	19.5	15.2	7.2	10.5	20.9	16.1	10.5	10.7
Financing	6.9	6.1	2.4	2.5	6.7	5.9	11.9	12.8	10.0	8.9	7.0	6.0	7.2
Business services	9.8	8.6	1.1	2.4	7.5	6.2	15.3	12.1	9.6	8.0	9.4	6.3	8.0
Real estate services	−34.7	−7.5	1.3	25.0	52.5	39.8	17.9	1.4	11.5	43.5	34.6	14.7	16.7
Insurance	5.1	7.0	3.8	3.5	3.5	5.7	7.8	9.9	7.8	7.2	8.6	4.2	6.2

Sources: Census and Statistics Department, *Annual Digest of Statistics* (various issues), and *Estimates of Gross Domestic Product, 1961 to 1996*; and IMF staff estimates.

Table 14. Productivity and Unit Labor Costs in Financing, Insurance, Real Estate, and Business Services
(Annual percentage changes)

	1983	1984	1985	1986	1987	1988	1989	1990	1991	1992	1993	1994	Average 1983–94
Labor productivity													
Total	3.5	2.7	1.4	–0.3	–5.5	–4.0	–7.5	0.0	8.3	–3.9	–3.3	–1.6	–0.8
Financing	–1.9	1.2	–3.6	20.1	12.8	–3.9	–6.1	–1.7	36.8	14.2	5.8	–5.9	5.7
Banks	–2.1	–10.2	–5.9	4.9	22.6	9.3	–3.8	10.4	30.2	9.6	4.2	–1.0	5.7
Nonbanks	–15.9	94.9	3.8	89.8	–8.1	–36.0	–4.6	–46.2	81.7	52.4	14.3	–15.8	17.5
Business services	3.2	1.1	5.6	9.9	10.0	14.4	–12.5	–13.0	4.6	–3.0	–4.2	–2.3	1.1
Real estate services	0.2	4.0	6.3	–10.2	–16.7	–14.3	–5.1	7.9	–15.2	–19.5	–18.4	2.6	–6.5
Insurance	10.9	–4.2	9.2	–8.5	9.9	0.5	–3.8	–14.5	7.7	8.3	28.9	20.9	5.4
Unit labor costs													
Total	4.1	5.6	6.8	9.2	15.4	20.0	29.1	16.5	3.9	15.5	16.0	10.4	12.7
Financing	10.2	8.4	11.6	–7.6	–3.9	24.1	23.4	18.7	–19.0	–4.6	5.4	12.5	6.6
Banks	10.4	22.0	14.3	5.8	–11.5	9.1	20.5	5.7	–14.9	–0.6	7.0	6.9	6.2
Nonbanks	28.4	–43.7	3.6	–41.5	18.0	86.2	21.5	117.0	–39.0	–28.5	–2.4	25.8	12.1
Business services	–1.1	3.7	0.6	–2.1	–1.1	–5.0	49.1	37.8	5.8	14.6	20.2	16.2	11.6
Real estate services	7.6	4.3	1.8	21.2	30.9	34.4	25.9	8.1	32.8	38.0	35.8	4.9	20.5
Insurance	–0.1	15.7	4.1	18.7	–1.5	13.5	27.6	30.6	3.8	4.3	–13.6	–12.1	7.6

Sources: Census and Statistics Department, *Annual Digest of Statistics* (various issues), and *Estimates of Gross Domestic Product, 1961 to 1996*; and IMF staff estimates.

ally eroded by the cumulative effects of high wage and property price inflation. As relocation options are more limited for these firms, they responded to eroding competitiveness by trying to restrain price increases, investing in labor-saving capital equipment, and, in some cases, reducing employment.

Intersectoral Resource Allocation

Trends in prices and wages of services industries relative to manufacturing prices and wages suggest that the intersectoral allocation of resources was, by and large, efficient. As prices of services relative to manufacturing prices rose rapidly across the services industries since 1990, the services sector expanded strongly while manufacturing stagnated. In particular, industries whose prices increased rapidly relative to manufacturing (air transportation, transportation services, communications, financing, restaurants, and hotels) were generally the ones that recorded the highest growth rates of real output (Table 17). Similarly, in all industries except restau-

Table 15. Community, Social, and Personal Services
(Annual percentage changes)

	1983	1984	1985	1986	1987	1988	1989	1990	1991	1992	1993	1994	Average 1983–94
Real output	2.6	2.9	6.6	4.0	4.9	5.0	3.1	2.8	4.4	5.9	8.4	4.8	4.6
Deflator	12.5	11.8	7.7	7.2	6.6	9.6	11.5	12.8	11.1	10.8	8.7	10.7	10.1
Employment	8.0	3.6	0.1	2.7	2.4	4.7	4.1	6.1	6.4	1.4	3.4	5.9	4.1
Wages	7.3	5.4	6.8	4.3	10.4	15.7	23.8	14.2	9.2	11.5	9.7	13.2	11.0
Productivity	–5.0	–0.7	6.5	1.3	2.5	0.2	–0.9	–3.1	–1.9	4.4	4.9	–1.0	0.6
Unit labor costs	12.9	6.1	0.3	2.9	7.7	15.4	24.9	17.9	11.3	6.8	4.6	14.4	10.4

Sources: Census and Statistics Department, *Annual Digest of Statistics* (various issues), and *Estimates of Gross Domestic Product, 1961 to 1996*; and IMF staff estimates.

Table 16. Gross Operating Surplus and Unit Labor Costs by Sector
(Annual percentage changes)

	1983	1984	1985	1986	1987	1988	1989	1990	1991	1992	1993	Average 1983–93
Gross operating surplus[1]												
Manufacturing	24.5	19.5	−17.4	31.3	25.4	9.2	0.7	0.2	4.0	6.3	−4.1	9.1
Total services	−5.1	10.7	0.6	9.9	21.3	12.5	0.4	2.5	12.4	10.8	9.6	7.8
Trade and tourism	0.5	33.2	−3.1	9.4	38.6	15.2	3.1	−0.5	7.8	14.3	12.1	11.9
Transportation	14.2	7.7	5.9	19.8	33.0	22.4	−5.4	5.2	11.9	10.4	6.7	12.0
Financing, real estate, and business services	−9.2	1.2	2.5	11.2	5.1	5.5	−0.1	6.8	19.5	7.4	5.5	5.0
Community, social, and personal services	7.0	−1.3	8.6	−4.2	0.7	8.6	−4.7	−2.9	−2.2	−4.1	7.3	1.2
Unit labor costs												
Manufacturing	−5.4	−3.5	6.4	−7.4	−4.9	−0.6	5.1	3.8	−1.2	−5.7	−2.0	−1.4
Total services	7.7	2.7	4.6	2.2	1.8	10.3	19.9	14.1	7.4	6.2	6.1	7.6
Trade and tourism	10.0	−2.5	9.0	4.9	−5.3	8.2	10.9	19.7	8.8	3.5	2.8	6.4
Transportation	2.0	8.9	6.3	−3.4	−10.7	−1.7	23.9	5.8	8.5	5.1	6.9	4.7
Financing, real estate, and business services	4.1	5.6	6.8	9.2	15.4	20.0	29.1	16.5	3.9	15.5	16.0	12.9
Community, social, and personal services	12.9	6.1	0.3	2.9	7.7	15.4	24.9	17.9	11.3	6.8	4.6	10.1

Sources: Census and Statistics Department, *Annual Digest of Statistics* (various issues), and *Estimates of Gross Domestic Product, 1961 to 1996*; and IMF staff estimates.

[1]In constant prices of the sector.

rants, wages grew faster than in manufacturing (Table 18). Relative wages grew especially rapidly in import/export trade, the industry that also experienced one of the highest growth rates of employment. Labor has thus moved away from manufacturing and certain declining services industries in a clear, predictable pattern.

There were some important exceptions, however. Relative prices in communications, the most productive service industry, declined steadily relative to manufacturing—and all other—prices, reflecting rapid technological progress in this industry. At the same time, the relative price increases in real estate services, community, social and personal services, and storage were among the highest, while real output and productivity growth in these industries were among the lowest of all industries considered. As the rapid price increases enabled wages to grow faster than in other industries and attracted labor from other, more productive industries, the resulting allocation of resources did not maximize the supply potential of the economy. However, given the absence of price distortions and generally competitive domestic markets, the observed price increases in these sectors essentially reflected the underlying demand conditions and intrinsic scarcity of land in Hong Kong. The resulting allocation of resources was thus

efficient from a general equilibrium perspective, although not necessarily optimal from the supply (i.e., growth) perspective.

Differential Productivity Growth, Inflation, and the Real Exchange Rate

Productivity Growth in Tradable and Nontradable Sectors

To gain further insight into determinants of sectoral performance, industries were divided into tradable and nontradable sectors. Manufacturing, wholesale and import/export trade, water, land freight, and air transportation, transportation services, and banks, nonbanks, and insurance were classified as tradable industries. Retail trade, restaurants and hotels, land passenger and government transportation, storage, communications, business services, real estate services, and community, social, and personal services were classified as nontradable.

Combined output of the above industries accounted for over 80 percent of GDP and total employment, so the sample covered is fairly representative of the Hong Kong economy. The share of tradables in combined output declined from the peak

Table 17. Output Prices by Sector Relative to Manufacturing Prices
(Annual percentage changes)

	1983	1984	1985	1986	1987	1988	1989	1990	1991	1992	1993	1994	Average 1983–94
Total services	−5.9	0.3	1.3	4.1	8.1	4.9	3.3	5.1	10.2	9.2	15.3	12.7	5.1
Trade and tourism	2.0	2.4	−2.0	0.7	1.3	0.3	−1.5	4.6	7.5	3.5	11.1	7.9	2.7
Wholesale	5.0	1.6	−5.9	3.3	0.9	−0.7	−5.5	4.0	5.5	1.2	9.4	6.8	1.7
Retail	1.8	0.0	−0.1	0.0	2.0	2.2	0.1	3.3	8.4	4.1	12.7	12.1	3.9
Import/export	4.2	2.9	−3.3	0.7	0.1	−1.8	−4.1	3.5	6.2	2.4	10.3	5.8	2.2
Restaurants	1.1	−1.0	2.4	−0.6	1.0	4.3	9.0	11.3	14.7	1.5	13.0	11.0	5.6
Hotels	5.5	4.3	3.7	3.0	6.1	4.6	1.0	3.3	7.8	6.2	14.2	15.4	6.3
Transportation, storage, communications	−2.4	−2.0	2.8	−2.5	−0.7	−1.2	2.5	2.0	7.9	1.2	6.9	9.3	1.3
Transportation	1.1	−0.8	1.9	−1.2	2.5	0.7	5.4	4.3	10.7	3.0	9.4	11.5	3.4
Land (passenger), government	4.2	2.0	4.8	0.4	3.0	0.2	5.8	10.3	14.6	6.2	15.2	15.4	6.1
Water, land (freight), services	−1.9	−2.4	0.3	−2.3	1.9	0.6	5.4	2.0	9.2	2.0	7.6	10.2	2.0
Air	2.9	2.1	2.9	12.6	11.7	11.1	−2.4	5.9	5.7	12.1	22.7	16.4	8.6
Storage	−23.4	−7.5	4.0	3.2	12.4	33.1	22.6	1.8	5.9	6.3	17.9	9.3	7.1
Communications	−16.7	−15.0	−7.9	−12.0	−16.7	−16.3	−14.3	−6.6	−0.1	−3.6	1.1	3.9	−8.7
Financing, real estate, and business services	−22.0	−7.6	0.5	11.6	22.5	13.6	8.7	4.0	12.7	19.7	24.1	17.1	8.7
Financing	−0.5	−1.8	1.6	−1.0	2.5	0.6	5.6	9.4	12.2	7.8	14.3	12.4	5.3
Business services	2.2	0.4	0.3	−1.0	3.2	1.0	8.8	8.7	11.8	7.0	17.0	12.7	6.0
Real estate services	−39.2	−14.5	0.6	20.8	46.5	32.9	11.2	−1.6	13.7	42.1	43.9	21.6	14.8
Insurance	−2.2	−1.1	3.0	0.0	−0.6	0.4	1.7	6.6	9.9	6.2	16.1	10.5	4.2
Community, social, personal services	4.7	3.4	6.9	3.6	2.4	4.2	5.2	9.4	13.3	9.8	16.2	17.3	8.0

Sources: Census and Statistics Department, *Annual Digest of Statistics* (various issues), and *Estimates of Gross Domestic Product, 1961 to 1996*; and IMF staff estimates.

of about 58 percent in 1984 to less than half in 1994, while the share of tradables in combined employment declined from two-thirds in 1982 to about 55 percent in 1994. This pattern of change is consistent with structural shifts observed in industrial countries, but the share of tradables in the economy is much higher in Hong Kong, reflecting the small size and openness of its economy.

Tradable industries exhibited much higher real output and productivity growth over the long run than nontradable industries (Table 19). At the same time, prices of nontradables increased about 5 percent per year faster relative to prices of tradables. The rising relative price of nontradables attracted considerably more labor into nontradable industries, where employment grew on average by 4¼ percent per year over 1982–94, compared with just ½ percent per year in tradable industries. The result was a predictable, large differential in labor productivity growth between tradable and nontradable industries, equivalent, on average, to 8¼ percentage points a year. The productivity differential was especially

large—up to 16 percentage points—in 1986–87 and 1991–93, when foreign trade also expanded at double-digit rates.

These results are consistent with the benchmark model of real exchange rate determination developed by Balassa (1964) and formalized by Samuelson (1964), according to which faster productivity growth in the tradable sector leads, via wage equalization and under the joint assumption of a small open economy and perfect capital mobility, to a decline in the relative price of tradables.

Inflation Differential Between Hong Kong and the United States

The above data are very useful in the analysis of the differential between inflation in Hong Kong and its major trading partners, notably the United States, given the link of the Hong Kong dollar to the U.S. dollar. With certain simplifying assumptions, the difference between the domestic and world rate of inflation can be expressed as the nontradable share

Table 18. Wages by Sector Relative to Manufacturing Wages
(Annual percentage changes)

	1983	1984	1985	1986	1987	1988	1989	1990	1991	1992	1993	1994	Average 1983–94
Wholesale	4.5	0.4	1.5	2.6	3.4	3.5	–3.2	1.6	–1.8	4.5	1.4	–1.4	1.4
Retail	–0.6	3.2	3.0	5.5	10.2	11.4	3.4	3.9	0.7	3.6	–0.7	–10.4	2.8
Import/export	4.2	9.3	2.0	5.8	5.3	5.8	0.1	5.3	–0.6	2.9	0.6	–3.0	3.1
Restaurants	–2.9	–2.6	–2.4	0.3	0.1	2.2	2.1	–3.0	–0.2	–2.1	–2.7	–2.5	–1.2
Hotels	0.5	3.5	2.0	4.7	–0.4	4.4	2.6	3.0	0.9	1.4	2.9	1.0	2.2
Transportation, storage, and communications	3.4	1.9	3.5	2.7	–0.5	0.7	3.5	2.0	3.1	2.4	0.9	1.7	2.1
Financing	0.5	0.9	1.1	5.1	–0.6	9.7	4.0	4.0	–0.2	–0.5	0.8	–2.8	1.8
Business services	–5.1	–3.6	–0.1	1.8	–0.2	0.0	17.0	6.8	–0.3	1.4	4.1	4.3	2.2
Real estate services	0.3	–0.2	1.7	3.0	0.0	6.0	7.2	3.9	1.5	1.4	0.1	–1.0	2.0
Insurance	3.0	2.0	6.8	2.8	–0.7	5.0	10.2	–0.6	0.7	3.1	0.6	–2.4	2.5
Community, social, and personal services	–0.2	–3.0	0.4	–1.3	1.2	6.4	11.0	1.7	–1.6	1.8	–0.9	4.1	1.6

Sources: Census and Statistics Department, *Annual Digest of Statistics* (various issues), and *Estimates of Gross Domestic Product, 1961 to 1996*; and IMF staff estimates.

multiplied by the difference in productivity growth in the tradable and nontradable sectors:

$$p - p^* = \alpha_N (q_T - q_N), \tag{1}$$

where p is the domestic (i.e., Hong Kong) and p^* the world (i.e., United States) rate of inflation, α_N is the share of nontradables in GDP, and q_T and q_N are growth rates of labor productivity in tradable and nontradable industries.[52]

In an empirical setting, one cannot expect the above relationship to hold exactly because the theoretical framework utilized is not intended to capture all the determinants of domestic inflation. In the case of Hong Kong, however, the relationship holds extremely well. Over 1983–94, the productivity differential between tradable and nontradable industries in Hong Kong explains, on average, 88 percent of the (annual) 4¼ percentage points inflation differential between Hong Kong and the United States; the average "unexplained" inflation differential is equivalent to just ½ percentage point per year. Such a result was generally assumed to hold in the policy literature on

Hong Kong's inflation (see, e.g., Goodhart (1983), and Hawkins and Kee (1996)), but was not previously quantified.

Real Exchange Rate and Differential Productivity Growth

Over the 1983–94 period, the real effective exchange rate of the Hong Kong dollar appreciated at an average annual rate of 1.8 percent. Over certain subperiods, however, the real exchange rate moved more substantially. Thus, from late 1983 to early 1985, the real exchange rate appreciated by close to 20 percent. Subsequently, it depreciated sharply, falling by 17 percent from its peak in early 1985 to the end of 1987. As inflation in Hong Kong rose sharply after 1987, the real exchange rate appreciated considerably—rising by 52 percent between the end of 1987 and the end of 1994.

A key question in this context is whether the observed trend appreciation of the real exchange rate is consistent with the "equilibrium" real appreciation that results from higher productivity growth between tradable and nontradable sectors in Hong Kong relative to its trading partners. If so, one could conclude that the long-run movements in the real exchange rate corresponded to the movements in the long-run "equilibrium" exchange rate.

While a rigorous test of this hypothesis would require a more complex analytical framework, a simple check can be performed on the basis of the above data. Defining the real exchange rate, R, as the rela-

---

[52]The following assumptions are used to derive this result: the inflation rate in the tradable goods sector in Hong Kong is equal to the U.S. rate of inflation, p^*; wages in tradable and nontradable sectors in Hong Kong are equalized; the GDP shares of nontradable sectors in Hong Kong and the United States are the same; and—given the absence of international competition—firms in the nontradable sector protect profit margins by means of a constant percentage markup on unit labor costs. For details, see Frisch (1983).

Table 19. Performance of Tradable and Nontradable Industries[1]
(Annual percentage changes)

	1983	1984	1985	1986	1987	1988	1989	1990	1991	1992	1993	1994	Average 1983–94
Real output													
Tradables	8.1	15.8	−0.4	15.0	22.1	11.1	4.0	5.4	11.4	10.1	10.8	5.6	9.9
Nontradables	3.1	6.5	8.2	3.9	4.7	7.4	4.3	4.5	4.2	3.5	3.4	7.8	5.1
Deflators													
Tradables	9.0	8.8	−0.3	3.6	6.1	5.5	5.3	5.8	3.3	3.9	1.1	1.0	4.4
Nontradables	−3.7	6.6	4.6	9.6	15.8	14.5	12.3	8.7	9.8	15.1	12.1	10.1	9.6
Relative price													
Nontradables–tradables	−1.6	−2.0	4.9	5.8	9.1	8.5	6.7	2.7	6.2	10.8	10.8	8.9	5.1
Employment													
Tradables	0.1	4.4	−0.6	2.7	3.8	2.3	0.7	−1.2	−1.8	−3.9	−1.0	1.7	0.6
Nontradables	5.4	3.3	2.4	2.2	3.0	5.2	5.1	6.8	5.5	3.3	2.3	5.7	4.2
Productivity													
Tradables	8.0	10.9	0.3	12.0	17.6	8.6	3.3	6.7	13.4	14.6	11.9	3.8	9.3
Nontradables	−2.1	3.2	5.7	1.6	1.6	2.1	−0.7	−2.1	−1.3	0.2	1.1	2.0	0.9
Productivity differential[2]													
Tradables–nontradables	10.1	7.7	−5.5	10.4	16.0	6.5	4.0	8.9	14.7	14.5	10.8	1.8	8.3
Inflation differential[2]													
Hong Kong–United States	6.6	4.2	−0.1	1.3	1.7	3.3	4.9	4.4	6.8	6.6	5.7	6.0	4.3

Source: IMF staff estimates.

[1] Tradable industries include: Manufacturing, wholesale, import/export trade, water, land (freight), and air transportation, transportation services, banks, nonbanks, and insurance.

Nontradable industries include: Retail, restaurants, hotels, land (passenger) and government transportation, storage, communications, business services, real estate services, and community, social, and personal services.

[2] Percentage points.

tive price of nontradables in Hong Kong, P_N, and abroad, P_N*:

$$R = P_N/P_N*, \qquad (2)$$

and log-differentiating yields

$$r = p_N - p_N*, \qquad (2')$$

where lower-case letters denote percentage changes. In the standard Balassa-Samuelson framework, the relative price of nontradables (i.e., the real exchange rate) depends on the productivity differential between tradable and nontradable sectors. Expanding equation (1) to capture the effect of differential productivity growth in trading partner countries (see, e.g., Aukurst (1977)), one obtains

$$r = \alpha_N (Q_T - Q_N) - \alpha_N* (Q_T* - Q_N*), \qquad (3)$$

where Q_T and Q_N denote total factor productivity (TFP) in tradable and nontradable sectors, respectively (stars denote trading partners' variables).

Estimates of TFP for tradable and nontradable sectors in Hong Kong are not available. Assuming a Cobb-Douglas production function, the TFP differ-

ential can be approximated as the labor productivity differential adjusted for the labor share. For the above classification of industries, the labor share in Hong Kong (i.e., compensation of employees as a percentage of value added) averaged about 53 percent over 1983–94. Thus, with $\alpha_N = 0.46$, a labor productivity differential of 8.3 percentage points, and the labor share of 0.53, one obtains a (weighted) TFP differential between tradable and nontradable sectors in Hong Kong equivalent to

$$\alpha_N (Q_T - Q_N) = 0.46 (8.3) 0.53 = 2.02 \text{ percentage points.}$$

Trading partner data can be approximated by the data for the OECD countries, which account for about 60 percent of Hong Kong's trade. The estimates for the OECD countries obtained by De Gregorio, Giovannini, and Wolf (1994) indicate a long-run TFP differential between tradable and nontradable industries of 1.24 percentage points, and an average share of nontradables of about 20 percent (the period covered was 1970–85). Thus, the TFP differential between tradable and nontradable sectors in Hong Kong's trading partners, weighted by the share of nontradables, is equivalent to

$$\alpha_N * (Q_T * - Q_N *) = 0.2 \,(1.24) = 0.25 \text{ percentage points.}$$

The long-run productivity differential was thus about 1.8 percentage points higher in Hong Kong than in the OECD countries. This figure is almost exactly equal to the average annual appreciation of the real effective exchange rate of the Hong Kong dollar (1.82 percent over 1983–94). Thus, the observed long-run real appreciation of the Hong Kong dollar was basically consistent with movements in the long-run equilibrium real exchange rate. It should be noted that this conclusion depends on two important assumptions:
- The rate of increase in the prices of internationally traded goods and services is the same in Hong Kong and its trading partners, so the real effective exchange rate index—which is CPI-based—correctly measures the movements in relative prices of nontradables in Hong Kong and abroad.
- In the long run, the movements in the equilibrium exchange rate reflect no factors other than the productivity differential in the tradable and nontradable sectors.

Policy Implications

Many observers in Hong Kong have been concerned that the rapid deindustrialization and the hollowing-out of manufacturing that took place over the past decade and a half will retard productivity and economic growth, increase the proportion of low-quality service jobs, and adversely affect income distribution. In response, two views have emerged (see Wong (1996)). According to the first view, a change in public policy from the present laissez-faire approach is necessary in order to reverse the decline of manufacturing. According to a second view, the transformation into a service economy is a natural outcome of market forces, and it is not unique to Hong Kong. In the long run, policies to support manufacturing industries would be inefficient, and could not reverse the loss of comparative advantage in such industries.

The above results indicate that many services industries in Hong Kong expanded strongly over 1982–94 and adjusted flexibly in periods of falling profitability and rising costs, as resources moved rapidly to their more efficient uses in response to relative price and relative wage changes. Tradable services generally performed much better than nontradable services, and the prices of nontradable services increased much faster. But overall, Hong Kong maintained a high real growth rate and a high growth rate of labor productivity, despite the decline of manufacturing. Inflation was, by and large, the result of faster productivity growth in tradable sectors, which include many service industries in addition to manufacturing.

An important question not addressed directly in this chapter is from where the sources of strong productivity growth in Hong Kong's tradable sectors came. In recent studies of growth in Asian newly industrialized countries, Hong Kong is generally an exception, showing significant increases in TFP.[53] However, introduction of technology that is, "new to the world" in the sense of providing superior best practices generally did not play a major role in Hong Kong's development (except perhaps in certain narrow segments of manufacturing), given the relatively low level of investment in research and development. Technical progress generally took the form of improved technical efficiency, that is, catching up with best practices available by introducing technology that was new to Hong Kong but already in use in other countries. Productivity of existing techniques was thus increased by a series of small improvements on otherwise unchanged technologies.[54] Finally, the results presented above suggest that improved allocative efficiency—shifting resources from low-productivity to high-productivity uses while remaining at the same technological level—may have been a significant source of TFP increases in Hong Kong.

The main policy implication of this analysis is that, left to its own devices, the private sector can successfully undergo a major structural transformation in a relatively stable macroeconomic environment and under the overall conditions of economic growth. The importance of stability in providing a level playing field cannot be underestimated. In the period considered, Hong Kong had a stable exchange rate. There have been only marginal changes in the tax system, which has been neutral in providing incentives to different activities. Major new public expenditure initiatives focused on improving physical infrastructure and human capital of the population, that is, programs with spillover benefits accruing more or less uniformly to all industries. To the extent that inflation had asymmetric effects on certain industries (e.g., property and personal and social services, which use relatively more nontradable inputs), the prevailing demand conditions were such that these industries were generally able to pass on the rising costs to consumers.

---

[53] See, for example, Young (1995).

[54] As noted by Davies (1996), these improvements most likely were made in the organization of work, the elicitation of effort from workers, and the compression of activities in time.

Looking ahead, these results imply that, in order to maintain competitiveness in services, industries, policymakers should avoid measures that may reduce the observed flexibility of factor prices or distort the price signals to which factor movements respond. While structural transformation hurts certain segments of the workforce more than others (for instance, workers with low skills or older workers), the best way to address such problems is by focusing on specific programs at the microeconomic level, without changing the noninterventionist framework of economic policy. At the same time, continued productivity gains will also require an expanding pool of highly skilled labor; hence, the importance of expanding and improving higher education cannot be underestimated.

Finally, much of Hong Kong's dynamism and competitiveness can be traced to the openness of its economy, and to the transfer of technology, information, and movements of labor and capital that this openness and the forces of globalization have encouraged. As Hong Kong develops and its comparative advantages change, it must ensure that the openness that has served it so well in the past is extended to the new trade frontiers, notably nontraded services. At the same time, it will be important to maintain transparency and the free flow of information on which the service sector—and, indeed, the modern economy—depend.

VI   Transition in 1997

This section reviews the key institutions and arrangements for economic policymaking that are expected to be put in place following the transfer of sovereignty over Hong Kong to China on July 1, 1997. The central point of the agreement between Britain and China on the future of Hong Kong is that Hong Kong's capitalist economic system would be preserved for 50 years. In the Sino-British Joint Declaration, China has undertaken to maintain many key aspects of Hong Kong's system: freedom of trade, freedom of capital movement, separate public finances, a separate convertible currency, common law, and basic freedoms such as speech, information, and travel. To implement these commitments, China has promulgated a constitutional document, the Basic Law, for Hong Kong. The Basic Law includes the provisions made in the Joint Declaration along with additional assurances on the continuity of Hong Kong's economic system. For instance, a low tax requirement was enshrined in the Basic Law in the belief that it was essential to Hong Kong's success. Recognizing Hong Kong's regional and international role, the Basic Law also committed the government of the future Hong Kong Special Administrative Region to maintain Hong Kong's status as an international financial center. As regards monetary policy, China has made important commitments that there will continue to be two separate monetary systems and currencies, as well as two mutually independent monetary authorities. In the international arena, Hong Kong will continue to participate in international organizations, including the IMF, and may subscribe to international treaties, under the name Hong Kong, China.

Historical Context

International treaties have featured prominently in Hong Kong's history. The Anglo-Chinese treaties of 1842, 1860, and 1898 established Hong Kong as a separate territorial and administrative unit. After July 1, 1997, Hong Kong's international position will be governed by the Joint Declaration, a Sino-British treaty signed in 1984 and registered with the United Nations. Unlike most treaties, the Joint Declaration has determined not only Hong Kong's international position, but also its constitutional structure, as the basic institutions and policies set down in the Joint Declaration and its annexes have been subsequently incorporated into the Basic Law, which will become Hong Kong's main constitutional document.

"Unequal" Treaties

Hong Kong was established as a separate territorial unit in 1842, as part of settlement between Britain and China following the First Opium War (1841–42). The original reason for the occupation of Hong Kong was the need for a base for trade with China (Box 14). Under the Treaty of Nanjing (1842), China ceded the Hong Kong Island to Britain "in perpetuity," opened up its ports to foreign trade, and conceded the right of extraterritoriality to British consuls. In 1860, following the Second Opium War (1858–60), China ceded the Kowloon peninsula to Britain. Finally, following the Japan-China war of 1894–95, Britain demanded the lease of the area north of Kowloon in order to secure control of the northern shore of the harbor and a wide area of land beyond for defense purposes. China leased this territory to Britain for 99 years under the Convention of Peking from July 1, 1898.

China has always regarded the treaties of 1842, 1860, and 1898 as "unequal" and refused to recognize their validity, claiming that Hong Kong was Chinese territory, which happened to be temporarily occupied by the British. But China did not officially repudiate the treaties. Hong Kong has provided a convenient center for trade contacts and financial negotiations, and a valuable outlet for China's exports and a place where China could earn foreign exchange to pay for its development program. China, in turn, provided much of the foodstuffs needed for Hong Kong's urban population, and was also a source of water, raw materials, and inexpensive manufactured goods.

When China was admitted to the United Nations in 1972, it asked that Hong Kong and Macau be re-

Box 14. Economic Background on the Establishment of Hong Kong

The Industrial Revolution and the broader trends in the developing international economy led to vastly increased demands for access to the Chinese market in the early nineteenth century. However, Chinese authorities at the time felt that the right to trade might be bestowed or tolerated, but it was not a subject for international negotiation (Cameron (1991)). Yet, fruitful trade was carried on in Guangzhou (Canton). China ran a large trade surplus on its exports of silk and tea, and there was a steady flow of silver to the local Chinese merchants and the treasury in Beijing that supported the continuation of trade (Endacott (1964)). However, the absence of official communication between the Chinese authorities and foreign traders and their national governments and, hence, of clear delineation of judicial jurisdiction in trading relations, meant that trade was always a potential source of friction.

Complicating the relations with China at the time was the expansion of the opium trade.[1] Importation of opium was banned in China in 1796, but it was a major economic activity of foreign traders in China at the time. In particular, Britain used exports of opium from India to pay for the vastly increased imports of tea, which became Britain's national beverage. Chinese traders along the southern coast developed a lucrative stake in the trade and frustrated the official attempts from Beijing to limit the transactions. In 1838, Chinese authorities adopted a tough line with the foreign traders as a whole to deal with the opium problem. Opium supplies were destroyed, but prices rose, increasing the incentives to continue the trade. In 1840, Britain sent a large fleet to enforce what it saw as its trading rights with China. The resulting conflict eventually led to the establishment of Hong Kong. The British government was initially uncertain whether to establish a permanent base on the Hong Kong Island. But the local traders moved faster and—as was to become common in Hong Kong's history—market forces were often far more important than government mandate.

---

[1]Opium was a vital part of the medicine in both Europe and China at the time. Consumption was regulated but not prohibited, much like alcohol (Segal (1993)).

---

moved from the list of territories that came under the supervision of the Special Committee on Colonialism on the grounds that they formed part of China:

> The settlement of the question of Hong Kong and Macau is entirely within China's sovereign right and they do not at all fall under the colonial territories. Consequently, they should not be covered by the declaration on the granting of independence to colonial countries and people. With regard to the questions of Hong Kong and Macau the Chinese government has consistently held that they should be settled in an appropriate way when conditions are ripe . . .[55]

This left the situation of Hong Kong vague. Although China did not regard itself as formally bound to respect the terminal date of the lease on the New Territories in 1997, Britain did, and it continued to regard the treaties of 1842, 1860, and 1898 as still in force. Consequently, it also considered itself bound to respect the terminal date of the lease of the New Territories (Miners (1995)).

Negotiations on the Future of Hong Kong

Until the early 1980s, the lack of certainty over the future of Hong Kong did not deter investors. But as 1997 approached, the British government became increasingly concerned that there might be a loss of confidence and withdrawal of investment if landowners could not be assured that their holdings would be extended beyond 1997. The British government approached the Chinese government on several occasions between 1979 and 1982 to discuss the subject of the land leases.

China's plans for the future of Hong Kong were first outlined in April 1982, when Mr. Edward Heath, a former British Prime Minister, met Mr. Deng Xiaoping in Beijing.[56] The plans provided for Hong Kong to become a special economic zone under Chinese sovereignty, governed by its own inhabitants, and retaining its existing capitalist way of life and its own system of laws and justice, but without any continuing British presence in the administration. In December 1982, China adopted a new constitution, which included provision in Article 31 for the establishment of Special Administrative Regions with a high degree of autonomy. During Mrs. Margaret Thatcher's visit to Beijing in September 1982, an agreement was reached to enter into talks "with the common aim of maintaining the stability and prosperity of Hong Kong." The talks in Beijing lasted for two years. In the first year, the British delegation attempted to persuade the Chinese that a continued British administration in Hong Kong was essential if its prosperity was to be safeguarded and investors were to stay in Hong Kong (Scott (1989)). However, the Chinese delegation remained unconvinced and reiterated its plans for the future Hong Kong Special Administrative Region.

---

[55]Speech by Mr. Huang Hua, China's Permanent Representative to the United Nations, quoted in *South China Morning Post,* March 13, 1972. Quoted in Miners (1995), p. 6.

[56]Speech by Mr. Edward Heath in *House of Commons Debates,* May 16, 1984, p. 427 (quoted in Miners (1995), p. 8).

The turning point in negotiations came in September 1983. The talks seemed to be near deadlock, and the Chinese government stated publicly that, unless agreement was reached by September 1984, China would announce its decision on the future of Hong Kong unilaterally. The lack of progress in the talks contributed to financial panic in Hong Kong and the value of the Hong Kong dollar dropped precipitously against the U.S. dollar. In the face of these events, the British side agreed to discuss how the stability and prosperity of Hong Kong might be assured without a continuing British administration. Progress was then made in elaborating the Chinese proposals, and in April 1984 the British Foreign Secretary, Sir Geoffrey Howe, publicly revealed for the first time that the British administration of Hong Kong would end in 1997. The talks were concluded in September 1984, when a Joint Declaration on the Question of Hong Kong was initialed by the heads of the two delegations.

The agreement leading up to the Joint Declaration was not put to the people of Hong Kong for their approval in a referendum. China had argued that the talks had only concerned Britain and China, and that the Chinese government would look after the interests of the Hong Kong people (Miners (1995)). In early 1985, China established a committee to draft the Basic Law, the constitution for the future Hong Kong Special Administrative Region. China emphasized the importance of ensuring that the Basic Law be acceptable to the Hong Kong people, and set up a Basic Law Consultative Committee to publicize the successive drafts of the law and collect public opinion on it. The final version of the Basic Law was adopted by the National People's Congress (China's parliament) in April 1990.

Implementation of the Joint Declaration

Although the Joint Declaration is almost entirely concerned with the way in which Hong Kong will be governed after 1997, it has been relevant to the institutional structure in the last 13 years of British sovereignty. In particular, the annexes to the Joint Declaration provided for the establishment of the Joint Liaison Group, which has had a major influence on the policies followed by the Hong Kong government since 1984.[57]

The Joint Liaison Group was established in 1985 to ensure the effective implementation of the Joint Declaration. It consists of five members each from Britain and China and is stationed in Hong Kong. Although the Joint Liaison Group is not an organ of power and does not have any supervisory role over the administration, Annex II of the Joint Declaration, which sets out the powers and duties of the Group, stated that if there is a disagreement, the matter "shall be referred to the two governments for solution through consultations." In practice, the British had agreed to consult the Chinese side on such issues as major franchises and contracts that straddle 1997 and that are of concern to the Chinese side.

The Joint Liaison Group worked out a number of agreements between 1985 and 1989, although discussions stalled following the events in Tiananmen Square in June 1989. In the past few years, cooperation between Britain and China has been restored.[58] Agreements have been reached on virtually all outstanding economic issues and a number of important legal issues (Box 15). However, there is continued disagreement about the future of Hong Kong's political institutions. In particular, China has not recognized the Legislative Council elections held in September 1995 according to revised electoral arrangements. China instead selected a provisional legislature in December 1996 that replaced the current, elected Legislative Council on July 1, 1997. It is expected that the main task of the provisional legislature will be to prepare new elections to be held within a year from the handover.

Hong Kong's Constitutional Arrangements

To assess the extent of continuity in institutional arrangements, and in particular the legal system embedded in the Joint Declaration and the Basic Law, it is helpful to review Hong Kong's early constitutional documents—the Letters Patent and Royal Instructions. These documents have laid out the basic structure of government that has been essentially preserved to this date. Of particular interest in the context of transition are intergovernmental relations between the Hong Kong government and the "central" government in London. These arrangements are then compared with those embedded in the Basic Law of the Hong Kong Special Administrative Region.

Current Constitutional Arrangements

The main emphasis of the Letters Patent ("patent" here means open to the public, not confidential) is on

---

[57]The activities of the Sino-British Land Commission, which was established under Annex III of the Joint Declaration to oversee the supply of land until 1997, are discussed later in this section.

[58]See Yahuda (1996) for factors leading to the decision to resume cooperation.

Box 15. Implementation of the Joint Declaration

From the signing of the Joint Declaration in 1984, through the end of February 1997, progress in the Joint Liaison Group has been achieved in four main areas.

1. Upholding the rule of law
   - Court of Final Appeal. The Sino-British Agreement (June 9, 1995) and the subsequent enactment of the Court of Final Appeal Ordinance ensure that this court will be set up in Hong Kong on July 1, 1997, in accordance with the relevant provisions of the Basic Law. Judicial continuity will thus be maintained.
   - Localization of laws. The government needs to localize about 150 U.K. enactments currently applied to Hong Kong in such areas as merchant shipping and civil aviation by way of 33 localization bills. So far, 23 ordinances have been enacted and agreements have been reached on 6 other proposals.
   - Bilateral agreements on legal and judicial issues. The Joint Liaison Group has agreed that Hong Kong should negotiate and conclude with other jurisdictions a series of bilateral agreements on the Surrender of Fugitive Offenders, Mutual Legal Assistance in Criminal Matters, and the Transfer of Sentenced Persons. A number of agreements have been signed. These bilateral agreements will continue to be valid after 1997.

2. Protection of rights and freedoms
   - Some of the multilateral international agreements that will continue to apply to Hong Kong after June 30, 1997, as agreed by the Chinese side in the Joint Declaration or the Joint Liaison Group, relate to human rights and the protection of individual rights and freedoms. These include the International Covenant on Economic, Social and Cultural Rights; the International Covenant on Civil and Political Rights; the UN Convention on the Rights of the Child; Conventions on the Political Rights of Women and the Elimination of Discrimination Against Women; the International Conventions on minimum age of work, maternity protection, right of association, and labor relations; and the International Convention on the Elimination of All Forms of Racial Discrimination.

3. Strengthening the economic infrastructure and institutions
   - Separate membership for Hong Kong in international finance, trade, and economic organizations, including the Asian Development Bank (agreement reached in 1985); GATT (1986)/WTO (1995); World Customs Organization (1987); and International Textiles and Clothing Bureau (1996).
   - The Memorandum of Understanding on the Airport was signed in September 1991. An agreement on the overall financial arrangements for the airport and the airport railway was signed in November 1994. The texts of the Financial Support Agreements for the airport and the airport railway were agreed in June 1995, and on the early commissioning of the second runway in May 1996;
   - The development of Container Terminal 9 was agreed in September 1996.
   - The Hong Kong shipping register will continue to be used after 1997.
   - Full agreement on the continuation of the intellectual property regulatory framework has been attained. Agreements have been reached on the localization of Hong Kong's registered designs law, patents law and copyright law, as well as the continued application of the Patent Cooperation Treaty and the Treaty establishing the World Intellectual Property Organization.
   - A network of 14 Investment Promotion and Protection Agreements have been concluded with third countries.
   - A network of 21 Air Services Agreements have been signed with third countries.
   - For major franchises and contracts that straddle 1997, a common view has been reached on 17 items, including subscription TV licenses, four fixed telecommunication network services licenses, the management contracts for various tunnels, China Motor Bus and Citybus Franchises, and six Personal Communications Services Licenses.

4. Ensuring a smooth transfer of government
   - Transfer of defense responsibilities. A comprehensive agreement in June 1994 on the future of the military estate stated that 14 sites will be handed over to the People's Liberation Army on July 1, 1997, exclusively for defense purposes. Twenty-five sites, which have excellent potential for housing and commercial development, will be returned to the Hong Kong government.
   - The civil service. A new civil service pension scheme was agreed in 1986. A civil service pension fund has also been established. More than a dozen informal meetings took place between Policy Secretaries and Heads of Departments in Hong Kong and their Chinese counterparts in 1995–96.
   - The transitional budget, which will cover the 1997 fiscal year from April 1, 1997, to March 31, 1998, in its entirety, was passed by the Legislative Council on April 16, 1997.
   - An agreement has been reached on the principles for the transfer of archives.
   - The Joint Liaison Group has also reached agreements on transitional arrangements for new identity cards and other travel documents, as well as the preparations for the issue of Special Administrative Region passports.
   - An Agreed Minute was also signed on the transfer of the Exchange Fund in its entirety to the Special Administrative Region government on July 1, 1997.

the need for the Governor to exercise all the rights in accordance with any instructions that may be given from London, and on the power of the Crown (i.e., the British government) to make laws for the colony and to reserve the right to disallow any ordinances passed by the Legislative Council (Miners (1995)). The Royal Instructions are almost entirely concerned with the details of the Executive and Legislative Councils. Because of the very wide powers given to the Governor and the Legislative Council, the Letters Patent and Royal Instructions are in all very short and simple. A large number of issues that are normally addressed in constitutions are omitted, including the organization of the court system and central and local government. These matters are regulated by ordinances passed by the Legislative Council or by administrative instructions issued by the Governor. The only specific limitation on the legislative powers of the Governor and the Legislative Council is contained in Clause XXVI of the Royal Instructions, which forbids the Governor to give his assent to any bill relating to 10 specified subjects—including the currency issue and the operation of the banking system—before obtaining permission from the Secretary of State.

Although the British Parliament has unlimited power to enact laws on any subject, it normally has not legislated on domestic Hong Kong affairs. And since the enactment of the Hong Kong Act 1985, the Legislative Council has been able to amend or repeal any Act of Parliament or any subordinate legislation issued under that Act which relates to Hong Kong.

Judging from these constitutional documents, the British government would appear to have substantial control over the way in which Hong Kong is run. However, as in any constitutional system, the way in which Hong Kong has been run has also been determined by established constitutional conventions—the rules that are recognized as binding by those who obey them but are not legally enforceable. The most important difference between the constitutional position as set out in the Letters Patent and Royal Instructions and what has actually happened is that the British government has very rarely exercised its legal right to give detailed instructions about the way the internal affairs of Hong Kong are to be conducted (Miners (1995)). In practice, the Hong Kong government has largely controlled its own affairs and determined its own policies, especially on economic and financial matters. In 1983, for example, a Public Finance Ordinance was passed by the Legislative Council that laid down comprehensive rules and procedures for the management and control of revenue and expenditure in Hong Kong that superseded the relevant parts of the Colonial Regulations, an early constitutional document that addressed important financial and civil service matters.

Constitutional Arrangements After 1997

On July 1, 1997, Hong Kong will become a Special Administrative Region of the People's Republic of China and the constitutional documents described above will be replaced by the Basic Law of the Region. The Basic Law incorporates the basic policies of the People's Republic in regard to Hong Kong as they were set down in the Joint Declaration and its annexes. In particular, the Basic Law provides that the Hong Kong Special Administrative Region has a high degree of autonomy—except in matters of foreign policy and defense—and enjoys executive, legislative, and independent judicial power, including that of final adjudication (Article 2). Of particular interest are the following general provisions of the Basic Law (see Appendix III for details):[59]

Economic system. The socialist system and policies shall not be practiced in the Hong Kong Special Administrative Region, and the previous capitalist system and way of life shall remain unchanged for 50 years (Article 5; JD 16, 42, 84).

Property relations. The Region shall protect the right of private ownership of property in accordance with law (Article 6; JD 18, 86).

Land and natural resources. The land and natural resources within the Region shall be State property. The government of the Region shall be responsible for their management, use and development and for their lease or grant to individuals, legal persons or organizations for use or development. The revenues derived therefrom shall be exclusively at the disposal of the government of the Region (Article 7).

Legal system. The laws previously in force in Hong Kong, that is, the common law, rules of equity, ordinances, subordinate legislation and customary law shall be maintained, except for any that contravene the Basic Law, and subject to any amendment by the legislature of the Region (Article 8; JD 10 and 53).

Rule of law. In accordance with Article 31 of the Constitution of the People's Republic of China, the systems and policies practiced in the Region, including the social and economic systems, the system for safeguarding the fundamental rights and freedoms of its residents, the executive, legislative and judicial systems, and the relevant policies, shall be based on the provisions of the Basic Law (Article 11; JD 42).

As discussed below, the Basic Law also provides for Hong Kong to retain the existing economic, financial, and monetary policies; the Hong Kong dollar will continue as an independent currency and will

---

[59]Parentheses contain references to the Articles of the Basic Law and cross-references to the corresponding articles of the Joint Declaration (JD).

remain fully convertible; Hong Kong's status as a free port and separate customs territory will not be altered; and the Chinese government will not levy taxes nor receive any revenue from the Hong Kong Special Administrative Region. Thus, it appears that in relations between the central authorities and the Region, the independent sphere of power assigned to the Region will be far greater than that normally exercised by member states of a federation. This is perhaps the most remarkable feature of the "one country, two systems" concept given that the People's Republic of China is a unitary state and not a federation.[60]

Institutions of Government

Hong Kong is administered by the Hong Kong government, which is headed by the Governor. The Governor has the ultimate direction of the administration of Hong Kong. An Executive Council offers advice to the Governor on important matters of policy. At the central level of the three-tier system of government, the Legislative Council legislates, controls public expenditure, and monitors the performance of the administration. At the regional level, the two municipal councils provide public health, cultural, and recreational services in their respective regions. At the district level, 18 district boards offer advice on the implementation of policies in their districts and provide a forum for public consultation.

As with constitutional arrangements, it is necessary to provide some background on the present system of government in Hong Kong in order to understand to what extent the continuity of existing institutional arrangements would be preserved in the Region. This section discusses the role of the Governor and the Executive Council in the present system and the future Hong Kong Special Administrative Region; the place of the Legislative Council in the present system of government; and the organization and roles of the civil service.

Governor and Executive Council

As the symbolic representative of the Queen's sovereignty over Hong Kong, the Governor exercises by delegation the powers of the royal prerogative. These powers include:
- Making laws for the peace, order, and good government of the colony;
- Making grants of land;
- Appointing judges and other officers of the government;
- Suspending or dismissing any officer (except judges of the Supreme and District Court, for whom a special procedure applies), and granting pardons;
- If the Governor has insufficient powers under existing legislation to deal with a crisis, having a bill be passed through all its stages at one sitting of the Legislative Council; and
- Giving immediate assent to a bill on one of the reserved subjects—including a bill concerning the currency issue or the operation of the banking system—so long as he "shall have satisfied himself that an urgent necessity exists that such a Bill be brought into immediate operation."

Recent constitutional changes have reduced somewhat the Governor's control over the Legislative Council. Since 1991, a majority of the members has been either directly or indirectly elected, but the Governor has retained the right to refuse his assent to any legislation passed and to dissolve the Council and order fresh elections at any time. The Governor's legal powers to exercise control over the civil service have also remained virtually unrestrained: all appointments, promotions, transfers, and dismissals are made by him or in his name; he can give directives to all civil servants as to the policy they must follow or actions they must take; and although he is required to consult the Executive Council on all major decisions, he is empowered to disregard its views and act according to his own judgment.

The Governor in practice rarely exercises the full extent of his powers. The main restraining forces have included the practical need to obtain cooperation of the civil service and to follow its established procedures; the likely reactions to new policy initiatives of organized groups; and public opinion in general. The Governor is also subject to British law (as far as it is applicable in Hong Kong) and to all the ordinances passed by the Legislative Council. Over the years, these restraining forces have proved effective: the Governor and administration have generally enjoyed a reasonable level of confidence of the population (Miners (1995)).

The powers and functions of the Chief Executive of the Hong Kong Special Administrative Region laid down in Article 48 of the Basic Law are broadly similar to those presently exercised by the Governor:[61]
- To lead the government of the Region;

---

[60]The independent powers of the Hong Kong Special Administrative Region are not formally part of the national constitution—they are set out in the Basic Law, which is an ordinary piece of legislation enacted by the National People's Congress. Moreover, under Article 18 of the Basic Law, the Central People's government is entitled to issue an order applying the relevant national laws to the Region, if the Standing Committee of the National People's Congress declares a state of war or, by reason of turmoil within the Region which endangers national unity or security and is beyond the control of the government of the Region, decides that the Region is in a state of emergency.

---

[61]The list is not exhaustive.

Box 16. Selection of the Chief Executive of the Hong Kong Special Administrative Region

The first Chief Executive of the Hong Kong Special Administrative Region was chosen by a 400-member Selection Committee comprising a broad range of representatives from Hong Kong. In particular, the Selection Committee comprised:

- 100 members from the industrial, commercial, and financial sectors;
- 100 members from the professions;
- 100 members from labor, grassroots, religious, and other sectors; and
- 100 former political figures, Hong Kong deputies to the National People's Congress, and the representatives of Hong Kong members of the National Committee of the Chinese People's Political Consultative Conference.

Members of these groups could apply in person to join the Selection Committee. In total, over 1,500 individuals applied. The Selection Committee was established in November 1996. The Selection Committee has itself been chosen by a 150-member Preparatory Committee appointed by the National People's Congress (China's parliament) in January 1996.

A total of 31 Hong Kong residents declared their bids for the Chief Executive's post. To be considered for appointment, these applicants had to satisfy the eligibility criteria as set out in the Basic Law and be nominated by at least 50 Selection Committee members. A total of three candidates passed this test. To be selected, the successful candidate needed more than half the votes of the Selection Committee in a secret ballot. In the event, the first Chief Executive-Designate, Mr. Tung Chee-Hwa, obtained 327 votes on December 11, 1996.

- To be responsible for the implementation of the Basic Law and other laws of the Region; to sign bills passed by the Legislative Council and to promulgate laws; to sign budgets passed by the Legislative Council and report the budgets and final accounts to the Central People's government for the record;
- To decide on government policies and to issue executive orders;
- To nominate and to report to the Central People's government for appointment of certain principal officials;
- To appoint or remove judges of the courts at all levels in accordance with legal procedures;
- To appoint or remove holders of public office in accordance with legal procedures;
- To implement the directives issued by the Central People's government in respect of the relevant matters provided for in the Basic Law;

- To conduct, on behalf of the government of the Region, external affairs and other affairs as authorized by the Central Authorities; and
- To approve the introduction of motions regarding revenues or expenditure to the Legislative Council.

Like the Governor, the Chief Executive may refuse to sign a bill passed by the Legislative Council and return it to the Council for reconsideration (Article 49). He or she may also dissolve the Council if it refuses to pass a bill proposed by the government or the annual budget (Article 50). But the Chief Executive may dissolve the Council only once during his or her term of office. To deal with an irreconcilable conflict between the Chief Executive and the Legislative Council—a situation that has never yet arisen—the Basic Law provides for resignation of the Chief Executive under certain circumstances (Article 52).

The first Chief Executive of the Hong Kong Special Administrative Region, Mr. Tung Chee-Hwa, was selected on December 11, 1996 under the procedures set out in Annex I of the Basic Law (Box 16).

The present Executive Council consists of three ex officio members—the Chief Secretary, the Financial Secretary, and the Attorney General—and ten other members appointed by the Governor with the approval of the Secretary of State. The Governor has almost always recommended the appointment of one of the senior nonofficial members of the Legislative Council when a vacancy occurs in the Executive Council. This overlap in membership has helped the Executive Council to anticipate the reactions of the nonofficial members on the Legislative Council and its Finance Committee. According to the Royal Instructions, appointed members, both official and nonofficial, may be appointed for a maximum period of five years and are eligible for reappointment.[62]

The Governor is required by the Royal Instructions to consult the Executive Council on all important matters of policy. The Governor in Council—the Governor acting after consulting the Executive Council—is Hong Kong's highest executive authority on policy matters. In practice, decisions are arrived at by consensus. It is a long-established convention that the Governor respects the majority view of the Council and generally does not act against the determined opposition of a minority composed of nonofficial members. The Governor in Council considers all principal legislation before it is introduced

---

[62]Unlike Britain, the Governor is in a weaker position vis-à-vis the official members of the Executive Council than is the Prime Minister vis-à-vis the cabinet ministers because the three ex-officio official members may have been in office under his predecessor and retain their seats as long as they hold their official positions (Miners (1995)).

into the Legislative Council, and is responsible for making subsidiary legislation. Its advice on policy matters involving the expenditure of public funds is subject to the approval of the funds by the Finance Committee of the Legislative Council.

According to the Basic Law, the Executive Council of the Hong Kong Special Administrative Region will be formally exactly the same as at present (Articles 54–56). All members are chosen and can be removed by the Chief Executive. The Basic Law specifies that members shall be principal officials of the government, members of the Legislative Council, and other public figures. The Chief Executive is required to consult the Executive Council on important policy decisions, but is not obliged to accept the opinion of the majority. If the Chief Executive decides to act contrary to the Executive Council, he or she is required to put his or her reasons on record.

Legislative Council

The present Legislative Council has 60 members. In the most recent elections, held in September 1995, 30 members were elected from functional constituencies, each representing an economic, social, professional, or other sector of the community; 20 were returned by direct elections in geographical constituencies which cover the whole territory; and 10 were elected by the Election Committee Constituency comprising members of the district boards. Legislative Councillors elected one of their fellow members as President. The Legislative Council thus became wholly elected for the first time in its history.[63]

The main functions of the Legislative Council are to enact laws, control public expenditure, and monitor the performance of the government by putting forward questions on matters of public interest. The government is responsible for initiating legislative and public funding proposals to the Legislative Council for consideration.

Legislation is enacted in the form of bills. A bill passed by the Legislative Council becomes law when it receives the Governor's assent. After the Governor's assent, a bill becomes an ordinance without being subject to external approval, although the Queen has reserve powers to disallow an ordinance.

Apart from the enactment of legislation, the Council holds two major debates in each legislative session: a wide-ranging debate on government policies which follows the Governor's address at the opening of the new session in October each year; and the budget debate on financial and economic affairs concerning the annual Appropriation Bill, which takes place in early March. Members of the Council may question the government on policy issues for which the latter is responsible, either seeking information on such issues or asking for official action on them.

All Legislative Council sittings and most meetings of its bills committees, subcommittees and panels are open to the public. The increased transparency of the Legislative Council has helped promote better awareness and understanding of the constitutional role and functions of the Council.

The Joint Declaration provided for the legislature of the Hong Kong Special Administrative Region to be constituted by elections, and for the executive authorities to be accountable to the legislature (JD 49–50).[64] The Basic Law and the decision of the National People's Congress of April 4, 1990, specified a method for the formation of the Legislative Council of the Region (Annex II). The Basic Law further provides that the Region may decide on its own the formation method of its legislature after 2007 (Annex II), and that the ultimate aim is the election of all members of the legislature by universal suffrage. Because of disagreement between Britain and China about the Legislative Council elections held in September 1995, a provisional legislature was selected in December 1996 by the Selection Committee which also chose the Chief Executive-Designate. The 60 members of the provisional legislature were selected from a list of 130 candidates previously nominated by members of the Selection Committee. Of the legislators chosen, 51 came from the Selection Committee itself, and 33 were members of the Legislative Council. As discussed above, one of the main tasks of the provisional legislature is expected to be to prepare for new elections to be held within a year from the transfer of sovereignty.

The powers and functions of the legislature of the Hong Kong Special Administrative Region as set out in Article 73 of the Basic Law are broadly similar to those currently exercised by the Legislative Council. These powers include:

• To enact, amend, or repeal laws in accordance with the provisions of the Basic Law and legal procedures;

---

[63]Before the 1995 elections, the Legislative Council was partially elected—18 members were elected by geographical constituencies with universal franchise, 21 were elected by functional constituencies with limited franchise, 18 were appointed by the Governor, and 3 were ex-officio principal administration officials.

[64]When the Joint Declaration was published, these provisions were widely assumed to mean "direct elections by universal suffrage" and "able to be dismissed by the legislature" (Miners (1995), p. 67).

- To examine and approve budgets introduced by the government;
- To approve taxation and public expenditure;
- To receive and debate the policy addresses of the Chief Executive, and any issue concerning public interests;
- To raise questions on the work of the government;
- To endorse the appointment and removal of the judges of the Court of Final Appeal and the Chief Judge of the High Court; and
- To receive and handle complaints from Hong Kong residents.

Civil Service

The Hong Kong government is organized into branches and departments. The branches, each headed by a policy secretary, collectively form the Government Secretariat. All suggestions for changing policy, including requests for new or modified forms of spending, have to be referred to the Government Secretariat. Secretariat officials may then take a decision themselves, or draft a paper for consideration by the Executive Council or the Finance Committee of the Legislative Council if a change in ambit or amount of expenditure is involved. This highly centralized system was designed to ensure that the Governor is kept fully informed and is in a position to exercise effective control, since he is constitutionally responsible for every executive act of government.

The Chief Secretary is principally responsible to the Governor for the formulation of government policies and their implementation. As the head of the Civil Service, the Chief Secretary is one of the Governor's principal advisers, along with the Financial Secretary and the Attorney General.

The Financial Secretary, who reports directly to the Governor, is responsible for the fiscal and economic policies of the government. He is an ex-officio member of the Executive Council and attends meetings of the Legislative Council as senior government representative. The Financial Secretary oversees the operations of the key economic policy branches of the Government Secretariat and the Hong Kong Monetary Authority. He also chairs the Exchange Fund Advisory Committee, and will oversee the management of the Land Fund of the Region after July 1, 1997. The Financial Secretary is responsible under the Public Finance Ordinance for laying before the legislature each year the government's estimates of revenue and expenditure. He delivers the annual budget speech, outlining the government's budgetary proposals and moving the adoption of the Appropriation Bill, which gives legal effect to the annual expenditure proposals contained in the budget.

The Efficiency Unit, established in May 1992, oversees and implements public sector reform. An important reform initiative is the performance pledge program, under which all departments directly serving the public have published performance pledges, informing their customers what services are available and the standards they can expect. The government has also introduced a system of program management, which has placed more emphasis on performance measurement, quality of service, value for money and accountability, thus leading to a more business-like approach to the delivery of services.

The Civil Service employs about 6 percent of Hong Kong's workforce. As of the end of 1996, the Civil Service had over 180,000 employees. Over 99 percent were local officers.

Recognizing that continuity in the civil service after 1997 is critical to achieving a smooth transition, in February 1997, the Chief Executive-Designate, Mr. Tung Chee-Hwa, appointed all 23 principal officials of the current government to serve on the first government of the Hong Kong Special Administrative Region.

The need for stability in the civil service is also recognized in the Basic Law. According to Article 100, "Public servants serving in all Hong Kong government departments, including the police department, before the establishment of the Region may all remain in employment and retain their seniority with pay, allowances, benefits and conditions of service no less favorable than before." To provide an additional assurance to civil servants on the security of pensions, a Civil Service Pension Reserve Fund was established in 1995.

Framework for Economic Policymaking

Process of Legislation

Almost all bills are traditionally drafted in the Government Secretariat and introduced by official members of the Legislative Council after consultations with interested parties. The finalized bills are put before the Executive Council for its approval. If the proposal is accepted in principle, a draft bill is introduced into the Legislative Council. This pre-legislative stage is by far the most important in the bill's formation—it has been rare for further substantial changes to be made during the passage of the bill through the Legislative Council. Bills normally take a month to complete their passage through the three readings in the Council. Controversial bills take longer, depending on the time needed for negotiations between the group of nonofficial members concerned with the bill and the official side. In an emergency, the bill can be passed through all its stages in a single session and receive the Governor's assent the same day. Apart from the need for the Governor's assent there are two other limitations on the legislative competence of the Legislative Council—the need for the Governor to obtain the consent of the Secretary of State on any bill on the "reserved subjects" list contained in Clause XXVI of the Royal Instructions; and the formal right of the British government to disallow the text of the bill.

In summary, unlike the United States Congress, the Legislative Council does not "make" laws; it normally endorses and formally ratifies (and only rarely challenges and amends) decisions that have already been taken in the Government Secretariat, after very extensive argument and consultation with all those interests thought likely to be concerned (Miners (1995)).

Members of the Legislative Council of the Hong Kong Special Administrative Region will continue to be allowed to introduce bills in accordance with the provisions of the Basic Law and legal procedures. Bills that do not relate to public expenditure or political structure or the operation of the government may be introduced individually or jointly by members of the Council. The written consent of the Chief Executive will be required before bills relating to government policies are introduced (Article 74).

Budget and Financial Control

This section describes current procedures for fiscal policymaking in Hong Kong and the provisions on public finances in the Basic Law. As discussed in Section IV, the Hong Kong government has in general maintained a broad balance of revenue and expenditure. A key to the success of these policies has been careful planning within the annual financial cycle and firm financial control exercised by the government and the legislature. According to the Basic Law, the spirit of these policies should be fully carried over to the Hong Kong Special Administrative Region.

Annual Financial Cycle

In May, the Financial Secretary determines the ceiling of permitted expenditure (both recurrent and capital) for the fiscal year which will commence on April 1 in the following year. This is done in accordance with the budgetary guidelines that, over time, government expenditure shall grow in real terms at a rate no faster than the forecast trend growth rate of the economy (measured in terms of GDP). At the same time, the Financial Secretary seeks the views of the Legislative Council on which areas they see as spending priorities. The difference between the expenditure ceilings determined by the Financial Secretary and the resources required to meet existing commitments represents the maximum "new money" available for new or improved services and new capital projects in the annual resource allocation exercise. Policy Secretaries are invited to submit bids for these additional resources. The bids are first considered by the Finance Branch and then by the "Star Chamber," which determines the new initiatives that are to be accorded priority, taking into account the views of the community and those of the Legislative Council members.[65]

In March, consolidated draft estimates are published in support of the Appropriation Bill, a few days before the Financial Secretary makes his budget speech. The Appropriation Bill is very short, merely listing the main heads of expenditure and the total sum to be authorized for the coming year. The budget speech provides the occasion for the Financial Secretary to set out his forecasts for the coming year and explain his proposals for changes in taxation. If there are to be any increases in taxes or government fees, the Governor is authorized by the Public Revenue Protection Ordinance to sign an order that brings these changes into force immediately without waiting for them to be approved by the Legislative Council.[66]

Financial Control

In addition to the passing of laws and the scrutiny and control of the acts of the executive, financial control or the "voting of money" is a major activity of Hong Kong's legislature. The main structural mechanism to control expenditure is the Finance Committee of the Legislative Council, which consists of all members of the Legislative Council except the President. The power of the Finance Committee derives from the fact that it has an absolute veto over all items of government expenditure. Section 8 of the Public Finance Ordinance stipulates that:

> No changes shall be made to the approved estimates of expenditure except with the approval of the Finance Committee upon a proposal of the Financial Secretary.

---

[65]The "Star Chamber" comprises the Chief Secretary, the Financial Secretary, the Secretary for the Treasury, and the Secretary for the Civil Service.

[66]The signing of this order does not prevent the Legislative Council from rejecting the proposed increase in taxation, nor does it prevent the Financial Secretary from withdrawing his proposal during the debate if he is convinced by the arguments brought against it.

Meetings of the Committee are open to the public and its proceedings reported in the press. The main limitations on the work of the Finance Committee are that it cannot vote to *increase* the sum requested by the government—it can only either approve, reject, or reduce it—and that it only discusses government expenditure, and not the ways in which revenue is raised and possible changes to taxation. In recent years, political parties have been keen on proposing actual decreases in taxation, in order to win support from the electorate. But the government is protected by Clause XXIV of the Royal Instructions, which states:

> Every ordinance, vote, resolution or question the object or effect of which may be to dispose of or charge any part of Our revenue arising within the Colony, shall be proposed only by the Governor, unless the proposal of the same shall have been expressly allowed or directed by him.

However, the formal ban on moving a motion to increase expenditure does not inhibit members of the Finance Committee from criticizing the proposals put before them. Similarly, members show no hesitation in suggesting modifications to taxation, both in the debates on the Appropriation Bill and at other times.

The Finance Committee is not directly concerned with broad questions of the balance of expenditure between different policy areas. Such strategic decisions on the allocation of resources are taken within the administration in the light of such considerations as the needs of the economy and the future growth and distribution of the population. The Finance Committee deals with the outcomes of these higher-level decisions in requests for specific spending approvals. However, these lower-level decisions have a cumulative effect in ensuring that waste is avoided and that the government obtains value for its money. Thus, over the period 1981–95, the Hong Kong government consolidated public sector expenditure (central government spending together with that of the Urban and Regional Councils, the Housing Authority, the government Trading Funds, and the Lotteries Fund) has averaged approximately 17 percent of GDP. While the small size of the public sector in Hong Kong is partly due to structural and political factors (including the small size and openness of the economy and the absence—until recently—of competitive elections), the institutionalized checks in the system of financial control have undoubtedly played an important role in restraining growth of the public sector.

Tax Policy

As discussed in Section IV, the basic approach of the Hong Kong government with regard to taxation

has been to maintain a simple tax system with low and stable tax rates. As the tax system has been adjusted only at the margin, especially by lowering or raising tax allowances under the income tax, there has been no need for elaborate institutional arrangements for tax policy—adjustments have been made almost exclusively by the Financial Secretary.

FY1997 Budget

As the fiscal year 1997/98 covers the last quarter of British administration (April 1–June 30, 1997) and the first three quarters of the Hong Kong Special Administrative Region administration (July 1, 1997–March 31, 1998), the FY1997 Budget was prepared by the Hong Kong government for the whole fiscal year in full consultation with an Expert Group set up under the Sino-British Joint Liaison Group.[67] To facilitate joint discussions on the preparation of the FY1997 Budget, it was necessary to familiarize the Chinese side with the Hong Kong government's budgetary policies and procedures in a series of seminars during 1995. The Hong Kong government also invited the Chinese side to observe the preparatory cycle for the FY1996 Budget.

The FY1997 Budget is the only budget that will be prepared in cooperation with the Chinese authorities. The reason for China's involvement was the unique nature of the transitional budget. The Chinese authorities have hitherto taken the position that the Central People's government will look after the interests of the government of the Hong Kong Special Administrative Region until it comes into being. From July 1, 1997, the preparation of the annual budget will fall within the scope of the Region's financial autonomy.

Public Finances of the Hong Kong Special Administrative Region

The financial autonomy of the Region is enshrined in the Basic Law. In particular, Article 106 of the Basic Law states that:[68]

• The Hong Kong Special Administrative Region shall have independent finances;
• The Region shall use its financial revenues exclusively for its own purposes, and they shall not be handed over to the Central People's government; and
• The Central People's government shall not levy taxes in the Region.

---

[67]For a discussion of the policy aspects of the FY1997 Budget, see Section IV.

[68]The corresponding Articles of the Joint Declaration are 23, 24, 79, 81, and 82.

Budgetary strategy and public expenditure policy of the Region should continue to abide by the traditional principles of fiscal prudence. Specifically, Article 107 states that the Region shall follow the principle of:

- Keeping expenditure within the limits of revenues in drawing up its budget;
- Striving to achieve a fiscal balance;
- Avoiding deficits; and
- Keeping the budget commensurate with the growth rate of the Region's GDP.

These principles closely resemble the budgetary approach followed by the Hong Kong government, which has generally been to limit, over time, the real growth in government expenditure to no more than the forecast trend growth of the GDP, and to raise sufficient revenue to meet the resulting expenditure.[69] Similarly, the provisions on the need to achieve a fiscal balance and avoid deficits suggest that budget deficits should continue to be regarded as more of a problem than budget surpluses, a position that is at the core of the current approach of the Hong Kong government. Of course, the precise definitions of the fiscal balance and deficits, and the period over which they are measured, would be important in this regard. Finally, the provision on keeping the budget commensurate with the growth rate of the GDP suggests that the relative size of the public sector in the Region should not expand unduly. In this context, it is also important to note that the Public Finance Ordinance, with its built-in system of financial control, would continue to apply in the Region subject to any necessary adaptation to bring it in line with the Basic Law.

Tax laws and tax policy of the Hong Kong Special Administrative Region should largely continue the present approach. Article 108 of the Basic Law states that:[70]

- The Region shall practice an independent taxation system.
- The Region shall, taking the low tax policy previously pursued in Hong Kong as reference, enact laws on its own concerning types of taxes, tax rates, tax reductions, allowances and exemptions, and other matters of taxation.

In terms of the continuity of the tax system, it should also be emphasized that all revenue ordinances that are currently effective have been localized and will continue to apply in the Region.

---

[69]The above-mentioned provisions in the Basic Law suggest that the level of revenue should be determined first, and that expenditure should not exceed that level of revenue.

[70]See also the Joint Declaration, Articles 24 and 81.

Monetary and Exchange Rate System

Hong Kong's linked exchange rate system occupies a unique position in the framework for economic policymaking in that its origins and role are closely tied to the transition itself. In 1983, a breakdown in the political and diplomatic dialogue between Britain and China on the future of Hong Kong exacerbated macroeconomic instability that developed in the early 1980s and led to an outflow of capital. These developments depressed the exchange rate, and began to generate sharply rising inflation, which further reinforced the outflow. Meanwhile, the decline in confidence weakened property prices and made banks hesitant to raise interest rates in response. At the height of this crisis, the Hong Kong dollar depreciated by 15 percent in two days, and rumors spread about the solvency of depository institutions. Fundamentally, however, the economy was sound, with efficient firms, strong public finances, and sizable foreign exchange reserves. Thus, the basic requirement for monetary policy was to give the public confidence in the *future* stability of the currency and the monetary system through whatever political adjustments and structural changes may lie ahead. To reestablish confidence, the authorities reverted to the trusted principles of the currency board. From October 1983, the note-issuing banks were thus required to pay U.S. dollars to the Exchange Fund as full cover for bank notes issued, at a fixed rate of HK$7.80 per US$1. This measure laid the foundation for the linked exchange rate system, which has proved in the past 13 years that it could maintain financial stability and absorb both political uncertainties (as it successfully did, for example, in 1989) and massive structural change in the economy.

Monetary Management Under the Present System

As discussed in Section IV, the main purpose of monetary policy under the linked exchange rate system is to maintain currency stability. The linked rate system has a high degree of built-in automaticity—money supply is determined endogenously by the banking system, and monetary conditions are essentially set by the U.S. monetary policy. However, the system that was originally set up in 1983 did not ensure that the monetary authorities' transactions with the banking system would have the desired impact on interbank liquidity and, hence, exchange rate stability (see Section IV). It was only in 1988, under the so-called Accounting Arrangements with the Hongkong and Shanghai Bank, that the monetary authorities acquired the power to influence the supply (or the price) of the base money, which is an essential feature of a central bank (Yam (1996a)). However, this power has been used almost exclusively for the purpose of supporting exchange rate stability.

Over the years, the authorities have built up and reorganized other central banking functions, and eventually established the Hong Kong Monetary Authority in April 1993. The Monetary Authority, with a staff of about 500, is now responsible for all the functions of a central bank, with the exception of the issue of bank notes and the role as banker to the government. In particular, the Monetary Authority performs the functions of:

- monetary management;
- banking policy and supervision;
- lender of last resort;
- payment and settlement systems; and
- reserves management.

In recent years, the Monetary Authority has also taken initiatives in developing the financial system, particularly in regard to the Hong Kong dollar debt market and promoting Hong Kong as an international financial center.

From an institutional perspective, the Monetary Authority operates under the provisions of the Exchange Fund (Amendment) Ordinance 1992, as a body that assists the Financial Secretary in the performance of his functions relating to the maintenance of currency stability and the safety and stability of the banking system. The highest policymaking body of the Monetary Authority is the Exchange Fund Advisory Committee, whose role is to advise the Financial Secretary as controller of the Exchange Fund on general policy relating to its deployment. The 10 members, appointed by the Governor, sit on the committee in a personal capacity. The Financial Secretary is ex officio chairman.

Monetary System After 1997

The structure of Hong Kong's monetary system after 1997 is laid out in Articles 110 and 111 of the Basic Law (Box 17). Article 110 provides for the legal foundation of the monetary system and monetary independence of the Hong Kong Special Administrative Region. Article 111 specifies that the Hong Kong dollar shall continue to circulate as the legal tender, that it must be backed by a 100 percent reserve, and that the authority to issue Hong Kong dollars shall rest with the government of the Special Administrative Region. The existing system of currency issue by private banks is allowed to continue, provided the stability of currency is maintained.

It is expected that the Exchange Fund Ordinance and the Banking Ordinance, as well as their amendments and accompanying legislation, will form the legal basis of the monetary system of the Region, as they have been brought into conformity with the Basic Law over the past few years.

The concept of monetary autonomy of the Hong Kong Special Administrative Region has been clarified in recent policy statements by China's senior officials as:

One country with two currencies, two monetary systems and two monetary authorities which are mutually independent (Chen (1996)).

Specifically, the relationship between the two currencies has been defined as "two currencies circulating respectively as the legal tender in two different social and economic systems" (Chen (1996)). The issue and management of the two currencies would remain the responsibilities of the two monetary authorities in accordance with their own arrangements. The Hong Kong dollar would be regarded as foreign currency in the mainland and the renminbi would be regarded as foreign currency in Hong Kong. Both the Hong Kong and the Chinese authorities have emphasized that the possible full convertibility of the renminbi would not affect the separate status of the two currencies (Yam (1996b)).

The mutually independent relationship between the two monetary systems and the two monetary authorities has been defined as one where neither of the two currencies, the two monetary systems, and the two monetary authorities has precedence over the other or is subsidiary to the other (Chen (1996)). The size of Hong Kong's monetary system relative to that of China is explicitly recognized in this context, and Chinese authorities have stated that the two monetary systems are of equal importance to China in its reform and liberalization.[71] The assets and liabilities between the two monetary systems would thus be considered as foreign assets and foreign liabilities, while Chinese banks operating in the monetary system of Hong Kong would be treated as if they were foreign banks, and vice versa. In an important move, the Bank for International Settlements recognized this commitment to separate the two monetary systems by offering separate membership to Hong Kong and China in 1996.

---

[71]Hong Kong's money supply is about 40 percent that of China; asset size of the banking system is 1.3 times that of China; foreign reserves, including the Land Fund, are about 80 percent as large as China's; and the stock market capitalization in Hong Kong is five times larger than that of Shanghai and Shenzhen combined.

**Box 17. Provisions on Monetary and Financial Autonomy
of the Hong Kong Special Administrative Region**

China's policies to maintain Hong Kong's autonomy in monetary and financial affairs and Hong Kong's status as an international financial center are clearly stated in the Joint Declaration and the Basic Law. In particular, these documents guarantee that:

- The monetary and financial systems of the Region shall be prescribed by law (BL 110);
- The Region shall, on its own, formulate monetary and financial policies, safeguard the free operation of financial business and financial markets, and regulate and supervise them in accordance with law (BL 110; JD 96, 97);
- The Hong Kong dollar shall continue to circulate as the legal tender (BL 111; JD 22, 100);
- The authority to issue Hong Kong currency shall be vested in the government of the Region. The issue of Hong Kong currency must be backed by a 100 percent reserve fund. The system regarding the issue of Hong Kong currency and the reserve fund system shall be prescribed by law (BL 111; JD 101);
- Designated banks may be authorized to issue Hong Kong currency. The arrangements for such issue must be consistent with the object of maintaining the stability of the currency (BL 111; JD 102);

- No foreign exchange controls shall be applied in the Region. The Hong Kong dollar shall be freely convertible. Markets for foreign exchange, gold, securities, futures, and the like shall continue (BL 112; JD 20, 22, 98, 99, 100);
- The Region shall safeguard the free flow of capital within, into and out of the region (BL 112; JD 21, 97);
- The Exchange Fund shall be managed and controlled by the government of the Region primarily for regulating the exchange value of the Hong Kong dollar (BL 113; JD 104); and
- The government of the Region shall provide an appropriate economic and legal environment for the maintenance of the status of Hong Kong as an international financial center (BL 109; JD 20, 94).

The fact that these principles are enshrined in constitutional documents rather than ordinary pieces of legislation indicates the importance attached by China to the maintenance of the present monetary system. In particular, Hong Kong is probably the only territory in the world with the commitment to remain an international financial center written into its constitution.

It has been pointed out that Hong Kong's monetary autonomy may actually increase after 1997 (Yam (1996b)). As mentioned previously, under the Royal Instructions,

> The Governor shall not assent to "any Bill affecting the Currency of the Colony or relating to the issue of Bank notes," or "any Bill establishing any Banking Association, or amending or altering the constitution, powers, or privileges of any Banking Association" without prior approval of the UK Secretary of State.

Under the Basic Law, the only general requirement is that "laws enacted by the legislature of the Hong Kong Special Administrative Region must be reported to the Standing Committee of the National People's Congress for the record." This higher degree of monetary autonomy has been put into effect by recent legislative amendments that allow the Financial Secretary or the Governor in Council to exercise certain powers that were previously subject to the prior approval of the Secretary of State, including: investment of the Exchange Fund in securities; determination of limits for borrowing for the account of the Exchange Fund; movement of foreign reserves surplus to the requirement of the Exchange Fund; authority to appoint banks to issue bank notes;

and authority to proclaim coins as legal tender, mint coins, and appoint the minting agency.

With regard to the exchange rate regime, Article 112 of the Basic Law prohibits any foreign exchange controls, directs that the Hong Kong dollar shall remain freely convertible, provides for the continuation of markets for foreign exchange, gold, securities, and other assets, and specifies free flow of capital. The Chinese authorities have endorsed the view of the Hong Kong government that the linked exchange rate system and the exchange rate of 7.80 Hong Kong dollars to the U.S. dollar are appropriate for the economic circumstances of Hong Kong. While emphasizing that the future government of the Region shall, on its own, formulate monetary and financial policies, the Chinese authorities have consistently stated that:

> For the small and open economy of Hong Kong, a stable exchange rate is the most important indicator of monetary stability. It is also where confidence in Hong Kong hinges to the various sectors of Hong Kong and to the international financial community. The linked exchange rate system of Hong Kong has in the past contributed greatly to the stability of the Hong Kong dollar, and played a very important role in maintaining monetary stability in Hong Kong. We support the linked ex-

change rate system of Hong Kong and the efforts made by Hong Kong to buttress that system.[72]

Many of these commitments have been backed up with concrete actions in the past few years. China has openly supported the issue of Exchange Fund Notes that straddle 1997 (the longest maturity of Exchange Fund Notes presently extends to ten years). In 1996, the People's Bank of China and the Hong Kong Monetary Authority signed a bilateral repurchase agreement for U.S. Treasury bills. The scope of this agreement is similar to those that the Hong Kong Monetary Authority has signed with nine other Asian central banks over the past two years. The Chinese authorities have expressed their readiness to offer liquidity support to the Hong Kong Monetary Authority and, if necessary, to use their foreign reserves to support the Hong Kong dollar (Chen (1996)).

Another safeguard concerning the continuity of Hong Kong's foreign exchange system is contained in Article 113 of the Basic Law, which specifies that the government of the Hong Kong Special Administrative Region, not the central government, shall be in control of the Exchange Fund. One concern that has been expressed in this regard is a possibility that the Hong Kong Monetary Authority could come under pressure to invest in Chinese debt securities before they are an acceptable credit risk (Yam (1996b)). However, both the Chinese and the Hong Kong authorities have emphasized that the Exchange Fund can only invest in high-quality debt denominated in currencies that are convertible on the capital account, and they have noted that the Exchange Fund's investment policy is highly transparent and is published for public scrutiny (Chen (1996); Yam (1996b)).

Regulatory Framework

As a leading international banking and financial center, Hong Kong has a vital interest in preserving the transparent rules and freedoms that are embedded in its regulatory institutions, and that have underlain much of its past success. The Basic Law contains many provisions that address the regulatory issues, including the specific commitments designed to protect freedom of trade and maintain Hong Kong's status as an international financial center.

Banking and Financial Markets

The financial market activity is regulated by two main institutions—the Hong Kong Monetary Au-

thority, which oversees the banking system, and the Securities and Futures Commission, which oversees the stock and futures exchanges and regulates a number of other nonbank financial intermediaries. The Stock Exchange of Hong Kong and the Commissioner of Insurance also participate actively in financial market regulation.

The legal framework for banking supervision is provided by the Banking Ordinance. The principal function of the Hong Kong Monetary Authority under this Ordinance is "to promote the general stability and effective working of the banking system." To this effect, the Monetary Authority seeks to establish a regulatory framework that is in line with international standards, while at the same time providing sufficient flexibility for banks to take commercial decisions. Hong Kong banks meet the supervisory standards recommended by the Basle Committee on Banking Supervision.

The firm financial regulatory framework developed by the Hong Kong Monetary Authority is expected to remain in place after 1997. According to the Basic Law, the Region will continue to regulate and supervise financial institutions (Article 110). The Hong Kong and the Chinese authorities have repeatedly stressed that the supervision will continue to be undertaken in accordance with international rules and practices (Carse (1996), Chen (1996)). In particular, financial institutions based in the mainland and Hong Kong setting up offices in each other's territory would be approved on the same basis as foreign financial institutions and regulated by the relevant supervisory authorities (Chen (1996)). To this effect, the Banking (Amendment) Ordinance 1995 has enhanced the Monetary Authority's central banking role by establishing the Monetary Authority as the licensing authority responsible for the authorization, suspension, and revocation of all types of banks. The Amendment Ordinance has also improved checks and balances in the authorization procedures by requiring the Monetary Authority to consult the Financial Secretary on important authorization decisions, such as suspension and revocation, and retaining the Governor in Council (Chief Executive in Council after the transition) as the body for hearing appeals against decisions made by the Monetary Authority.

Over the years, the financial regulators from Hong Kong and China have cooperated closely on concrete matters concerning banking supervision and financial market infrastructure, including, most recently, linking of the payments systems.

With regard to financial market regulation, the regulatory activities of the Securities and Futures Commission and the Stock Exchange of Hong Kong will continue unchanged in the Hong Kong Special Administrative Region. Article 112 of the Basic Law

---

[72]Quoted in Yam (1996c), pp. 3–4.

provides for the continuation of markets for foreign exchange, gold, securities, futures, and the like, and Article 111 charges the Region with the responsibility for safeguarding the free operation of financial businesses and financial markets.

A concrete example of the application of these provisions has been the issuance of H shares on the Stock Exchange of Hong Kong, which has been a major engine of market development since 1993. The listing of H shares reflects the strategic goal of both regulators and market participants to make Hong Kong the main conduit for equity investment in China. As discussed in Section IV, the Securities and Futures Commission, the Stock Exchange of Hong Kong, and the Chinese authorities jointly established a framework for listing of H share companies, under which these companies are required to meet all the listing and reporting standards that apply to Hong Kong listings.

Another strategic goal of the Hong Kong and Chinese authorities in the area of financial markets has been to uphold Hong Kong's world-class financial status. Article 109 of the Basic Law directs the government of the Region to "provide an appropriate economic and legal environment for the maintenance of the status of Hong Kong as an international financial center." Although specific factors underlying such environment have not been defined, the Hong Kong and Chinese authorities have clarified one of its key aspects, the relationship between Hong Kong and Shanghai. The Chinese authorities have rejected as groundless speculations that Shanghai would replace Hong Kong as China's main international financial center (Chen (1995)). Rather, the relationship between the two centers is seen as one of "complementarity and mutual reinforcement": it is recognized that, before the renminbi becomes fully convertible, it will not be possible for Shanghai to become an international financial center, and that, given the size of China's economy, there is sufficient room for more than one financial center.

Markets for Goods and Services

As a fully open economy with no tariff barriers or other restrictions on trade, Hong Kong has been a strong supporter of free trade and the multilateral trading system. Hong Kong actively participates in various trade fora, including the WTO and APEC. The authorities regard Hong Kong's separate membership in these forums is an important manifestation of Hong Kong's autonomy in trade and economic affairs.

Both the Joint Declaration and the Basic Law provide strong guarantees on the continuity of Hong Kong's free trade policies. The relevant provisions state that:

- The Region shall maintain the capitalist economic and trade systems previously practiced in Hong Kong (JD 84; BL 5);
- The Region shall decide on its own economic and trade policies (JD 85, 86);
- The Region may on its own maintain and develop economic and trade relations with all states and regions (JD 88);
- The Region shall maintain the status of a free port and shall not impose any tariff. It shall pursue the policy of free trade and safeguard the free movement of goods, intangible assets, and capital (JD 19, 87; BL 114, 115);
- The Region shall be a separate customs territory and may participate in relevant international organizations and trade agreements under the name "Hong Kong, China" (JD 19, 89, 90; BL 116);
- Export quotas and tariff preferences obtained by the Region shall be enjoyed exclusively by the region (JD 91; BL 116); and
- The Region may issue its own certificates of origin for products (JD 92; BL 117).

The Basic Law also contains important provisions on the continuity of Hong Kong's existing system of shipping and civil aviation management and regulation (see Appendix III). In addition, the government of the Region is directed in the Basic Law to provide an economic and legal environment for encouraging investments, technological progress, and the development of new industries (Article 118); to formulate appropriate policies to promote and coordinate the development of various trades (manufacturing, commerce, tourism, real estate, transport, public utilities, services); and to pay regard to the protection of the environment (Article 119). The Region shall continue to recognize the existing professions and professional organizations (Article 142), and formulate and protect by law its own policies on intellectual property rights (Articles 139 and 140). In the non-traded sectors, agreements have been reached that all current franchises for utilities and public transportation will continue after June 30, 1997, and in the telecommunications industry, the Joint Liaison Group has agreed the granting of licenses for fixed telecommunication network services and personal communications services. In accordance with the Basic Law (Article 160), other telecommunications licenses issued before July 1, 1997 will continue to be valid.

There has been every indication that autonomy in trade policies will be upheld after the transition. In particular, it has been agreed in the Joint Liaison Group that the Hong Kong Special Administrative Region will continue to participate on its own as a separate contracting party in the WTO and the APEC forum as well as five other international organizations (Asian Development Bank, World Customs Organization, International Textiles and Clothing Bureau, World Meteorological Organization, and Network of Aquaculture Centers in Asia and the Pacific). Agreement has also been reached on the continued application of some 200 multilateral agreements to Hong Kong after June 30, 1997, in areas including trade and finance and conventions establishing a number of international organizations (including the Articles of Agreement of the IMF, the World Bank, and the IFC). Hong Kong has also concluded a series of bilateral agreements with other governments in areas covering air services and investment promotion and protection.

As a dependent territory of the United Kingdom until June 30, 1997, and a Special Administrative Region of the People's Republic of China from July 1, 1997, Hong Kong is not eligible to become a member of the IMF. However, in view of Hong Kong's importance as a major international trading and financial center, and acting at the request of the United Kingdom and with support of the Chinese authorities, the IMF staff team has visited Hong Kong regularly since October 1990 for Article IV consultation discussions with the authorities. Against the background of Hong Kong's enviable record of economic success, these discussions have focused on conditions necessary to maintain stability and confidence in the economy in the lead up to and beyond the transfer of sovereignty. Under a 1989 agreement reached in the Joint Liaison Group, the Hong Kong Special Administrative Region will continue to participate in the activities of the IMF. In February 1997, the Chinese authorities have formally requested the continuation of the Article IV consultation discussions with respect to Hong Kong, China, after the transfer of sovereignty on July 1, 1997. The Executive Board of the IMF has approved that request. In addition, the Hong Kong Monetary Authority announced its intention in December 1996 to participate in the IMF's New Arrangements to Borrow.

Factor Markets

Labor Market

The Hong Kong government has generally refrained from intervening in the labor market. The labor market is on the whole highly flexible, in part because the price mechanism has not been constrained by strong labor unions, business and labor regulations, and high taxes and transfer payments. Labor legislation does not impose a statutory minimum wage. Earnings of most workers fluctuate with overall economic activity, although it is customary to award each worker an extra month's salary at Chi-

nese New Year. Workers generally respond quickly to alternative market opportunities, partly owing to structural factors (geographical compactness, efficient communication network). In the face of an economic downturn, it has been customary among workers to accept a reduction in hours worked rather than face forced layoffs. Although Hong Kong has labor legislation not unlike that of industrial countries and has signed a large number of International Labour Organisation conventions, these regulations have not affected the underlying flexibility of the labor market.

According to Article 147 of the Basic Law, the Hong Kong Special Administrative Region shall on its own formulate laws and policies relating to labor. Other provisions related to the labor market include those on labor immigration (Articles 22 and 154), and those on education, science, culture, sports, and social services (Articles 136–49) (see Appendix III). For example, Article 144 stipulates that the policy of subventions for nongovernmental organizations in education, medicine and health, culture, art, recreation, sports, social welfare, and social work shall be maintained, while according to Article 145, the Region shall formulate its own policies on the development and improvement of the social welfare system in the light of the economic conditions and social needs.

Land Market

Virtually all land in Hong Kong is owned by the Hong Kong government, which has maintained a policy of retaining the freehold of the territories ceded by the Chinese government in the last century, and a reversionary interest in the leased territories. Land disposed of by the government is subject to a lease term. Land for noninstitutional uses is generally leased to the highest bidder at public auctions, with lease terms of 75 years or longer (up to 1,000 years). Most leases are transferable, and the land market is a market for land leases.

As discussed above, the subject of land leases has played a critical role in Hong Kong's history. All leaseholds in the New Territories and New Kowloon expire on June 27, 1997, and without the Joint Declaration and the Basic Law, owners of land and property in this area, which represents 92 percent of the land mass of Hong Kong, would have had no guarantee that their leases would be renewed after that date.

Until 1996, the government controlled the supply of new land for development and, hence, could affect the market price through timing and size of land releases. The Land Commission was set up in 1985 in order to implement Annex III of the Joint Declaration, which contains provisions on land leases extending beyond the transfer of sovereignty. According to the agreement, the Land Commission has monitored the amount of land sold each year and could allow sales in excess of the limit of 50 hectares a year laid down in the Joint Declaration. Revenue from land transactions that confer a benefit that extends beyond June 30, 1997 and are completed on or before May 27, 1985, has been shared equally between the Hong Kong government and the future government of the Hong Kong Special Administrative Region, after deducting the cost incurred by the Hong Kong government in developing the new sites. The Hong Kong government's share of land revenue has been credited to a special capital account of the budget, and could be used only to finance capital works projects (see Section IV). The share of the future government has been transferred to the Hong Kong Special Administrative Region Government Land Fund, which was established in 1986 to receive, hold, and manage in trust for the future government its share of land premium income. In May 1997, the Chief Executive-Designate of the Hong Kong Special Administrative Region proposed that the Land Fund be consolidated with fiscal reserves as of July 1, 1997.

Besides Article 7 of the Basic Law—which specifies that land will be state property, and that the government of the Region will manage and lease land, and dispose of land revenues on its own—other relevant provisions are:

• Land leases and related rights granted before the establishment of the Region and extending beyond June 30, 1997 shall continue to be recognized and protected under the law of the Region (Article 120);

• Land leases extending beyond June 30, 1997 shall not be subject to additional premium, but to an annual rent equivalent to 3 percent of the rateable value of the properties concerned (Article 121);

• Indigenous villagers holding rural properties shall continue to pay the previous rent; and

• Land leases that expire after July 1, 1997 without a right of renewal shall be dealt with in accordance with laws and policies of the Region on its own (Article 123).

One important implication of these provisions is that, from July 1, 1997, onward, land revenues that previously accrued to the Land Fund will be included in the budget of the Special Administrative Region. The assets of the Land Fund itself will be consolidated with fiscal reserves, and, in addition, the government of the Region will collect rents equivalent to 3 percent of the rateable value from all leases of land expiring after June 30, 1997. Also, the 50 hectares limit on land sales provided for in the Joint Declaration will no longer be applicable. As a result, fiscal reserves are projected to jump to HK$359 billion (27 percent of GDP) by the end of FY1997, representing more than two year's worth of current expenditure.

Appendix I   Estimates

This appendix describes the econometric estimates of the consumption function and the export supply and import demand functions discussed in Section III.

Consumption Function Estimates

The consumption equations are based on the rational expectations forward-looking model of consumption as discussed in Hall and Taylor (1993). Forward-looking behavior is captured empirically by constructing a measure of permanent income that depends on rational expectations of actual future income. The consumption equations also include the real interest rate, which depends on the expected rate of inflation.

Consumption was broken down into durables, nondurables, and services. This disaggregation was chosen because durables are more volatile than services and more sensitive to interest rates. Nondurables tend to lie in between in terms of their volatility and sensitivity.

The general form for the equations is given by:

$$CX = a + bCX(-1) + dYP + eRRL, \qquad (1)$$

where CX becomes consumer durables, CD; consumer nondurables, CN; and consumer services, CS; and where $CX(-1)$ denotes consumption lagged by one period; YP is permanent income; and RRL is the real interest rate.

The permanent-income variable is defined as

$$YP = Y + 0.9Y(+1), \qquad (2)$$

where Y and $Y(+1)$ denote current and next-period real income, respectively. Real GDP is used as a proxy for real income.

The real interest rate variable is defined as the difference between the Best Lending Rate, BLR, and the expected rate of inflation, LP:

$$RRL = BLR - LP. \qquad (3)$$

The expected rate of inflation was obtained by fitting the following price equation:

$$LP = f + gLP(-1) + hLW + iLIMP + jT + U,$$
$$U = \rho U(-1) + V, \qquad (4)$$

where LP is the log of the GDP deflator, LW is the log of the real wage index, $LIMP$ is the log of the unit value index for imports, T is a time trend, and U is the first-order autoregressive term. The estimated price equation for the period 1967–94 is shown below:[73]

$$LP = 0.114 + 0.381LP(-1) + 0.216LW$$
$$\quad (0.148)\,(1.385) \qquad\quad (1.699)$$
$$\quad + 0.177LIMP + 0.038T, \qquad (5)$$
$$\quad\;\; (1.899) \qquad\;\; (1.723)$$

$$\bar{R}^2 = 0.999, \quad DW = 1.777, \quad F = 837.7$$

The estimated coefficients of the price equation have the expected signs and are statistically significant at the 5 percent test level, except for the coefficient on lagged inflation (which is significant at the 10 percent level) and the constant term. The estimates suggest that changes in the GDP deflator are most sensitive to real wage and import price changes. Compared with similar estimates for the Group of Seven countries (Taylor (1993)), the wage elasticity and especially the import price elasticity of the aggregate price level are both very high in Hong Kong.

The consumption equations are linear in the levels of the variables and were estimated using the generalized method of moments (GMM) estimator for the period 1969–94.[74] The details of the estimated consumption equations are presented in Table 20, and the elasticities associated with the estimated coefficients in Table 21. The elasticities of consumption

---

[73]Values of t-statistics are shown in parentheses. The estimate for the autocorrelation coefficient ρ was 0.599 ($t = 1.856$). The estimates were obtained by the Cochrane-Orcutt iterative method. The Durbin-Watson statistic of 1.77 indicates absence of autocorrelation.

[74]The GMM estimator gives consistent estimates of both the parameters and the standard errors of the estimates. The instruments used were: $CD(-1)$, $CN(-1)$, or $CS(-1)$, as appropriate; lagged real GDP; lagged interest rate; lagged inflation; and a time trend.

Table 20. Estimates of Consumption Equations, 1969–94

Dependent Variable	Constant	Lagged Consumption	Real Income	Real Interest Rate	$\bar{R}^2$	DW
Durables	−3,944.81 (−3.86)	0.928 (17.41)	0.013 (4.00)	−470.97 (−2.76)	0.99	1.78
Nondurables	3,640.58 (1.40)	0.782 (5.11)	0.029 (1.81)	−463.10 (−1.87)	0.99	1.55
Services	−3,206.05 (−2.18)	0.142 (0.63)	0.121 (4.01)	572.38 (2.56)	0.99	1.92
Domestic consumption by residents	−1,701.86 (−0.88)	0.743 (6.30)	0.096 (2.78)	−927.11 (−2.31)	0.99	1.45

Source: IMF staff estimates.
Note: t-value are in parentheses.

with respect to lagged consumption and permanent income, and the semielasticities of consumption with respect to the interest rate (i.e., the percentage changes in consumption associated with a percentage point change in the real interest rate) were calculated for the 1993 sample points.

All estimated coefficients on real income and real interest rate, and all but one on lagged consumption (in the equation for services), are statistically highly significant. In particular, the real interest rate enters significantly in all equations, confirming the view that consumption in Hong Kong is highly sensitive to real interest rate changes.

The interest rate semielasticity is highest for durables. The impact is about one half as large for nondurables, and about a third as large for overall consumption by domestic residents. The long-run semielasticity of durables consumption is very high: an increase in real interest rate of 1 percentage point lowers consumption of durables by 1.12 percent after adjustment lags. The positive sign of the interest rate semielasticity for services suggests that the substitution effect of interest rate changes is stronger than the income effect.[75] Services also have the highest elasticity with respect to income: a 1 percent increase in real income raises consumption of services by about ½ percent.

Compared with the estimates of consumption equations for the Group of Seven countries presented in Taylor (1993), these results suggest that consumption in Hong Kong is highly sensitive to both real income and real interest rate changes. For example, the highest long-run semielasticity of inter-

est rate in the sample studied by Taylor was −0.96 (for France and Japan), compared with −1.12 for Hong Kong. These results probably reflect the fact that, compared with the Group of Seven countries, in Hong Kong there are few possibilities for smoothing consumption outside the family budget.

Estimates of Export Supply and Import Demand Functions

The following description of the econometric estimates of export supply and import demand functions for Hong Kong during 1960–95 is based on a small macroeconomic model developed by IMF staff. The demand for Hong Kong's exports is assumed to depend on the price of Hong Kong's exports relative to those in trading partners, and the volume of world merchandise imports weighted by Hong Kong's export shares. Domestic exports, net reexports (i.e., reexports less nonretained imports), and exports of services have been included in total exports to obtain a full measure of Hong Kong's export performance. Net reexports are important in this context because Hong Kong firms realize large gains from reexport trade—the rate of reexport margin is on average about 17 percent of the value of reexports (16 percent of GDP).[76] This substantial margin reflects the value of intermediary production services such as product design, quality control, packaging, and marketing that are applied to products imported into Hong Kong (e.g., from China) and subsequently exported to overseas markets.

---

[75]In theory, the impact of interest rate changes on consumption is ambiguous, as it depends on the relative strength of the substitution vs. the income effect.

[76]The rate of reexport margin is defined as the ratio of net reexports to total reexports for a given product category.

Table 21. Consumption Demand Elasticities, 1969–94

Dependent Variable	Lagged Consumption	Real Income		Real Interest Rate	
		Short run	Long run	Short run	Long run
Durables	0.452	0.188	0.343	–0.612	–1.117
Nondurables	0.423	0.189	0.328	–0.275	–0.477
Services	0.118	0.472	0.535	0.317	0.359
Domestic consumption by residents	0.409	0.233	0.394	–0.217	–0.367

Source: IMF staff estimates.

The export supply equation was estimated on annual data from 1960–95 using the maximum likelihood iterative technique. The estimated equation is shown below:[77]

$$\log X_t = 6.718 - 0.462 \log PX_t + 0.900 \log FD_t \quad (6)$$
$$(59.58) \quad (-3.33) \quad (31.79)$$

$$\bar{R}^2 = 0.991, \quad DW = 1.597, \quad F = 1,070.80$$

where:

X_t = domestic exports of goods, net reexports of goods, and exports of nonfactor services in constant prices ("total exports");

PX_t = deflator for total exports expressed in U.S. dollars, divided by the weighted average of partner country prices in U.S. dollars using Hong Kong's export weights; and

FD_t = weighted average of partner country total import volumes, using Hong Kong's export weights.

The above results show that relative prices and foreign activity have strong and significant effects. Specifically, a 1 percent increase in the relative price of Hong Kong's exports leads to a ½ percent fall in export volume, whereas a 1 percent rise in the import volumes of trading partners generates an almost equivalent increase in export volume. The lower elasticity of export price compared with foreign demand may reflect the composition of Hong Kong's exports, which are increasingly geared toward high-quality goods and high-value added services. These characteristics would tend to make Hong Kong's exports nonessential items in foreign markets and, hence, one would expect the demand for such products to be more sensitive to changes in foreign incomes than prices of Hong Kong's exports.

The demand for imports is estimated as a function of real total domestic demand and the ratio of import prices to the consumer price index. To provide a precise account of the import demand of the Hong Kong economy, nonretained imports are excluded from total imports of goods, that is, only retained imports of goods and imports of nonfactor services are included. As above, the import demand equation was estimated on annual data from 1960 to 95 using the maximum likelihood iterative technique. The equation is estimated as[78]

$$\log M_t = -0.978 - 0.452 \log PM_t + 1.049 \log DD_t \quad (7)$$
$$(-1.91) \quad (-2.65) \quad (22.02)$$

$$\bar{R}^2 = 0.996, \quad DW = 1.626, \quad F = 1987.84$$

where:

M_t = retained imports of goods and imports of nonfactor services in constant prices ("total imports");

PM_t = deflator for total imports expressed in U.S. dollars, divided by the consumer price index (CPI(B)) expressed in U.S. dollars; and

DD_t = total real domestic demand in constant prices.

These estimates indicate that the volume of imports is about equally sensitive as that of exports to relative price movements, with a 1 percent rise in the relative price of imports leading to a fall in import volume of about ½ percent. Import demand is roughly homogeneous with respect to real domestic demand, with a 1 percent rise in domestic demand implying a slightly greater than 1 percent increase in volume of retained imports and imports of nonfactor services.

---

[77]Values of t-statistics are shown in parentheses. The estimate for the autocorrelation coefficient ρ was 0.526 ($t = 3.59$).

[78]Values of t-statistics are shown in parentheses. The estimate for the autocorrelation coefficient ρ was 0.723 ($t = 6.34$).

Appendix II   Data Sources and Description

This appendix describes data used in Section V to derive estimates of real growth, output and input prices, and labor productivity and unit labor costs in manufacturing and services.

Data Sources

- Publications of the Census and Statistics Department:
  Estimates of Gross Domestic Product, 1961 to 1996 (March 1997) (EGDP).
  Quarterly Report of GDP Estimates (various editions) (QGDP).
  Annual Digest of Statistics (various editions) (ADS).
  Monthly Digest of Statistics (various editions) (MDS).
- Data on retained imports in current and constant prices were provided by the Census and Statistics Department.

Description of the Data

Nominal Value Added

- Annual production-based GDP at current prices by economic activity (EGDP, 11).
- Breakdown of value added in *wholesale, retail, import/export trades, restaurants and hotels* was published for the first time in 1996 (EGDP, 13). Gross output in wholesale, retail, and import/export trades is measured by the gross margin realized on trading (i.e., the sales value less the cost of goods sold). To a lesser extent, trading establishments also provide agency services to their clients, so the income from commissions, fees, service charges, and rentals is also included in gross output. The intermediate consumption comprises rentals, operating expenses on materials and supplies, and the cost of services such as advertising, insurance, and transportation.
- Breakdown of value added in *transportation, storage, and communications* is obtained from prin-

cipal statistics for all transport and related services by major industry group and value added (ADS 5.8). The coverage in the ADS is not comprehensive: the production-based estimates of GDP for this sector are on average 5 percent higher than the total obtained from the ADS. Gross output in transportation, storage, and communications is measured by the service charges received (passenger and freight revenue, warehousing rental, sales of postal, courier, telephone and other communication services). The intermediate consumption comprises standard expense items (fuel, materials and supplies, repair and maintenance costs, rentals).

- Breakdown of value added in *financing, insurance, real estate, and business services* was published for the first time in 1996 (EGDP, 13). For the purpose of this study, value added in financing was split between banks and nonbank financial institutions. The share of banks was assumed to correspond to imputed bank services charge ("financial intermediation services indirectly measured"), which is used to calculate production-based estimates of gross domestic product (EGDP, 11). The share of nonbank financial institutions was obtained by subtracting the imputed bank services charge from value added of financing. Gross output of banks is measured by net interest receipts (i.e., total interest received from loans less total interest paid out to depositors and creditors) and other service charges. For nonbank financial institutions (investment and holding companies, stockbrokers, brokers and dealers in foreign exchange, gold bullion, commodity futures), the value of output is measured by the amount of management fees, service charges, and commissions and brokerages. The intermediate consumption of the financial services comprises the same cost items as in other industries, except that interest payments are not included (they are netted out from gross output).

- Gross output of *community, social, and personal services* is estimated as the sum of operating expenses (including imputed rentals for government owned or subsidized premises) and compensation of employees. The operating expenses are treated as intermediate consumption, and compensation of employees as value added.

Exports and Imports of Services

- Exports and imports of services by component at current and constant (1990) market prices (EGDP, 8).
- Breakdown includes exports and imports of the following services:
    Transportation (sea, air, and land transportation);
    Travel (business and personal travel);
    Insurance (direct insurance and reinsurance);
    Financial (banking, financial assets dealing, brokerage services);
    Trade-related (off-shore trading, purchasing services, other trade related services); and
    Other business services (communication, legal, advertising, marketing research, management consultancy, accounting, industrial, construction, real estate, architectural, computer, information, news transmission, production and distribution of films, hotel management, and other business services).

Employment

Average of end-quarter estimates of the number of persons engaged by major industry group (MDS 2.4). Recently, the Census and Statistics Department introduced a set of composite employment estimates (Census and Statistics Department (1997)) that provides a more complete coverage of employment by sector; however, these estimates are not available prior to 1986.

Wages

Average of semiannual (March and September) wage indices by industry sector (MDS 2.7).

Deflators

- *Manufacturing:* Derived from nominal value added and index of industrial production (MDS, 4.1).
- *Wholesale trade:* Implicit price deflator for retained imports (derived from the data supplied by the Census and Statistics Department). Wholesalers mostly distribute imported goods in the domestic market, including foodstuffs, consumer goods, machinery and equipment, and production inputs (fuels, raw materials and semimanufactures). Over the long run, wholesale prices should broadly reflect movements in prices of retained imports, which form the basis for cost calculations in this industry.
- *Retail trade:* Derived from indices of value and volume of retail sales (ADS, 5.15). Given the comprehensive coverage of the indices of value and volume of retail sales, this deflator should provide a good indicator of the price changes in the retail sector.

- *Import/export trade:* Weighted average of the deflators for domestic exports (EGDP, 3), retained imports and net reexports (i.e., reexports less nonretained imports) (derived from the data supplied by the Census and Statistics Department), and exports and imports of trade-related services (derived from EGDP, 8). The weights used were the nominal shares of these five components in their sum. The rationale for the use of the deflators for domestic exports and retained imports is obvious. Net reexports (reexports less nonretained imports) represent "gross output" or reexport margin realized in reexport trade, normally accounting for 15–18 percent of GDP. Although value added in reexport trade (that is, reexport margin less the cost of intermediate goods and services used up in reexport trade) is lower, it nevertheless makes up a substantial amount. Finally, the deflators for trade related services represent the price movements relevant for companies engaged in off-shore trading.
- *Restaurants:* Derived from indices of volume and value of restaurant receipts (ADS, 5.18). The implicit deflator should provide a good indicator of price changes in restaurant business.
- *Hotels:* Implicit price deflator for expenditure of nonresidents in Hong Kong (EGDP, 5). This deflator is essentially custom-designed to measure price changes in tourism industry.
- *Land (passenger and supporting services) and government transportation:* Transportation subindex of the composite consumer price index (CPI) which covers: fares for ferries, trains, taxis, and public transportation; motor fuel; purchases of and repairs to motor vehicles; and motor licenses, insurance, parking fees, and tunnel tolls. Land (passenger and supporting services) and government transportation are for the most part nontradable services, so their prices generally move in line with underlying costs, which should be adequately captured by the transportation component of the CPI.
- *Land (freight), water, and air transportation and transportation services:* Weighted average of the deflators for exports and imports of transportation services (derived from EGDP, 8). The weights used were nominal shares of exports and imports of transportation services in total trade in such services. Water and air transportation and related services are tradable, so their prices are expected to move in line with export and import prices.
- *Storage*: Rental index for private flatted factories (MDS, 5.12). A separate warehousing rental index is not available.
- *Communications:* Derived from the data on international telephone calls, in millions of minutes (ADS, 12.16). Although a relatively crude proxy for real growth, the use of this index yielded, inter alia, a time series of falling output prices, which has indeed

been a characteristic of this industry. The use of alternative deflators (e.g., exports of business services, which cover communications services) did not yield plausible results (for example, real growth decelerated sharply in 1993, when, by all accounts, there was a boom in communications business).

• *Banks and nonbank financial institutions:* Given the high mobility of financial capital and absence of restrictions on capital flows, all financial services were treated as tradable and, hence, a weighted price deflator for exports and imports of financial services (derived from EGDP, 8) was used. The weights used were nominal shares of exports and imports of financial services in total trade in such services. For nonbanks, a number of alternative deflators were tried, including the Hang Seng share price index, and total turnover on the Stock Exchange of Hong Kong deflated by the Hang Seng index. The results indicate the same pattern of real growth as those obtained from the deflator for exports and imports of financial services, the difference being mostly a scale effect.

• *Real estate services:* Implicit price deflator for real estate developers' margin, derived from the breakdown of gross domestic fixed capital formation by public/private sector (EGDP, 7). Real estate developers' margins are estimated as the value of the work in progress less all project outlays incurred during the year.[79] This deflator is essentially custom-designed, as the survey on investment from which it is obtained also is used to derive the GDP estimates for construction and real estate services.

• *Business services:* Implicit price deflator for exports of other business services (derived from EGDP, 8). Business services comprise accounting and auditing, legal services, architectural design, engineering and similar firms. The value of their output is measured by the fees, commissions, and other service charges received. Although many business services are nontradable, the high level of competition among domestic service providers ensures more or less competitive pricing, so a deflator for exports of such services was used to obtain value added in constant prices.

• *Insurance:* Weighted average of the deflators for exports and imports of insurance services (derived from EGDP, 8). The weights used were nominal shares of exports and imports of insurance services in total trade in such services.

---

[79]For buildings that are completely built within a year and sold in the same year, the real estate developers' margin is equal to the selling price of the building less total costs incurred by the developer (excluding interest payments). Otherwise, the margin is equivalent to value of the work in progress less all project outlays incurred during the year.

• *Community, personal, and social services:* "Miscellaneous services" subindex of the composite CPI, which covers school fees and educational charges, medical services, entertainment expenses, household services, hairdressing, repairs to personal and household goods, subscriptions, and postal and telephone services.

Labor Productivity

Measured as the (change in) value added in constant prices per worker. Data on person hours are not available.

Unit Labor Costs

Measured as the (change in) the nominal wage bill (wL) per value added in constant prices (pQ) (equivalent to dividing the nominal wage index by the labor productivity index).

Gross Operating Surplus

Defined as value added less compensation of employees (EGDP, 12).

Relative Prices

Defined as the (change in) the output price deflator for industry i divided by the price deflator for manufacturing output.

Relative Wages

Defined as the (change in) the nominal wage index for industry i divided by the nominal wage index for manufacturing.

Profitability

Measured as gross operating surplus in constant prices of the sector.

Tradable Industries

Manufacturing, wholesale and import/export trade; water, land freight, and air transportation; transportation services; banks, nonbanks, and insurance companies were classified as tradable industries.

Nontradable Industries

Retail trade, restaurants and hotels, land passenger and government transportation, storage, communications, business services, real estate services, and community, social, and personal services were classified as nontradable.

Estimates of Real Growth in Manufacturing

Until recently, the Census and Statistics Department compiled regularly only an index of *gross* output in manufacturing at constant prices (quarterly index of industrial production). Recently, the Department started publishing estimates of value added in manufacturing at constant prices (Census and Statistics Department (1996)); this index is, however, only compiled on an annual basis and it is available with a long delay. Finally, as most of the manufacturing output is exported, the deflator for domestic exports can be used as a proxy for changes in manufacturing prices to deflate nominal value added inmanufacturing.

Real growth estimates derived from the index of value added at constant prices and the domestic exports deflator are closely correlated (Table 8). Until 1990, the two indices also tracked closely the movements in the index of industrial production. Since then, however, the growth path derived from these two indices has diverged from the one derived from the index of industrial production. In particular, estimates based on the index of industrial production imply that (gross) output did not respond much to a decline in manufacturing prices in 1991 and 1993, while estimates based on the index of value added at constant prices imply that, as manufacturing prices rose in 1991 and 1993, value added declined sharply. For an industry consisting of price-taking firms, such a response would not be rational. Moreover, partner-county data confirm that manufacturing prices actually declined in 1991 and 1993.[80] For these reasons, the analysis in this paper was based on the index of industrial production.

---

[80]The World Economic Outlook database indicates that, for partner countries that together account for 95 percent of trade of Hong Kong, export and import deflators for manufactured goods declined by ½ percent in 1991, and 6 percent in 1993.

Appendix III   Joint Declaration and the Basic Law

This appendix provides a summary of some key provisions in the Joint Declaration and the Basic Law that are discussed in Section VI.[81]

I. General Provisions

1. **Economic system**
   (JD 16, 42, 84; BL 5)

   The socialist system and policies shall not be practiced in the Region, and the previous capitalist system and way of life shall remain unchanged for 50 years.

2. **Property relations**
   (JD 18, 86; BL 6)

   The right of private ownership of property shall be protected.

3. **Land and natural resources**
   (BL 7)

   The land and natural resources within the Hong Kong Special Administrative Region shall be state property. Land shall be managed, developed, and leased by the Region and revenue derived therefrom shall be left with the Region.

4. **Legal system**
   (JD 10, 53; BL 8)

   The laws previously in force in Hong Kong—the common law, rules of equity, ordinances—shall be maintained, except for any that contravene the Basic Law.

II. Provisions on the Economy

1. **Legal and economic framework**
   (JD 18, 86; BL 105)

   The rights of private ownership of property and investments shall be protected by law.

   (JD 20, 94; BL 109)

   The Region shall provide an appropriate economic and legal environment for

   (BL 118)

   (i) the maintenance of the status of Hong Kong as an international financial center;

   (BL 119)

   (ii) encouraging investments, technological progress, and the development of new industries;

   (BL 119)

   (iii) the development of various trades; and
   (iv) the protection of the environment.

---

[81]Based on *The Joint Declaration of the Government of the United Kingdom of Great Britain and Northern Ireland and the Government of the People's Republic of China on the Question of Hong Kong* [Initialed on September 26, 1984; Signed on December 19, 1984; Ratified on May 27, 1985] (Hong Kong: Government Printer); and *The Basic Law of the Hong Kong Special Administrative Region of the People's Republic of China* [Signed on April 4, 1990] (Hong Kong: Government Printer, 1993). Parentheses contain cross-references to the corresponding Articles of the Joint Declaration (JD) and the Basic Law (BL). The summary presented is not exhaustive. The Hong Kong Special Administrative Region is referred to in this appendix as "the Region."

2. Public finance

Independent finances
(JD 23, 24, 79, 81, 82;
BL 106)

The Region shall have independent finances and use its resources exclusively for its own purposes. Central government shall not levy taxes in the Region.

Budget policy and public expenditure
(BL 107)

The Region shall follow the principle of keeping expenditure within the limits of revenues in drawing up its budget, and strive to achieve fiscal balance, avoid deficits, and keep the budget commensurate with the growth rate of its GDP.

Tax laws and tax policy
(JD 24, 81; BL 108)

The Region shall practice an independent taxation system. Taking the low tax policy as reference, it shall enact its own tax laws.

3. Monetary and financial systems

Legal foundation
(BL 110)

The monetary and financial systems of the Region shall be prescribed by law.

Monetary independence
(JD 96, 97; BL 110)

The Region shall, on its own, formulate monetary and financial policies, safeguard the free operation of financial business and financial markets, and regulate and supervise them in accordance with law.

Legal tender
(JD 22, 100; BL 111)

The Hong Kong dollar shall continue to circulate as the legal tender.

Currency issue and backing
(JD 101; BL 111)

The authority to issue Hong Kong currency shall be vested in the government of the Region. The issue of Hong Kong currency must be backed by a 100 percent reserve fund. The system regarding the issue of Hong Kong currency and the reserve fund system shall be prescribed by law.

(JD 102; BL 111)

Designated banks may be authorized to issue Hong Kong currency. The arrangements for such issue must be consistent with the object of maintaining the stability of the currency.

**Foreign exchange controls,
convertibility, financial markets**
(JD 20, 22, 98, 99, 100; BL 112)

No foreign exchange controls shall be applied in the Region. The Hong Kong dollar shall be freely convertible. Markets for foreign exchange, gold, securities, futures, and the like shall continue.

Capital flows
(JD 21, 97; BL 112)

The Region shall safeguard the free flow of capital within, into, and out of the region.

Exchange Fund
(JD 104; BL 113)

The Exchange Fund shall be managed and controlled by the government of the Region primarily for regulating the exchange value of the Hong Kong dollar.

4. Trade and industry

Free port status and free trade policy
(JD 19, 87; BL 114, 115)

The Region shall maintain the status of a free port and shall not impose any tariff. It shall pursue the policy of free trade and safeguard the free movement of goods, intangible assets, and capital.

Separate customs territory
(JD 19, 89, 90; BL 116)

The Region shall be a separate customs territory and may participate in relevant international organizations and trade agreements under the name "Hong Kong, China."

(JD 91; BL 116)

Export quotas and tariff preferences obtained by the Region shall be enjoyed exclusively by the region.

(JD 92; BL 117)

The Region may issue its own certificates of origin for products.

5. Land leases

Protection of land leases
(JD 18, 86, 202; BL 120)

Land leases and related rights granted before the establishment of the Region and extending beyond June 30, 1997, shall continue to be recognized and protected under the law of the Region.

Payment of rent
(JD 203, 204, 207, 208; BL 121)

Land leases extending beyond June 30, 1997, shall not be subject to additional premium, but to an annual rent equivalent to 3 percent of the rateable value of the properties concerned.

Rural properties (JD 205; BL 122)

Indigenous villagers holding rural properties shall continue to pay the previous rent.

6. Shipping

(JD 105; BL 124)

Hong Kong's existing system of shipping management and regulation shall be maintained-

(JD 108; BL 125)

Hong Kong shall continue to maintain a separate shipping register.

(JD 109; BL 126)

Ships (except foreign warships) shall continue to enjoy access to the ports of the Region.

(JD 107; BL 127)

Private shipping and port businesses may continue to operate freely.

7. Civil aviation

(JD 112; BL 129)

The Region shall continue the previous system of civil aviation management in Hong Kong.

(JD 118–122; BL 133)

The Region, acting under authorization from the Central People's Government, may renew or amend, negotiate and conclude air services agreements and provisional arrangements to regulate all air services to, from, or through the Region that do not operate to, from, or through the mainland of China.

(JD 114; BL 131)   The Central People's Government shall, in consultation with the government of the Region, make arrangements for air services between the Region and other parts of China.

8. Immigration and labor

(JD 165; BL 22)   For entry into the Region, people from other parts of China must apply for approval. Among them, the number of persons who enter the region for the purpose of settlement shall be determined by the competent authorities of the Central People's government after consulting the government of the Region.

(JD 166; BL 154)   The government of the Region may apply immigration controls on entry into, stay in, and departure from the Region by persons from foreign states and regions.

(BL 147)   The Region shall on its own formulate laws and policies relating to labor.

(JD 129; BL 142)   Hong Kong's previous system of assessing and certifying professional qualifications shall be maintained. The Region shall continue to recognize the existing professions and professional organizations.

9. Social services

(BL 144)   The policy of subventions for nongovernmental organizations in education, medicine and health, culture, art, recreation, sports, social welfare, and social work shall be maintained.

(BL 145)   The Region shall formulate its own policies on the development and improvement of the social welfare system in the light of the economic conditions and social needs.

References

Aukurst, Odd (1977), "Inflation in the Open Economy: A Norwegian Model," in *World-Wide Inflation: Theory and Recent Experience*, ed. by Lawrence B. Krause and Walter S. Salant (Washington: Brookings Institution), pp. 107–53.

Balassa, Bela (1964), "The Purchasing-Power-Parity Doctrine: A Reappraisal," *Journal of Political Economy* (December), Vol. 72, pp. 584–96.

Cameron, Nigel (1990), *An Illustrated History of Hong Kong* (Oxford: Oxford University Press).

Carse, David (1996), "The Hong Kong Banking Industry: To 1997 and Beyond," Speech at the Banker of the Year Awards, July 18, 1996.

Census and Statistics Department, Hong Kong (1997), "Introduction to Composite Employment Estimates," *Hong Kong Monthly Digest of Statistics* (March).

_____(1996), "Labor Productivity of the Manufacturing Sector in Hong Kong, 1982–1994," *Hong Kong Monthly Digest of Statistics* (December).

Chai, Joseph C.H. (1992), "Economic Relations with China," in *The Economic System of Hong Kong*, ed. by H.C.Y. Ho and L.C. Chau (Hong Kong: Asian Research Service), pp. 140–54.

Chau, L.C. (1992), "Public Housing," in *The Economic System of Hong Kong*, ed. by H.C.Y. Ho and L.C. Chau (Hong Kong: Asian Research Service), pp. 169–89.

Chen Yuan (1995), "Financial Relations between Hong Kong and the Mainland," *HKMA Quarterly Bulletin*, No. 4, pp. 25–31.

_____(1996), "Monetary Relations between China and Hong Kong," *HKMA Quarterly Bulletin*, No. 9 (November), pp. 36–40.

Cheung, Anthony B.L. (1996), "The Civil Service in Transition," in *The Other Hong Kong Report 1996*, ed. by Nyaw Mee-kau and Li Si-ming (Hong Kong: The Chinese University Press), pp. 67–88.

Ching, Frank (1996), "From the Joint Declaration to the Basic Law," in *The Other Hong Kong Report 1996*, ed. by Nyaw Mee-kau and Li Si-ming (Hong Kong: The Chinese University Press), pp. 33–50.

Consumer Council (1994), *Are Hong Kong Depositors Fairly Treated?* (Hong Kong: Consumer Council, February).

_____(1995), *Assessing Competition in the Domestic Water Heating and Cooking Fuel Market* (Hong Kong: Consumer Council, July).

_____(1996a), *Ensuring Competition in the Dynamic Television Broadcasting Market* (Hong Kong: Consumer Council, January).

_____(1996b), *Achieving Competition in the Liberalized Telecommunications Market* (Hong Kong: Consumer Council, March).

_____(1996c), *How Competitive Is the Private Residential Property Market?* (Hong Kong: Consumer Council, July).

_____(1996d), *Competition Policy: The Key to Hong Kong's Future Economic Success* (Hong Kong: Consumer Council, November).

Davies, Howard (1996), "High IQ and Low Technology: Hong Kong's Key to Success," *Long Range Planning*, Vol. 29, No. 5, pp. 685–91.

Davies, Ken (1996), *Hong Kong after 1997* (London: Economist Intelligence Unit).

Endacott, G.B. (1964), *An Eastern Entrepôt: A Collection of Documents Illustrating the History of Hong Kong* (London: Her Majesty's Stationery Office).

Enright, Michael, E. Scott, J. West, and D. Dodwell (1997), *The Hong Kong Advantage: A Study of the Competitiveness of the Hong Kong Economy* (Hong Kong: Oxford University Press).

Frisch, Helmut (1983), *Theories of Inflation* (Cambridge: Cambridge University Press).

Fu, Y. (1995), "Housing Market and Housing Policies," in *The Other Hong Kong Report, 1995*, ed. by S.Y.L. Cheung and S.M.H. Sze (Hong Kong: The Chinese University Press), pp. 261–86.

General Agreement on Tariffs and Trade (1994), *Trade Policy Review Mechanism—Hong Kong* (GATT: Geneva, September).

Goodhart, Charles (1983), "The Role of Monetary Management in an Economy," in *Monetary Management in Hong Kong* (Hong Kong: HKMA), pp. 5–14.

Government Secretariat, Hong Kong (1996), *The Services Sector Support and Promotion*, Addendum to the 1996–97 Budget (Hong Kong: Government Printer, March).

_____(1997), *Hong Kong at Your Service: Final Report of the Government Task Force on Services Promotion*, Addendum to the 1997–98 Budget (Hong Kong: Government Printer, March).

Government Secretariat, Housing Branch (1997), *Homes for Hong Kong People: The Way Forward*, Long-

Term Housing Strategy Review Consultative Document (Hong Kong: Government Secretariat, January).

De Gregorio, Jose, Alberto Giovannini, and Holger C. Wolf (1994), "International Evidence on Tradables and Nontradables Inflation," *European Economic Review*, Vol. 38, pp. 1225–44.

Grey, Jack (1990), *Rebellions and Revolutions* (Oxford: Oxford University Press).

Haddon-Cave, Sir Charles Philip (1982), "Public Policy and Economic Success." *Hong Kong Manager*, Vol. 18 (May), pp. 15–19.

Hall, Maximilian (1984), *Banking Regulation and Supervision: A Comparative Study of the United Kingdom, the United States, and Japan* (Aldershot: Edward Elgar).

Hall, Robert E., and John B. Taylor (1993), *Macroeconomics: Theory, Performance, and Policy*, 4th edition (New York: Norton).

Hawkins, John (1995), "The Best of Times, the Worst of Times: Developments in Productivity," *HKMA Quarterly Bulletin* (August), pp. 11–21.

_____, and Dorcas Kee (1996), "Analysis of Inflation in Hong Kong," *HKMA Quarterly Bulletin* (August), pp. 2–23.

Hawkins, John, and Matthew Yiu (1995), "Real and Effective Exchange Rates," *HKMA Quarterly Bulletin* (November), pp. 1–11.

Hewitt Associates LLC and GML Consulting (1995), *Report of the Consultancy on the Mandatory Provident Fund System* (Hong Kong: Hewitt Associates LLC and GML Consulting Ltd., April).

Hong Kong Government (1996), *Hong Kong 1996: A Review of 1995* (Hong Kong: Hong Kong Government).

Hong Kong Monetary Authority (1994), *Study on the Consumer Council Report "Are Hong Kong Depositors Fairly Treated?"* (Hong Kong: HKMA, July).

_____(1995), "Hong Kong as an International Financial Center: A Strategy Paper," *HKMA Quarterly Bulletin* (August), pp. 37–48.

International Monetary Fund (1996), *United Kingdom–Hong Kong: Recent Economic Developments*. IMF Staff Country Report No. 96/29 (Washington: IMF, April).

_____(1997a), *United Kingdom–Hong Kong: Recent Economic Developments*. IMF Staff Country Report No. 97/49 (Washington: IMF).

_____(1997b), *United Kingdom–Hong Kong: Selected Issues*. IMF Staff Country Report No. 97/50 (Washington: IMF).

Jao, Y.C. (1990), "From Sterling Exchange Standard to Dollar Exchange Standard: The Evolution of Hong Kong's Contemporary Monetary System, 1967–1989," in *Money in Hong Kong: Historical Perspective and Contemporary Analysis*, ed. by Y.C. Jao and Frank H.H. King (Hong Kong: Centre of Asian Studies, University of Hong Kong), pp. 51–175.

_____(1992), "Monetary System and Banking Structure," in *The Economic System of Hong Kong*, ed. by

H.C.Y. Ho and L.C. Chau (Hong Kong: Asian Research Services), pp. 43–85.

_____(1994), "Money and Banking," in *The Economic System of Hong Kong*, 2nd ed., ed. by H.C.Y. Ho (Hong Kong: Asian Research Services).

Latter, Anthony (1994), "The Currency Board Approach to Monetary Policy," in *Monetary Management in Hong Kong* (Hong Kong: HKMA), pp. 26–43.

Lo, Chi-kin (1996), "Constitution and Administration," in *The Other Hong Kong Report 1996*, ed. by Nyaw Mee-kau and Li Si-ming (Hong Kong: The Chinese University Press), pp. 1–12.

Miners, Norman (1995), *The Government and Politics of Hong Kong*, Fifth Edition (Hong Kong: Oxford University Press).

Nugée, John (1995), "A Brief History of the Exchange Fund," *HKMA Quarterly Bulletin* (May), pp. 1–17.

OECD (1993), "Hong Kong's Economic Relations with China," paper presented at the OECD Workshop on Economic Integration of OECD Economies, Dynamic Asian Economies, and Central and Eastern European Countries, Budapest, September.

Peng, Ruijie, and William C. Wheaton (1994), "Effects of Restrictive Land Supply on Housing in Hong Kong: An Econometric Analysis," *Journal of Housing Research*, Vol. 5, No. 2, pp. 263–92.

Planning, Environment and Lands Branch (1994), *Report of the Task Force on Land Supply, and Property Prices* (Hong Kong: Environment, Planning and Lands Branch, June).

Samuelson, Paul A. (1994), "Theoretical Notes on Trade Problems," *Review of Economic Studies* (March), Vol. 46, pp. 145–54.

Scott, Ian (1989), *Political Change and the Crisis of Legitimacy in Hong Kong* (Hong Kong: Oxford University Press).

Segal, Gerald (1993), *The Fate of Hong Kong* (London: Simon and Schuster).

Siu, Yat-Ming (1996), "Population and Immigration: With a Special Account on Chinese Immigrants," in *The Other Hong Kong Report 1996*, ed. by Nyaw Mee-kau and Li Si-ming (Hong Kong: Chinese University Press), pp. 325–48.

Smith, Alan (1997), "Statistics Provide Evidence of Hong Kong's Great Leap Forward." *South China Morning Post*, Internet Edition, May 5, 1997.

Szczepanik, Edward (1958), *The Economic Growth of Hong Kong* (London: Oxford University Press).

Taylor, John B. (1993), *Macroeconomic Policy in a World Economy: From Econometric Design to Practical Operation* (New York: Norton).

Welsh, Frank (1993), *A History of Hong Kong* (London: Harper Collins).

Wong, Richard Y.C. (1996), "The Growth of Manufacturing and Services in Hong Kong," *HKCER Letters* Vol. 40 (September), pp. 1–4.

World Bank (1995), *The Emerging East Asian Bond Market—Hong Kong* (Washington: The World Bank, East Asia and Pacific Region, June).

Yahuda, Michael (1996), *Hong Kong: China's Challenge* (London: Routledge).

Yam, Joseph (1995), "Hong Kong as an International Financial Center," *HKMA Quarterly Bulletin* (August), pp. 32–36.

———(1996a), "One Country, Two Systems," *HKMA Quarterly Bulletin*, No. 6 (February), pp. 19-21.

———(1996b), "Monetary Relationship between Mainland China and Hong Kong after 1997," Speech to the British Chamber of Commerce, Hong Kong, September 18, 1996.

———(1996c), "Hong Kong's Monetary Scene: Myths and Realities," *HKMA Quarterly Bulletin*, No. 9 (November), pp. 45–51.

Young, Alwyn (1995), "The Tyranny of Numbers: Confronting the Realities of the East Asian Growth Experience," *Quarterly Journal of Economics* (August), pp. 641–80.

Recent Occasional Papers of the International Monetary Fund

152. Hong Kong, China: Growth, Structural Change, and Economic Stability During the Transition, by John Dodsworth and Dubravko Mihaljek, 1997.

151. Currency Board Arrangements: Issues and Experiences, by a staff team led by Tomás J.T. Baliño and Charles Enoch. 1997.

150. Kuwait: From Reconstruction to Accumulation for Future Generations, by Nigel Andrew Chalk, Mohamed A. El-Erian, Susan J. Fennell, Alexei P. Kireyev, and John F. Wison. 1997.

149. The Composition of Fiscal Adjustment and Growth: Lessons from Fiscal Reforms in Eight Economies, by G.A. Mackenzie, David W.H. Orsmond, and Philip R. Gerson. 1997.

148. Nigeria: Experience with Structural Adjustment, by Gary Moser, Scott Rogers, and Reinold van Til, with Robin Kibuka and Inutu Lukonga. 1997.

147. Aging Populations and Public Pension Schemes, by Sheetal K. Chand and Albert Jaeger, 1996

146. Thailand: The Road to Sustained Growth, by Kalpana Kochhar, Louis Dicks-Mireaux, Balazs Horvath, Mauro Mecagni, Erik Offerdal, and Jianping Zhou. 1996.

145. Exchange Rate Movements and Their Impact on Trade and Investment in the APEC Region, by Takatoshi Ito, Peter Isard, Steven Symansky, and Tamim Bayoumi. 1996.

144. National Bank of Poland: The Road to Indirect Instruments, by Piero Ugolini. 1996.

143. Adjustment for Growth: The African Experience, by Michael T. Hadjimichael, Michael Nowak, Robert Sharer, and Amor Tahari. 1996.

142. Quasi-Fiscal Operations of Public Financial Institutions, by G.A. Mackenzie and Peter Stella. 1996.

141. Monetary and Exchange System Reforms in China: An Experiment in Gradualism, by Hassanali Mehran, Marc Quintyn, Tom Nordman, and Bernard Laurens. 1996.

140. Government Reform in New Zealand, by Graham C. Scott. 1996.

139. Reinvigorating Growth in Developing Countries: Lessons from Adjustment Policies in Eight Economies, by David Goldsbrough, Sharmini Coorey, Louis Dicks-Mireaux, Balazs Horvath, Kalpana Kochhar, Mauro Mecagni, Erik Offerdal, and Jianping Zhou. 1996.

138. Aftermath of the CFA Franc Devaluation, by Jean A.P. Clément, with Johannes Mueller, Stéphane Cossé, and Jean Le Dem. 1996.

137. The Lao People's Democratic Republic: Systemic Transformation and Adjustment, edited by Ichiro Otani and Chi Do Pham. 1996.

136. Jordan: Strategy for Adjustment and Growth, edited by Edouard Maciejewski and Ahsan Mansur. 1996.

135. Vietnam: Transition to a Market Economy, by John R. Dodsworth, Erich Spitäller, Michael Braulke, Keon Hyok Lee, Kenneth Miranda, Christian Mulder, Hisanobu Shishido, and Krishna Srinivasan. 1996.

134. India: Economic Reform and Growth, by Ajai Chopra, Charles Collyns, Richard Hemming, and Karen Parker with Woosik Chu and Oliver Fratzscher. 1995.

133. Policy Experiences and Issues in the Baltics, Russia, and Other Countries of the Former Soviet Union, edited by Daniel A. Citrin and Ashok K. Lahiri. 1995.

132. Financial Fragilities in Latin America: The 1980s and 1990s, by Liliana Rojas-Suárez and Steven R. Weisbrod. 1995.

131. Capital Account Convertibility: Review of Experience and Implications for IMF Policies, by staff teams headed by Peter J. Quirk and Owen Evans. 1995.

130. Challenges to the Swedish Welfare State, by Desmond Lachman, Adam Bennett, John H. Green, Robert Hagemann, and Ramana Ramaswamy. 1995.

129. IMF Conditionality: Experience Under Stand-By and Extended Arrangements. Part II: Background Papers. Susan Schadler, Editor, with Adam Bennett, Maria Carkovic, Louis Dicks-Mireaux, Mauro Mecagni, James H.J. Morsink, and Miguel A. Savastano. 1995.

128. IMF Conditionality: Experience Under Stand-By and Extended Arrangements. Part I: Key Issues and Findings, by Susan Schadler, Adam Bennett, Maria Carkovic, Louis Dicks-Mireaux, Mauro Mecagni, James H.J. Morsink, and Miguel A. Savastano. 1995.

127. Road Maps of the Transition: The Baltics, the Czech Republic, Hungary, and Russia, by Biswajit Banerjee, Vincent Koen, Thomas Krueger, Mark S. Lutz, Michael Marrese, and Tapio O. Saavalainen. 1995.

126. The Adoption of Indirect Instruments of Monetary Policy, by a staff team headed by William E. Alexander, Tomás J.T. Baliño, and Charles Enoch. 1995.

125. United Germany: The First Five Years—Performance and Policy Issues, by Robert Corker, Robert A. Feldman, Karl Habermeier, Hari Vittas, and Tessa van der Willigen. 1995.

124. Saving Behavior and the Asset Price "Bubble" in Japan: Analytical Studies, edited by Ulrich Baumgartner and Guy Meredith. 1995.

123. Comprehensive Tax Reform: The Colombian Experience, edited by Parthasarathi Shome. 1995.

122. Capital Flows in the APEC Region, edited by Mohsin S. Khan and Carmen M. Reinhart. 1995.

121. Uganda: Adjustment with Growth, 1987–94, by Robert L. Sharer, Hema R. De Zoysa, and Calvin A. McDonald. 1995.

120. Economic Dislocation and Recovery in Lebanon, by Sena Eken, Paul Cashin, S. Nuri Erbas, Jose Martelino, and Adnan Mazarei. 1995.

119. Singapore: A Case Study in Rapid Development, edited by Kenneth Bercuson with a staff team comprising Robert G. Carling, Aasim M. Husain, Thomas Rumbaugh, and Rachel van Elkan. 1995.

118. Sub-Saharan Africa: Growth, Savings, and Investment, by Michael T. Hadjimichael, Dhaneshwar Ghura, Martin Mühleisen, Roger Nord, and E. Murat Uçer. 1995.

117. Resilience and Growth Through Sustained Adjustment: The Moroccan Experience, by Saleh M. Nsouli, Sena Eken, Klaus Enders, Van-Can Thai, Jörg Decressin, and Filippo Cartiglia, with Janet Bungay. 1995.

116. Improving the International Monetary System: Constraints and Possibilities, by Michael Mussa, Morris Goldstein, Peter B. Clark, Donald J. Mathieson, and Tamim Bayoumi. 1994.

115. Exchange Rates and Economic Fundamentals: A Framework for Analysis, by Peter B. Clark, Leonardo Bartolini, Tamim Bayoumi, and Steven Symansky. 1994.

114. Economic Reform in China: A New Phase, by Wanda Tseng, Hoe Ee Khor, Kalpana Kochhar, Dubravko Mihaljek, and David Burton. 1994.

113. Poland: The Path to a Market Economy, by Liam P. Ebrill, Ajai Chopra, Charalambos Christofides, Paul Mylonas, Inci Otker, and Gerd Schwartz. 1994.

112. The Behavior of Non-Oil Commodity Prices, by Eduardo Borensztein, Mohsin S. Khan, Carmen M. Reinhart, and Peter Wickham. 1994.

111. The Russian Federation in Transition: External Developments, by Benedicte Vibe Christensen. 1994.

110. Limiting Central Bank Credit to the Government: Theory and Practice, by Carlo Cottarelli. 1993.

109. The Path to Convertibility and Growth: The Tunisian Experience, by Saleh M. Nsouli, Sena Eken, Paul Duran, Gerwin Bell, and Zühtü Yücelik. 1993.

108. Recent Experiences with Surges in Capital Inflows, by Susan Schadler, Maria Carkovic, Adam Bennett, and Robert Kahn. 1993.

107. China at the Threshold of a Market Economy, by Michael W. Bell, Hoe Ee Khor, and Kalpana Kochhar with Jun Ma, Simon N'guiamba, and Rajiv Lall. 1993.

Note: For information on the title and availability of Occasional Papers not listed, please consult the IMF Publications Catalog or contact IMF Publication Services.